# THE ADHD HAND BOOK

**Stuart Passmore** is a psychologist in private practice, with extensive experience in working with individuals, couples and families. Stuart specialises in parenting children with behavioural disorders and non-compliant behaviour. He also specialises in the treatment of post-traumatic stress disorder (PTSD). When Stuart is not in the office, he is busy writing a series on evidenced-based parenting or spending time with his wife and children.

# THE ADHD HAND BOOK

*Stuart Passmore*

BSc (Psych.), Honours (Psych.), Cert. Psych. Counsel.

EXISLE
PUBLISHING

First published 2014

Exisle Publishing Pty Ltd
'Moonrising', Narone Creek Road, Wollombi, NSW 2325, Australia
P.O. Box 60–490, Titirangi, Auckland 0642, New Zealand
www.exislepublishing.com

A CiP record for this book is available from the National Library of Australia

ISBN 978 1 921966 11 8

Design and typesetting by Tracey Gibbs
Illustrations by Rebecca Mills
Cover images courtesy of iStock.com © Perkmeup Imagery, © Jaroslaw Wojcik, © gbh007; background pattern adapted from vectorstock.com © SelenaMay
Typeset in Miller Text 10/16 and DIN
Printed in Shenzhen, China, by Ink Asia

This book uses paper sourced under ISO 14001 guidelines from well-managed forests and other controlled sources.

10 9 8 7 6 5 4 3 2 1

**Disclaimer**
This book is a general guide only and should never be a substitute for the skill, knowledge and experience of a qualified medical professional dealing with the facts, circumstances and symptoms of a particular case. The information presented in this book is based on the research, training and professional experience of the author, and is true and complete to the best of their knowledge. However, this book is intended only as an informative guide; it is not intended to replace or countermand the advice given by the reader's personal medical team. Because each person and situation is unique, the author and the publisher urge the reader to check with a qualified healthcare professional before using any procedure where there is a question as to its appropriateness. The author, publisher and their distributors are not responsible for any adverse effects or consequences resulting from the use of the information in this book. It is the responsibility of the reader to consult a qualified healthcare professional regarding their personal care. This book contains references to products that may not be available everywhere. The intent of the information provided is to be helpful; however, there is no guarantee of results associated with the information provided. Use of brand names is for educational purposes only and does not imply endorsement.

*Thank you to my wife and children for the blessing that you are.*

# Contents

# CHAPTER 1

# Defining attention deficit hyperactivity disorder (ADHD)

A child receiving a diagnosis of attention deficit hyperactivity disorder (ADHD) is often very difficult for the parents and it can be even harder to come to terms with. After what seems to be a lengthy assessment process, that final diagnosis can be met with hurt, anger, disappointment and even self-blame. In my experience, parents often feel scared, vulnerable and very confused and have lots of questions that need to be answered about the assessment process and the results. 'What is ADHD, how did it start, is it something we did or didn't do, can it be fixed, how is it fixed, does our child have to take medication, and will he have to take medication for the rest of his life?' are just some of the most common questions asked by parents.

Attention deficit hyperactivity disorder is defined as a neurodevelopmental disorder that begins to show signs and symptoms in young children. According to the *Diagnostic and Statistical Manual of Mental Disorders* (or the DSM), which provides the standard criteria for the classification of mental disorders for mental health professionals, symptoms of ADHD can be visible in the kindergarten-aged child. Often there will be certain behaviours that alert the kindergarten teacher, schoolteacher or the parents that something about the child's behaviour is not quite right, or as some people say, 'not quite normal'. ADHD has three core symptoms — inattention, hyperactivity and impulsivity — and these are revealed by a number of different behaviours the child constantly engages in. The DSM also categorises ADHD into three types based on these core symptoms:

1. **ADHD, Combined Type:** both inattention and hyperactivity–impulsivity.
2. **ADHD, Predominantly Inattentive Type:** inattention, but not enough (at least six out of nine) hyperactivity–impulsivity symptoms.
3. **ADHD, Predominantly Hyperactive–Impulsive Type:** hyperactivity–impulsivity, but not enough (at least six out of nine) inattention symptoms.

CASE STUDY

A ten-year-old boy was referred to my clinic by his school as his teacher was quite concerned with his behaviour and she believed he had ADHD. The first time I met the boy I invited him to sit down and have a chat with me. He could only sit in the chair for maybe a couple of minutes at a time (and that was stretching it!). He constantly got out of his chair to investigate my bookshelf; he kept on pulling out a number of books at a time to read the title, but without completely reading one title he would grab for another book. He investigated the window blinds and pulled them up and down and up and down, then while he was still pulling the window blinds up and down he saw someone had left their pushbike outside and he was more than happy to go and ride it for them. He played with the tissue box on the desk, the phone, the pens, and the permanent whiteboard markers (which he offered to use to draw me a picture on the office wall). When he did sit down he was fidgety, he wildly swung his legs back and forth, and he constantly changed topics. When I asked him a question, he would try to answer it, but then get sidetracked by something else in the office he hadn't investigated yet and so he never quite finished answering the question. But he was never short of a word or a topic to talk about. And all this happened in the first 10 minutes of meeting him.

# The three core symptoms of ADHD

## INATTENTION

As you read through this book you will discover that ADHD is not a simple disorder but a complex one that has quite a few problems associated with it. Inattention is one of the core symptoms of ADHD and is evident in a number of different places, such as at school and at home. But ADHD is not the same as a child being distracted or daydreaming for a few minutes. Children struggling with ADHD fail to pay close attention to details and tend to make 'silly' or careless mistakes with their schoolwork and chores at home. Their schoolwork usually has pretty messy handwriting and the work often appears as though the child really hasn't put much effort into completing it. This is because the child has such enormous difficulties maintaining their attention for more than a few minutes in almost any environment or activity, including playtime. This obviously makes it extremely difficult to maintain attention long enough to complete almost any task to a satisfactory level. I have often heard parents say 'he just doesn't listen' or 'he's always in another world', 'he's just lazy' or 'he doesn't care about his schoolwork'. This is mostly because of the difficulty in keeping their attention or sustaining attention for any length of time.

One of the biggest problems for children with ADHD trying to do their schoolwork is their inability to complete one task before they move onto the next. You can begin to understand why children (and adults) might be labelled as 'naughty' and 'lazy' because they often don't follow through with requests or instructions from their parents, teachers or bosses. Also, they consistently fail to complete most tasks such as homework to a satisfactory level. Children with ADHD will consistently put off their chores and their homework because of how easily they are distracted by almost anything. It seems that almost any noise or event that most people ignore with ease are major distractions for the child with ADHD. Then there's the forgetfulness. Children and adults with ADHD tend to be very forgetful with virtually all of their responsibilities, such as taking their homework to school or forgetting to take their lunch to work or missing important appointments. And imagine how inattention might interfere with social or personal relationships. For instance, inattention could be expressed by constant changes in conversation topics, or not listening to the person speaking to you, not paying attention to the conversation, not waiting for your turn to talk, and failing to follow the rules during game play. Imagine the difficulties an adult with ADHD would experience in the workforce trying to complete one task at a time. In fact, failing to complete tasks due to inattention is one of the behaviours that is considered when making a diagnosis.

Children (and adults) with ADHD experience quite a lot of difficulty organising tasks and activities and if the task requires a lot of attention, the child typically responds as though that task or activity is unpleasant, and they try to avoid it. The child's desk at school is constantly in a state of chaos with their pens, paper and books scattered everywhere, or lost somewhere or even damaged. It begins to make sense that these children try to avoid activities, such as homework, that require sustained concentration. You may even begin to understand why these children develop an intense dislike for certain activities and try to avoid them. Again, when it comes to diagnosing ADHD, avoidance is taken into account, but with ADHD the avoidance must be *directly related* to the child's inability to pay attention.

## HYPERACTIVITY

The hyperactive symptoms of ADHD are generally pretty obvious to the onlooker as the child constantly fidgets and squirms in their seat. It's as if they just can't sit still. They twist and itch and shrug their shoulders, get up and down from their chair, or appear to have enough energy to run a marathon or climb Mt Everest and always at the most inappropriate moment. Actually, this is one of the most defining characteristics of the hyperactive symptoms. The child with ADHD tends to talk a million miles an hour and obviously finds it very difficult to sit quietly and play. The thing to remember here, though, is that the hyperactivity may differ with age and the child's developmental level. As such, the DSM warns that an ADHD diagnosis in young children should be made cautiously. The young child, such as the toddler or kindergarten-aged child, with

ADHD displays behaviours that are very, very different to children the same age. For instance, one father described his hyperactive son as 'he's like a steam train, he just keeps on going and going. He's into everything. You pull him away from one thing and he's straight into something else'. Other parents have described feeling awkward when their young one jumps up and down on a friend's furniture or constantly runs through their house. At bedtime or at kindergarten these little ones aren't very good at sitting still long enough to listen to a story and they don't do very well participating in quiet activities.

Some parents reading this book might think this description is almost describing their school-aged child. Well, that's because the school-aged child can display similar behaviours. School-aged children might experience some difficulty remaining in their seat, as they do tend to get up and down from their chair or they might squirm about in their seat. But the behaviours aren't nearly as frequent or with the same intensity as with the child with ADHD.

## IMPULSIVITY

The impulsiveness of ADHD makes it look as if the child is impatient, or that they just can't wait their turn to respond to a question. Their answers seem to burst out even before you have finished asking the question and as they can't seem to wait for their turn so they just keep on interrupting people. They talk before being invited to, they certainly don't seem to be listening to anything you or anybody else says, and they tend to try to talk with you when the moment is untimely. In addition, they seem to just grab from others whatever they like, get into things they are not allowed to touch, and as one father stated, 'he constantly makes a nuisance of himself'. Unfortunately, because of this aspect of ADHD, childhood (and even adult) accidents seem to be fairly common. Things are knocked over and broken or the child may even grab a hot pot on the stove and get burned. The problem of the child getting hurt from being involved in dangerous activities is quite real. To make matters worse, such children rarely if at all consider there could be serious consequences for their actions. It can get to a point where the impulsivity can cause problems with friends and family and in some cases even in sporting clubs because little Johnny won't keep quiet long enough for the coach to provide his instruction without being constantly interrupted. In fact, impaired peer relationships or peer rejection, neglect and poor friendship stability is common in children with ADHD. Generally, this is because the child with ADHD has obvious problems in their abilities to engage in positive social interactions and tends to be more aggressive than children of the same age. The bottom line is that children with ADHD tend to be more disliked by other children. The impulsivity interferes with school-based learning with a common complaint from teachers being 'he just doesn't stop talking, he constantly interrupts me, and he's a constant distraction to all the other kids in the classroom'.

Unfortunately, peer relationships are not the only relationships that experience a great deal of pressure. For children and adolescents with ADHD, family conflict is fairly common. Such family conflict can increase, particularly as the teenager consistently fails to accept responsibility for their negative behaviours or for not finishing things like their chores. This is because children and adolescents with ADHD are far less likely to comply with requests, they are more pessimistic, and less able to sustain compliance than children and adolescents without ADHD. It also seems that parents cannot trust their child to be at home on their own for fear the child or adolescent will not obey their rules. It is fairly well known that interactions between children with ADHD and their family members can be very negative. So it's not surprising that parents of children with ADHD report significantly greater problems in the family, which also produces stress in their parenting efforts compared to parents of children without ADHD.

It seems one of the most frustrating and embarrassing aspects of ADHD is that the attention deficits along with the hyperactive behaviours are not limited to just the home. It can be seen in multiple places such as school, the grandparents' place, a friend's place and just about anywhere else you can think of. However, the DSM states that it is unusual for a child or adolescent to exhibit the same level of problems with the same intensity across all settings or even within the same settings all the time. The symptoms typically get worse when the child has to maintain sustained concentration or is in situations that aren't terribly appealing or don't offer something unique. So sitting in the same classroom day after day, listening to the same teacher hour after hour teaching the same thing would hardly be described as appealing or stimulating for the child with ADHD, nor would sitting quietly in the nursing home visiting Grandma. This would be equally true of completing homework or pretty much any chore that doesn't offer unique changes.

There are a number of other observed behavioural difficulties associated with ADHD that also depend on the child's age and developmental stage. For example, your child may seemingly become frustrated very quickly and over 'little things'. We call this low frustration tolerance. There may be temper tantrums, or explosive behaviour, wanting to be the boss at home or with friends, or during playtime. Some parents have reported that their child seems to be totally inflexible and frequently demands their needs or their desires are met. The parents are also aware that their child seems to feel down or sad and has very low self-esteem. Some parents have suggested they feel their child's own sense of worth is taking a pounding. Possibly one of the more difficult aspects of this disorder is the hurt and frustration these children feel at being rejected by their peers.

Children with ADHD usually struggle academically and really don't place too much value in education. Many parents have described the nightmarish interactions that often occur when it comes to getting their child to actually sit down and do some homework and then trying to deal with the conflict that follows. Then there is facing the frustrated teacher who again informs you that your child has not submitted any homework for the past month and that if this keeps up your child will have to repeat the year. It stands to reason that children with ADHD may leave school early and because of their poorer academic achievements they may have significantly reduced employment opportunities.

If you and others around you don't know what is going on with your child, you can begin to believe you have a child who is just being lazy or naughty, who rejects responsibility at every turn and who is simply being rebellious. Consequently, family relationships and particularly the parent–child relationship are often strained. You battle each night to get your child to do any homework and even then it is rushed and messy and you know the teacher will complain about it and his poor behaviour in class — again! And one thing that tends to bother you the most is that your child really doesn't seem to have many friends, if any at all, and is rarely invited to birthday parties or only has a few of his classmates turn up to his. Eventually the schoolteacher tells you to get your child tested for ADHD and it really knocks you when after all the assessments are complete you are told he has ADHD. Your mind shoots back to all those media reports that show 'horrible' kids on a rampage, which question the use of medication and even suggest that ADHD is only a modern phenomenon. Understandably you begin to wonder if ADHD is real and whether or not it is a modern-day phenomenon.

# CHAPTER 2

## The history of ADHD

How long has ADHD been around? Is it a new phenomenon or has it been a problem in societies for some time? With the growing interest by the media and its frequent coverage of ADHD, it seems as though it might be a fairly 'new' disorder. But is that really the case? Some researchers and authors have suggested that the professional literature has a number of case reports that indicate ADHD was recognised as early as the 19th century. Other authors have reported that the non-professional field has described ADHD as a modern disorder that has particularly resulted from varied influences at the end of the 20th century. However, a simple search of the scientific or psychiatric literature from the 19th century yields a great number of case reports indicating the existence of this syndrome at that time.

Historically, in the 1930s and 1940s, some of the behaviours currently associated with ADHD, such as restlessness and inattentiveness, were then referred to as minimal brain dysfunction (MBD) that was due to brain damage as a result of an injury to the frontal lobe. However, as researchers started focusing more and more on understanding ADHD, such theories began to lose ground and were eventually recognised as inaccurate as the research results failed to provide support for MBD. At times it seems that many people questioned the very existence of attention deficit hyperactivity disorder (ADHD), rather implying that it is only a modern condition. Other arguments seem to be fuelled by media reports of the escalating rates with which ADHD is diagnosed across the world, with a tendency to either suggest or infer it is little more than a conspiracy between doctors and drug companies to make millions of dollars from prescribing drugs to children. Still questions remain, however, over the 'realness' of ADHD and whether or not it is a legitimate diagnosable disorder, and if it is real, is it just a modern phenomenon, and if it isn't, then how long has it been around for?

The name 'attention deficit hyperactivity disorder' and the abbreviated term ADHD are, indeed, modern. In fact, some authors have suggested that the term 'attention deficit hyperactivity disorder' was first used in the revised third edition of the *Diagnostic and Statistical Manual of Mental Disorders* published by the American Psychiatric Association in 1987. However, we need to be careful not to get hung up on the use of terms, as in this instance the term itself is irrelevant as it has little bearing on the question of whether or not the condition is real, or how long the condition has been around. This is simply because the symptoms of ADHD have been noted and recorded for much longer than most people are aware of. In fact, as you read this chapter you will see that the symptoms associated with ADHD have been observed for more than two centuries. Simply stated, the modern condition referred to as attention deficit hyperactivity disorder has its origins dating as far back as the 18th century, yet was described under different names (for example, simple hyperexcitability, minimal brain dysfunction, hyperkinetic disorder, attention deficit disorder).

There is evidence that ADHD symptoms in children were first noticed in the 1800s and were, in fact, documented by Dr Heinrich Hoffmann in his well-known poem, *The Story of Fidgety Philip*. There does, however, appear to be some differences of opinion as to exactly when Dr Hoffmann wrote the poem. Some have suggested the poem was written in 1863, while others have proposed 1844 and still others submit it was written in 1848. While it appears there is little consensus on the exact date the poem was written, there is agreement it was written in the middle of the 1800s and has astounding similarities to 'modern' ADHD symptoms in children. Have a read and see what you think.

## The Story of Fidgety Philip by Heinrich Hoffmann

'Let me see if Philip can
Be a little gentleman;
Let me see if he is able
To sit still for once at table':
Thus Papa bade Phil behave
And Mamma looked very grave.
But fidgety Phil,
He won't sit still;
He wriggles,
And giggles,
And then, I declare,
Swings backwards and forwards,
And tilts up his chair,
Just like any rocking horse —
'Philip! I am getting cross!'

See the naughty, restless child
Growing still more rude and wild,
Till his chair falls over quite.
Philip screams with all his might,
Catches at the cloth, but then
That makes matters worse again.
Down upon the ground they fall
Glasses, plates, knives, forks, and all.
How Mamma did fret and frown,
When she saw them tumbling down!
And Papa made such a face!
Philip is in sad disgrace.

Where is Philip, where is he?
Fairly covered up you see!
Cloth and all are lying on him;
He has pulled down all upon him.

*What a terrible to-do!*
*Dishes, glasses, snapt in two!*
*Here a knife, and there a fork!*
*Philip, this is cruel work.*
*Table all so bare, and ah!*
*Poor Papa, and poor Mamma*
*Look quite cross, and wonder how*
*They shall have their dinner now.*

While it has been argued that Hoffmann's poem refers to a child with ADHD, there are others who have also written on the subject. What is considered to be one of the earliest written accounts of ADHD dates back to 1798 in the writings of physician, Dr Alexander Crichton. In his book, *Mental Restlessness*, Dr Crichton is argued to have been the first to note and document ADHD symptoms of the inattentive subtype in children. Crichton defined the condition as 'the incapacity of attending with a necessary constancy to any one object' or, to put it another way, these children appeared to have a heightened distractibility and an inability to maintain attention for any longer than a minute or two. Crichton's focus turned to the age of the individual, as he suggested that children may well have been born with the condition. Interestingly, he also noticed these children were likely to encounter problems at school:

> *When born with a person it becomes evident at a very early period of life, and has a very bad effect, inasmuch as it renders him incapable of attending with constancy to any one object of education. But it seldom is in so great a degree as totally to impede all instruction; and what is very fortunate, it is generally diminished with age.*

For Crichton this was not just a theory, he was able to provide examples of just how debilitating this condition can be:

> *Every impression seems to agitate the person, and gives him or her an unnatural degree of mental restlessness. People walking*

*up and down the room, a slight noise in the same, the moving [of] a table, the shutting [of] a door suddenly, a slight excess of heat or cold, too much light, or too little light, all destroy constant attention in such patients, inasmuch as it is easily excited by every expression. The barking of dogs, an ill-tuned organ, or the scolding of women, are sufficient to distract patients of this description to such a degree, as almost approaches to the nature of delirium.*

John Haslam in his book, *Observations on Madness and Melancholy*, described the case of a young boy who, from the age of two, was:

*Mischievous and uncontrollable ... a creature of volition and a terror of the family ... he had limited attention span, being only attracted by 'fits and starts'. He had been several times to school and was the hopeless pupil of many masters, distinguished for their patience and rigid discipline.*

Now while there were potentially a number of other behaviours that would have an experienced clinician considering a comorbid diagnosis (discussed later in Chapter 6) with ADHD, it seems fairly clear this boy demonstrated ADHD symptoms. In 1870, the British Parliament passed the *Education Act* that made it compulsory for children to attend school. It has been suggested that it was this compulsory school attendance that brought to light the extent to which ADHD symptoms of inattention and hyperactivity were prevalent among children rather than it being little more than extremes of normal childhood behaviour. Perhaps as a consequence of the prevalence rate of ADHD symptoms being observed and being reported in schools, the medical profession gradually became more and more involved.

While there are a number of references to ADHD symptoms recorded throughout history, the psychiatric literature tends to credit the paediatrician George Still as the first person to formally account for the hyperactive symptoms of ADHD in children. In 1902, Still presented a series of papers to the Royal College of Physicians in

London about certain behaviours of children he had observed. During his presentation, Still provided his audience with examples from as many as 43 different children he had observed displaying what he referred to as insufficient 'moral control'. According to Still, the children were exhibiting behaviours that included restlessness, problems with sustained attention, and difficulties with self-regulation:

> *Another boy, aged six years, with marked moral defect was unable to keep his attention even to a game for more than a very short time, and as might be expected, the failure of attention was very noticeable at school, with the result that in some cases the child was backward in school attainments, although in manner and ordinary conversation he appeared as bright and intelligent as any child could be.*

Still also noted the children could be aggressive, defiant, and were resistant to discipline. They were described as having poor impulse control, and did not learn from the consequences of their behaviour. These behaviours or deficits in moral control were typically first displayed in the early school years and were more likely to be evident in boys with far greater frequency than in girls. The descriptions are remarkably close to what we refer to today as attention deficit hyperactivity disorder.

In 1913, Robert Stein recorded his theory of ADHD as being 'children saturated with insanity while still in the womb' with 'badly built minds' and a 'kind of partial moral dementia'. Stein noted these children seemed to present with persistent disruptive behaviour problems that again were evident during the early school years. Interestingly, Stein noted that these children not only struggled academically but also had difficulty making and maintaining social relationships. Another author suggested that the children Stein referred to would most likely fulfil the criteria for a diagnosis of ADHD today. He further suggested that Stein's reference to 'badly built minds' could well compare to the current neurobiological findings that are implicated in the disorder.

Medical references of ADHD were published in the British journal, *The Lancet* in 1902 and 1904, and in the *Journal of the American*

*Medical Association* in 1921. According to one author, the behaviours of inattentiveness, distractibility, overactivity and impulsiveness were considered to be a result of head injuries that occurred due to a complication of a viral infection known as encephalitis. Encephalitis is the swelling of a person's brain, which has two common causes: either an infection invading the brain or the immune system mistakenly attacking the brain. Encephalitis was said to have occurred in 1918 because of an influenza epidemic following World War I. Following the encephalitis epidemic, the distractibility and overactivity of children was later described as 'organic drivenness' and was said to be the result of damage to the child's brainstem. Since then the disorder we now know as ADHD went under a number of different names in the medical profession over the course of history, beginning in 1922 with the term 'postencephalitic behaviour disorder', which was later changed in 1947 to the 'brain-injured child'. In 1963 it was changed again and replaced with the term 'perceptually handicapped child', and in 1966 was changed again to 'minimal brain injury'.

In 1968 when the American Psychiatric Association released the second edition of the *Diagnostic and Statistical Manual for Mental Disorders* (DSM-II), the focus on ADHD had changed and attention was directed toward the hyperactive symptoms. The DSM-II provided a categorisation of the symptoms of overactivity, restlessness and inattention and named the condition the hyperkinetic reaction of children. However, there remained continued debate about the obvious differences in the expression of symptoms in some children. For instance, it was well documented that some children with this condition were hyperactive and impulsive, while other children were simply inattentive and were nothing like their hyperactive and impulsive peers. In 1980, the American Psychiatric Association published the third edition of the DSM (DSM-III), with an attempt to address these two apparent incompatible states of the same condition. The term 'hyperkinetic reaction of childhood' was replaced with a new category called 'attention deficit disorder' (ADD). This new category recognised the two different types of the condition (now called a disorder) by classifying the two distinct types as ADD with hyperactivity and ADD without hyperactivity. However, in 1987, when the DSM was revised again (DSM-III-R), the lack of research support for the two types found the disorder being regarded as a single categorical disorder, and it was not until the fourth edition of the DSM that the disorder was classified as attention-deficit/hyperactivity disorder.

As you can see, ADHD or, more appropriately, ADHD symptoms have a long history, one that extends well beyond the current controversies to a time when little was gained by concocting stories or making up disorders of childhood for financial gain by global drug companies. It is also interesting to note that professionals of different fields — from educators to philosophers to the medical field, including doctors, psychiatrists and paediatricians — have all attempted to understand the condition by developing and testing theories as to the underlying causes of children *without moral control* from as early as the 1700s. If ADHD has been with us for potentially hundreds of years, how come there seems to be so much controversy today surrounding whether it is a real disorder or not? Well, part of the problem could be the way it is diagnosed, who does the diagnosis, and the myths that we encounter almost on a daily basis.

# CHAPTER 3

## The myths and facts of ADHD

It is completely understandable that members of the public are totally confused about ADHD or even doubt the existence of ADHD as a real behavioural disorder. There appears to be a number of solid arguments against the existence of ADHD, including the contention it is simply a term used to describe normal childhood behaviour that has now been labelled as deviant and non-conformative. Others maintain that ADHD is nothing more than an elaborate scheme devised by powerful drug companies to make bigger profits through the sale of their medications. Certainly, in recent times, there has been an occasion where a high-profile professional was found to have been accepting money from drug companies and the implication has been one of bribery and deception — for the critics such a revelation is a goldmine. For them this one individual is the personification of their argument that doctors and paediatricians are on the drug companies' payroll and accept all sorts of benefits just to prescribe their medications. It is true that corruption has the potential to develop where there is big money involved. However, such an argument says nothing of the existence of the disorder itself but really speaks of the individual accepting such gratuities. To argue that a professional taking a bribe is the evidence needed to disprove the existence of ADHD is akin to suggesting that evolution is an untruth and a worldwide conspiracy because there is a lack of evidence of any animals found in archaeological digs in the transformative stage (for example, ape to man, whale to cow).

However, there are people with genuine concerns that simply cannot be ignored who call into question the validity of ADHD as a real disorder and the way in which it is diagnosed. For instance, one critic has argued:

*Behaviours that were once considered normal range are now currently defined as pathological by those with a vested interest in promoting the widespread use of psychotropic drugs in child and adolescent populations. (Stolzer, 2007)*

This critic began her argument with a very brief historical account of ADHD in America. Apparently ADHD did not exist at all in America in the 1950s, but by 1970 some 2000 children had been diagnosed as hyperactive and by 2006, 8 to 10 million American children had received a diagnosis of ADHD. The critic further argued against ADHD by stating:

*What was once an unheard of 'psychiatric disorder' is now commonplace in America. Millions of American children are diagnosed with a mythical disease, and the vast majority of these children are prescribed dangerous and addictive drugs in order to control normal-range, historically documented child behaviours. (Stolzer, 2007)*

This critic suggested that American children, particularly boys, were disproportionately diagnosed with ADHD as compared to the rest of the world and asked the question: 'Why has this disease not been recorded across time [or] across cultures?' It would appear this critic is not a student of history or such a question would not have been raised. You may recall from the previous chapter that ADHD has been a recognised disorder for hundreds of years with documented symptoms — a fact this critic appeared to neglect in her historical accounts. Furthermore, ADHD is, in fact, recognised and diagnosed across the world and in many, many cultures, not just in Western societies.

With the current advances in neuro-imaging, scientists today are able to explore deep regions of the brain and their functions that were completely unknown in the 1950s, let alone some 200 years ago. The neurology of ADHD is covered in depth in this book. When you read Chapter 4 you will begin to understand why professionals all over the world refer to ADHD as a neurological disorder. In fact, the growing evidence from the accumulating research from around the globe is so overwhelming that hundreds of professionals signed a consensus statement outlining their concern over the few individuals who continue to cast doubt on the existence of ADHD as a real disorder. The International Consensus Statement on ADHD states:

> *We cannot overemphasise the point that, as a matter of science, the notion that ADHD does not exist is simply wrong. All major medical associations and government health agencies recognize ADHD as a genuine disorder because the scientific evidence indicating it is so overwhelming.*
>
> *... The central psychological deficits in those with ADHD have now been linked through numerous studies using various scientific methods to several specific brain regions (the frontal lobe, its connections to the basal ganglia, and their relationship to the central aspects of the cerebellum). Most neurological studies find that as a group those with ADHD have less brain electrical activity and show less reactivity to stimulation in one or more of these regions. And neuro-imaging studies of groups of those with ADHD also demonstrate relatively smaller areas of brain matter and less metabolic activity of this brain matter than is the case in control groups [children without ADHD] used in these studies.*
>
> *... Occasional coverage of the disorder casts the story in the form of a sporting event with evenly matched competitors. The views of a handful of nonexpert doctors [or those that have not received medical or psychiatric training] that ADHD does not exist are contrasted against mainstream scientific views that it does, as if both views had equal merit. Such attempts at balance give the public the impression that there is substantial scientific disagreement over whether ADHD is a real medical condition. In fact, there is no such disagreement — at least no more so than there is over whether smoking causes cancer, for example, or whether a virus causes HIV/AIDS. (Barkley, 2002).*

The author picks up on an important point here when he notes that it appears media coverage of ADHD pits the non-believing professional against the scientific world to infer or even suggest that perhaps the medical and psychiatric world really aren't too sure whether ADHD exists or not. In fact, as the author states, this could not be further from the truth. But it is interesting to note how sometimes certain professionals are not even consulted when a story about ADHD is going to air. For instance, a current affairs program in Australia recently aired the story of a woman who was reported to have three children with ADHD. They did the typical camera shots of the children at their worst and then approached a 'professional' for his opinion. Here's what he said:

> Worldwide the numbers of children diagnosed each year with ADHD is mysteriously growing ... [Naturopath and osteopath says there's help beyond medication. He believes a clean diet can turn little lives around. The camera turns to the naturopath/ osteopath.] She can start by taking the sugars away and the gluten products away. She'll see a change in the children, I'll guarantee it.

The author of the International Consensus Statement on ADHD was very much aware of such media reports when he further stated:

> To publish stories that ADHD is a fictitious disorder or merely a conflict between today's Huckleberry Finns and their caregivers is tantamount to declaring the Earth flat, the laws of gravity debatable, and the periodic table in chemistry a fraud. ADHD should be depicted in the media as realistically and accurately as it is depicted in science — as a valid disorder having varied and substantial adverse impact on those who may suffer from it through no fault of their own or their parents and teachers.

It would be fair to say the author of this consensus takes ADHD very seriously, so much so he approached leading professionals all over the world to sign it. To list the number of people who included their name would take some time, as there are 86 signatories on the consensus. The range of such individuals includes professors of clinical psychiatry, psychology, neurology, paediatric psychopharmacology, physiology, social behaviour and clinical paediatrics. These professors and associate professors are positioned in departments of psychiatry, neurology, paediatrics, cognitive neuroscience, clinical neuropsychology, the clinical training of psychologists, child and adolescent psychiatry, child behaviour programs, colleges of physicians and surgeons, substance abuse research departments, children's national medical centres and preventative and social medicines just to name a few. And they come from the United States, United Kingdom, Israel, Sweden, Canada, England, Australia, New Zealand, Puerto Rico, the Netherlands and Norway. If ADHD really is a myth, it is now a worldwide conspiracy. It really is hard to imagine that such an impressive list of professionals from all different departments of mental and physical health from all over the world would be caught up in such a conspiracy. Let's take a look at some of the most common myths concerning the causes of ADHD.

## Myth 1: ADHD is only a Western phenomenon

It is a fact that ADHD is a disorder causing a lot of concern in Western societies, but is it limited to Western cultures only or do other countries have the same or similar rates of ADHD? It appears some proponents of this myth like to argue that the United States, for instance, has the greatest number of children diagnosed with ADHD as compared to the rest of the world and that this number is growing every year. On the surface this is one of the better arguments, as it sounds quite convincing. After all, when we watch media reports covering the prevalence of ADHD and the ever-growing rate, we never seem to hear about any culture other than our own or some other Western country. Nevertheless, it is well documented that ADHD is not just an American problem; in fact it doesn't even appear to be restricted to just Western countries either.

However, the question of whether or not ADHD is a Western phenomenon has been raised and has prompted numerous investigations to answer this question. As a result of this research, there have been a number of factors identified that would explain the apparent differences in ADHD rates across the different cultures. A number of investigators set out to test whether or not ADHD was truly an American epidemic and whether or not ADHD was prevalent in both Western and non-Western countries across the world. They also wanted to know whether the prevalence rates of ADHD in US children were similar to children in other countries around the world. Some of the key questions they set out to answer were:

- Is ADHD common to children worldwide?
- Is ADHD common to a large number of races and societies?
- Are the apparent differences in prevalence rates between countries due to confusion regarding its diagnosis?

This last question is really quite important as differences in prevalence rates across countries may partly lie in the fact that different cultures have different diagnostic criteria and/or different names that all appear to be essentially describing the common symptoms of ADHD. It seems there are cross-cultural differences in the way in which ADHD is assessed, as well as the name by which it is referred to.

The investigators reminded us of the history of ADHD and the different names it has been known under (for example, minimal brain dysfunction and organic brain dysfunction). Other terms such as hyperkinetic disorder (HKD) and 'deficits in attention, motor control and perception' (DAMP) are still used today. For instance, the United Kingdom and a number of other European countries use the term HKD, while Scandinavia refers to ADHD as DAMP. Equally, while some countries use the *Diagnostic and Statistical Manual of Mental Disorders* (DSM), other countries use the *International Classification of Diseases* (ICD). While there are some minor differences in the diagnostic criteria between the two manuals, it is recognised they are describing the same disorder.

The investigators reviewed 50 studies of ADHD that only used the criteria as set out in the DSM-IV to diagnose the disorder. Of the 50 studies, only twenty were conducted in the United States, while the remaining 30 were conducted in other countries. The results of these studies revealed that the prevalence of ADHD in other countries was the same as or similar to that in the United States. A further nine studies were excluded from the review as they had been conducted in countries that included Hong Kong, Germany, France, India, the USA, the UK, Sweden, Canada, and China because they used a slightly different criteria set from the International Classification of Diseases version 10 (ICD-10) in their diagnostic procedure. The ICD is still measuring ADHD, just under a different name.

Other investigators have also suggested that the prevalence rate for ADHD is the same in many other countries as it is in the United States; that the apparent disparity in rates between various countries has been primarily attributed to the way in which ADHD is diagnosed across the globe (DSM versus ICD). It has also been found that studies on ADHD conducted outside the United States were almost predictably similar with those conducted within the United States. Furthermore, it has been found that the patterns of adaptive impairments, neuropsychological deficits, ADHD prevalence within family members, genetic influence, and functional and molecular imaging findings, along with response to medication, were all strikingly similar to the US. It has also been pointed out that there is a lack of studies coming out of developing countries, which suggested that ADHD might in fact have higher rates in certain countries due to some of the severe social risk factors found in those countries.

One possible example of this was provided by some other researchers who compared the prevalence rates of ADHD symptoms in a sample of 600 Ukrainian children between the ages of ten and twelve years to 443 North American children of the same age. The researchers found that the ADHD prevalence rate for the Ukrainian children was 19.8 per cent compared to 9.7 per cent for the US children. The Ukrainian children were at the time living within 30 kilometres of the Chernobyl nuclear power plant. They had been evacuated to Kiev where they stayed for ten years after their evacuation. The researchers suggested that they were unaware as to why the prevalence of ADHD for this group of children was so high. It was noted that one possible explanation for such high rates of ADHD might be due to the environmental adversity of the Chernobyl disaster under which the children were living and the fact that they had also been evacuated from their homes and community. However, the researchers suggested that no firm conclusions could be drawn about this until it had been properly researched.

## Myth 2: Drug companies made up the term ADHD just so they could increase their profits

There are a number of variations on this myth but they all seem to come back to a central point of drug companies trying to increase their profits. One such variation implicates doctors (and therefore paediatricians and child psychiatrists) as being part of a worldwide conspiracy to only prescribe medications from certain pharmaceutical companies because they get 'kick-backs' from that company. Unfortunately there have been isolated cases where a trusted individual has sold out ethically, professionally and morally in favour of the almighty dollar. But when you take into account the prevalence rates of ADHD across the world there are tens, if not hundreds of thousands of doctors, paediatricians and child psychiatrists who are being accused of accepting bribes. This is just a ridiculous argument. Another variation of this myth is that there is really no effective treatment that works for ADHD. Evidence from around the world suggests that medication is the frontline therapy or first choice of therapy for ADHD. However, there are also a number of effective non-medicinal therapies available. Such therapies include behavioural interventions, school classroom interventions, cognitive behavioural therapy, and parent management training to name just a few. Chapter 8 outlines all the different alternative therapies.

## Myth 3: The medications they use for ADHD are dangerous

Again this issue is covered in a lot of detail in Chapter 8. However, before leaving this myth there is just one point that is very important to remember. It is true that some children may experience side effects while taking ADHD medication, but it is equally true that people react differently to different drugs. Some people even have a reaction to or experience side effects from non-prescription medications such as paracetamol. There are a lot of factors a psychiatrist or paediatrician must take into account before placing a child on medication for ADHD. In the hands of a competent practitioner the child will be monitored carefully and, if required, the dose can or will be adjusted or the medication itself will be changed. For more information see Chapter 7, which covers ADHD medications.

## Myth 4: Giving stimulant medication to children puts the child at risk of becoming a drug user or an addict later in life

Yes, it is true that medication for ADHD is a controlled substance and in most countries is restricted and requires a prescription to allow the patient access to the medication. However, according to the professional research that has studied this issue, as it currently stands there is no evidence to suggest there is a relationship between children being prescribed medication for ADHD and later substance use and/or abuse. While stimulant medication can have abuse potential, stimulants are not addictive if they are used as directed by your paediatrician. This means that children and adults can stop taking the medication with little difficulty if taken as prescribed. Stimulants can become addictive if taken for the wrong reason, such as consuming excessive amounts to get a high because of the mood-elevating effects or to stay awake. Using stimulants for these purposes increases the risk of addiction. It is for these reasons that stimulant medication is *not* recommended for individuals who have a history of drug abuse.

The issue at hand is the possible confusion between ADHD and substance abuse and the comorbid conditions commonly found in people with ADHD. Just to be clear: there has been no causal relationship found between ADHD and later substance use or abuse. Investigations have found that, according to the majority of studies, delinquent behaviour is associated with substance use and abuse. There have been some studies that have found where ADHD is comorbid with conduct disorder there is a greater risk of substance abuse. The end result of this research suggested that individuals with both ADHD and conduct disorder were at higher risk of using tobacco products, alcohol, marijuana and 'other street drugs'. This research also found that individuals with ADHD and conduct disorder were more at risk of developing a dependence on marijuana and other hard drugs.

Researchers have also examined the results of longitudinal studies for substance abuse potential. Longitudinal studies typically require a research project that has been designed to involve and follow a group of participants over a number of years. The researchers will continue to follow the participants and collect all relevant data to their research design at certain time intervals such as when the child turns eight, ten and twelve years of age and so on. Such research designs are a vital component in the field of mental health as the results can inform us of such benefits as:

- The most successful forms of treatment.
- Whether or not the symptoms of a disorder change over time.
- How a disorder might affect an individual's personal, social and professional life.
- Whether or not the disorder might predispose an individual to more adverse life conditions compared to people without the disorder.

Such longitudinal studies follow groups of children who have been diagnosed with ADHD in childhood through to adulthood in an attempt to determine how the disorder might affect them as adults. According to the investigators, the results of such studies initially indicated a very poor outcome as there had been significant increases in substance abuse, trouble with the law, and the individuals experienced difficult relationships and problems with employment. However, when the results were examined a little more closely it was found that generally the groups could be divided in two: those with ADHD only and those with ADHD plus conduct disorder. It was found the individuals with ADHD plus conduct disorder had the poor outcomes, with significant increases in substance abuse, problems with the law, difficult relationships and problems with employment. On the other hand the outcome for those with ADHD only was not terribly different from individuals without ADHD. The investigators suggested this has been a consistent pattern in many studies for the last 50 years.

## Myth 5: If ADHD does exist it disappears in adolescence and is very rare in adulthood

This myth has been around for quite some time, and for a number of years even a lot of professionals were unsure if adults could really have ADHD. This was because it was thought that by the time the individual reached adolescence, they had all but outgrown the disorder. However, today it is readily recognised from longitudinal studies that ADHD exists into adulthood. One longitudinal study investigating whether the symptoms of ADHD decline with age followed a large group of children with the disorder over a four-year period. The results indicated that about 72 per cent of the children still displayed enough ADHD symptoms to have received a diagnosis at twenty years of age. The researchers concluded, 'our results also indicate that a majority of subjects continue to struggle with a substantial number of ADHD symptoms and high levels of dysfunction ... by the age of 20'. This myth is dealt with in more detail in Chapter 10.

## Myth 6: ADHD is a result of bad parenting

This myth has been circulating since the days of Noah and surprisingly it is still a popular one. While it may not be true, in a way it makes sense. If you believe that ADHD is nothing more than a child misbehaving, the logical conclusion is to point the finger of blame at the parents. Obviously, if the parents had just bothered to control their child and put some boundaries in place the kid wouldn't be misbehaving. However, the fact is that parenting, whether good or bad, *does not* cause ADHD. So to all the parents out there who believe that somehow, in some way, you are responsible for your child developing ADHD because of some failure in your parenting skills, you can relax. ADHD *is not* caused by parenting styles. When you read Chapter 4 on the causes of ADHD, you will see that ADHD is a neurological disorder. But, and it is a big BUT, certain parenting practices are known to increase the frequency and the intensity of the presentation of certain ADHD symptoms. This is one of the reasons why parent management training is usually a very helpful tool for parents dealing with their ADHD child. The issue of parenting is discussed further in Chapter 8 on alternative therapies for ADHD.

## Myth 7: Diet causes ADHD

Before we begin looking at diet as a potential cause of ADHD, we need to understand that a child's diet *can* have a negative impact on their behaviour. However, it is not typically in the sensationalist fashion that many might have us believe. There appear to be two separate issues at the core of this argument that have somehow merged into one big misunderstanding. As will be discussed below, the idea that diet causes ADHD has not received any scientific support. It is true that children can have reactions to some foods or that the child may have chemical sensitivities and it is these reactions that have been found to have a negative impact on the child's behaviour. This does not, however, mean the food or the chemical has *caused* ADHD.

That diet causes ADHD is a really popular myth and has many proponents who are very happy to argue that all a parent need do is change the child's diet and their child will be cured of ADHD, or that there will be amazing changes to their behaviour. Just as an interesting exercise, Google the phrase 'ADHD and diet' and see just how many hits are listed — you will be surprised. On that one phrase alone there are about 18,000,000 hits. Of course, not all of those sites are suggesting that diet causes ADHD; there are sites that refute the myth. However, the point is that ADHD and diet is currently a hot topic of debate for many people from all walks of life.

The argument of diet influencing a child's behaviour can be dated back to the 1970s with the release of the popular Feingold diet. Dr Benjamin Feingold argued that food additives such as azo dye food colours and naturally occurring salicylates (salicylates are a compound found in some medications such as aspirin and are naturally occurring in some foods) and preservatives found in certain foods were fundamentally responsible for a child's hyperactive behaviour. Feingold claimed that placing children on a strict diet would treat the disorder and without any documented evidence he also claimed he had around a 50 per cent success rate with hyperactive children who had been placed on the diet. And, yes, it is true there have been a handful of studies that reported improvement in a child's behaviour following Feingold's strict diet. However, it appears not all is as it seems. The improvements were noted in only a small number of children who appeared to have allergic reactions to certain food additives. Decades of independent research have produced no support for Feingold's claim. In fact, the results of systematic studies have shown what appears to be the exact opposite; that is, placing a child on a strict diet is ineffective and such a diet does not seem to alter the core symptoms of ADHD such as inattention, hyperactivity and impulsivity. Furthermore, it seems that the Feingold diet has regularly failed to receive any consistent scientific support since its inception. In spite of all this evidence (or the lack thereof), many people still choose to place their child with ADHD on a strict diet. In 2005 a couple of researchers surveyed parents of children with ADHD. Surprisingly, they found that the majority of parents they surveyed had placed their child on a strict diet. The second most common approach was to place the child on a vitamin/mineral diet.

That diet may have a negative impact on a child's behaviour is a separate issue all together. To be a little more precise, that a child might be intolerant to certain food additives that can influence a child's behaviour has had support from scientific research all over the world. One paediatric neurologist in America reported the results of a huge study conducted in the UK, where 18,000 people participated in the study. The results of the study indicated that 7 per cent of the participants reported having a reaction to a food additive. In this study, the boys had higher rates of behavioural and mood changes compared to the girls. This same paediatrician described a second study conducted at the Royal Children's Hospital, Victoria, Australia, where 25 per cent of the children involved in the study were identified as the most likely to have a reaction to additives. In a study of 200 hyperactive children, 150 noted a change in their behaviour when placed on a diet free of synthetic colourings. Other investigations have found that a child's attention problems were not evident following the consumption of food colourings, but severe irritability, restlessness and sleeping problems were found to be the common complaints.

There are many, many other myths regarding diet just about everywhere one looks. To provide an exhaustive list of such myths is not worth the time it would take. However, just to give you an idea of how extensive the diet myths are, here is a small list of foods and food products that are said to *cause* ADHD: dairy products and animal products in general because they reportedly contain hormones, pesticides and antibiotics and, of course, the animal itself is said to be diseased; caffeine; sweets and sugar; processed food and fast food; MSG and foods that contain food preservatives, food dyes and 'other' chemicals; white bread; white rice; and peanut butter.

Such a list is not necessarily a bad thing as, within reason, it may promote a healthy diet not just for the child but for the family in general to reduce their intake of such foods. And any parent who permits their child to consume caffeine drinks (for example, energy drinks, coffee and frequent consumption of Coca Cola) really should recognise this is just not a healthy option.

## Myth 8: Sugar causes ADHD

Not so long ago I was interviewing an adult female at my clinic who was really quite concerned about her friend's five-year-old child who reportedly had ADHD. The woman was seeking ways in which she might help support her friend with an ADHD child. Of course, one of the first questions asked of this lady was, 'What makes you think the child has ADHD?' The woman responded indignantly, 'I know she has ADHD and it was caused by the amount of sugar in her diet'. According to this woman, the child was not yet at school and would therefore spend her days at home with her mum. The mother was a very social woman who would often have friends visit during the day and they would sit at the kitchen table drinking coffee. The kitchen table was where the mother kept a bowl of white sugar. Apparently the child would frequently help herself to a teaspoon of sugar throughout the day as she pleased and, according to the woman, within minutes the child would be running around the house almost uncontrollably. As disturbing as this report is, it is most likely inaccurate as there is currently no evidence to suggest that sugar causes ADHD. In fact, it has been shown that certain sugar products do not even affect the behaviour of a child with ADHD.

One doctor reported on the results of sixteen published studies conducted by Vanderbilt University on the effects of sucrose on the behaviour and cognitions of children with ADHD. According to the doctor, the studies 'failed to demonstrate a significant adverse effect in the group as a whole ... NutraSweet (aspartame) used as a control was considered to have no adverse effect on behaviour or cognition'. Other investigators have reported that even when aspartame consumption was more than 10 times the usual level, it still had no adverse effect on the cognitive or behavioural functioning of children with ADHD. It seems fairly clear that sugar does not cause ADHD, but please be aware of the effects sugary products do have on a child's health in general. If sugary products are not kept in check they can bring on other health-related problems.

There are so many myths about the causes of ADHD that we could just about devote an entire book to them. Most of these myths are plain ridiculous (for example, fluorescent lighting, tar and pitch, soaps and detergents, yeast and insect repellents and, of course, poor teaching and poor parenting are all on the list) and do not deserve the effort it would require to write them down. It seems everywhere we go someone has an opinion or a conspiracy theory to 'prove' ADHD is not a real disorder. Some of these myths sound incredibly believable, like the myths of poor parenting or diet causing ADHD, yet there is no real evidence to support these claims. So, is there a cause for ADHD, and if there is, what is it? The next chapter answers these questions at length.

# CHAPTER 4

## The causes of ADHD

Neuroscience is, by its very nature, a complex area to study and understand. Many of the world's finest professionals have dedicated their entire careers to studying the brain, so because of its complexity, only the bare essentials for understanding those regions of the brain that are implicated in ADHD will be presented in this chapter. This chapter will also discuss one of the most influential theories on the causes of ADHD to date. While it might initially seem a bit complex, including this type of information in a book about ADHD is necessary for one reason: to answer the single most asked question of so many worried and distressed parents — 'How is ADHD caused?' So, before we begin on the neuroscience, let's take a look at some of the other known causes of ADHD.

## What are the causes of ADHD?

Just recently I had a young couple in my clinic really quite concerned about the behaviour of their soon-to-be seven-year-old son. At the time he was in first grade at a local primary school and things hadn't been going so well for him. In fact, in the first six months of the school year he had fallen behind in his reading, writing and maths and the teacher had raised concerns about his social interactions and his classroom and playground behaviour. At the end of a long process of gathering information from the parents and the schoolteachers, I suspected the boy might have ADHD. As such, I referred him to a clinic that specialises in childhood assessments to determine exactly what was going on for the boy. However, before making such a referral I like to discuss with parents my suspicions and take the time to answer any questions they might have. When I told the parents that I suspected their son had

ADHD, the first question his mother asked was, 'What causes ADHD?'

The simplest answer to such a question is that most likely there are a number of potential causes of ADHD. In fact, the causes of ADHD are considered to be an extremely complex interaction between biological and environmental factors. Think about it this way, heart disease is a killer of thousands of people every year. The Australian Heart Foundation has reported heart disease as:

> ... the leading cause of death in Australia, accounting for 33% of all deaths in Australia in 2009. Cardiovascular disease kills one Australian every 11 minutes. Cardiovascular disease is one of Australia's largest health problems.

Heart disease does not necessarily have a single cause either. For instance, we know lifestyle choices such as diet can be a cause of heart disease, and smoking cigarettes is also a known cause, and we can't deny the role hereditary factors play as well. Like ADHD, heart disease can also be an extremely complex interaction between biological and environmental factors.

So, getting back to the parents in my clinic, I informed them that there are a number of causes of ADHD, such as smoking during pregnancy, alcohol consumption during pregnancy, and genetics. Stunned, the mother looked over at her husband and peered deep into his eyes, then looking back at me, she reported with a tremor in her voice, 'Most of my family on my mother's side have ADHD and I smoked about ten to fifteen cigarettes a day all through my pregnancy'.

## SMOKING AND ADHD

Most of us would understand that exposing a pregnant mother or an infant to environmental toxins, such as carbon monoxide and toluene, is extremely dangerous, as toxins can cause birth defects in the unborn baby and numerous diseases in children. Exposing a baby to environmental toxins both during pregnancy and after the birth may cause abnormalities in the baby's brain and nervous system. Certain toxins are also known to dramatically increase the risks of the child developing distractibility, hyperactivity, restlessness and inattention. One such extremely poisonous toxin, which is found in cigarettes, that has been linked to ADHD is lead. Now most of us might readily recognise that this is a rather serious toxin to be exposed to and the evidence clearly shows that prenatal exposure to lead is very, very dangerous to the baby.

A mother smoking during pregnancy places her unborn child at risk of developing a number of problems. Because of this, researchers have turned their attention to smoking during pregnancy in an effort to answer the question: 'Is smoking a possible cause of ADHD?' What researchers have found is that smoking during pregnancy has been associated with a greater risk of developing ADHD symptoms. Remember that each time the pregnant mother inhales the smoke from a cigarette, she is literally sucking in over 4000 chemicals (such as warfarin (rat poison), ammonia and arsenic) along with nicotine, the addictive substance of the cigarette. Smoking during pregnancy is also a known cause of hypoxia, which is a pathological condition where the whole body or a region of the body, such as the brain, is deprived of oxygen. Hypoxia is thought to be linked to ADHD. Many researchers have found links between maternal smoking and children being born with ADHD, with one study documenting that smoking during pregnancy placed the unborn child at a threefold risk of having hyperkinetic disorder compared with non-smoking mothers.

## ALCOHOL CONSUMPTION

Alcohol consumption during pregnancy has not escaped the attention of the professional world either as it is a known cause of birth defects in children, such as in foetal alcohol syndrome (FAS). FAS carries with it a number of associated problems for the child including:

- poor growth *in utero* and post birth
- heart defects
- cognitive deficits
- behavioural problems, and
- learning difficulties and disorders to name just a few.

The effects of FAS are far reaching, as it also often has dramatic consequences on the child's facial features such as small eye openings, large folds in the skin of the upper eyelid at the corners of the eyes, a small head, a small upper jaw, a low nasal bridge, a short nose, and a thin upper lip.

Alcohol is considered to be one of the top three toxins to the unborn baby as it creates considerable risks for ADHD. In fact, consuming alcohol during pregnancy increases the risk of the unborn child developing ADHD to about three times the amount it would have been had the mother not consumed alcohol at all. This is because alcohol is known to bring about behavioural and structural changes in the growing baby *in utero*. In addition, alcohol can lead to the malformation of the frontal lobe of the baby and can affect the development of the baby's nervous system. These issues combined provide the possible link to ADHD. One researcher found that mothers who consumed alcohol during their pregnancy had high rates of children with ADHD symptoms, such as a decreased attention span, hyperactivity, impulsive behaviour and learning difficulties. The issue here is that although it doesn't happen to every child and no one knows exactly how much consumed alcohol may cause ADHD, the reality is that any amount of alcohol consumed during pregnancy can be dangerous for the baby. However, alcohol is not the only poison unborn children can be exposed to. Drug use and abuse also has catastrophic consequences on the unborn infant and such children often show signs of hyperactivity, impulsivity and inattention.

There are no safe levels of alcohol consumption or smoking during pregnancy. The fact is that both of these substances are drugs (socially sanctioned or not is irrelevant) and place the unborn baby at high risk of physical, mental, social and developmental disorders. Most parents I see emphatically state that they would never put their beautiful baby in harm's way. But a mother who drinks alcohol or smokes during her pregnancy is doing just that. In addition, expectant fathers should never smoke around their wives — pregnant or not — as passive smoking (inhaling another's expired cigarette smoke) is a proven killer.

## OTHER ENVIRONMENTAL TOXINS

Exposure to toxins, such as lead, has been linked to the development of hyperactive and inattentive behaviour in children. There is evidence that high levels of lead in the body of a young child, particularly between the ages of twelve and 36 months of age, may place the child at a higher risk of developing ADHD. Some investigators have established that lead contamination can cause distractibility, hyperactivity, restlessness, and poorer intellectual functioning. However, not every child who has been exposed to lead, even at high levels, develops ADHD. In fact, the relationship between lead exposure and ADHD is considered to be very weak. So while we are aware that illicit drug use, alcohol consumption, cigarette smoking and exposure to lead is dangerous to the baby, we cannot argue that exposure to toxins is entirely responsible for every case of ADHD.

## GENETIC FACTORS

Many years ago the parents of a twelve-year-old boy sat in my office terribly worried about their son's ever-increasing aggression and violence. He was verbally abusive and, at times, became physically aggressive toward other children and both parents. The parents felt that, unless there was an immediate intervention, their son's behaviour would only continue to get worse and he would wind up in trouble with the police.

One of the common factors I see with people who have anger problems is their denial of having any control over their anger and thus a denial of being responsible for their aggressive behaviour. Typically, such individuals make lots of excuses for their behaviour like 'it's her fault I got angry', or 'if she just did what I told her to do in the first place I wouldn't have punched her' and so on. Accepting responsibility for one's behaviour means there are no more excuses and angry people don't like this. In therapy, this is one of the first issues I deal with, as the individual must learn to accept responsibility for their behaviour.

I met with the boy who tried to impress me with how 'tough' he was. He glared at me, swore at me and told me quite bluntly he did not like me and didn't want to be in my office. After all his efforts failed to impress, he tried blaming his parents, his teachers, his school and just about everybody else in his life for his behaviour until he realised he was without excuse. Eventually he turned his attention toward me and in an effort to unsettle and undermine my efforts he accused me of swearing at him and he told me that he would tell his parents he didn't want to return because I had been nasty to him. At that, I stood up, called his parents into the office and, turning to the boy, I said, 'Here's your chance to tell your parents'. When he realised I wasn't buying into his games he defiantly glared at me and stated:

> There is nothing I can do. I cannot control my anger and you need to f****n' accept it. I'm sick of your shit ... do you remember last week when you said that I am responsible for my anger — well, I know I'm not because it's genetic. I have an angry gene and because of that I can't control my anger.

Needless to say the boy wasn't impressed when I told him this just wasn't true. While everybody might have heard about genes or hereditability, intimate knowledge of our genes is quite intricate and complex.

Research has found that up to 40 per cent of true ADHD cases are genetic. For the genetic group there is a very strong family history of ADHD in a parent, grandparent or a first-degree relative. The evidence for a genetic basis of ADHD is undeniable and is found by researchers studying families and twins and through molecular genetic studies that may identify a number of individual genes that would account for ADHD. But the evidence for a genetic basis isn't necessarily just derived from studies focused on particular genes that might be responsible for ADHD. Instead, the evidence for a genetic basis comes from familial studies where the focus is on *patterns of inheritance*. In fact, around 10 to 35 per cent of immediate relatives of children with ADHD also have the disorder, while about 32 per cent of siblings will also have the disorder, and if a parent has ADHD, there is a 57 per cent chance the child will have ADHD as well. The statistics for twins are just as alarming.

Study designs using twins have been a valuable source of information for both the medical and psychological professions. Studies focusing on the genetic inheritance of disorders such as ADHD will often try to involve twins where possible. In this instance, the researchers would want to involve both monozygotic (identical) and dizygotic (fraternal) twins. Monozygotic twins are genetically identical and share 100 per cent of their genes, whereas dizygotic twins share only 50 per cent of their genes. Because monozygotic twins are genetically the same, if one of the twins were to have ADHD, one could expect the other twin to have ADHD too. Such an expectation would not necessarily eventuate with dizygotic twins. Twin studies have also looked at twins raised together and apart. Such research is very influential in clarifying a genetic basis for ADHD because if ADHD was caused by environmental factors alone there would be no differences between both the monozygotic and dizygotic twins in rates of ADHD. However, this is simply not the case.

To try to explain why the results of such studies are statistically significant would be to complete a university degree in statistics. However, it is important to understand research results and why they are significant. One investigator put it like this:

> ... *Heritability estimates are statistics about the variance of a characteristic in a population that can be accounted for by genetics. They cannot provide a precise breakdown in individual cases: suggesting, for example, that in any one individual the ADHD is 75 per cent genetic and 25 per cent environmental.*

What does all this mean and why is it important? Well, when we begin to consider large-scale twin studies with an average heritability of ADHD at 0.80, we begin to realise just how significant such results are. It's really like saying there is an 80 per cent heritability factor. To put this into perspective a little further, an average of 0.80 is about the same for height. Everyone knows that tall parents 'breed' tall children; in fact, the degree of heritability is 0.80–0.91, about the same as ADHD. Finally, these studies have consistently found that the twins' environment has very little effect on the traits of ADHD. Such results firmly refute the idea that poor parenting, diet, sugar or other myths are the cause of ADHD.

There is also something very important we must remember: we are not just an expression of our genes. The development or expression of behaviour is the result of complex interactions between genetics, our environment such as the family we grew up in, our experiences and our perceptions, and our interpretations of events. What this means is that the behaviour of a child with ADHD might well be influenced by their genetic make up but this is not predestination, so all is not lost. We must remember that an individual should not and must not ever be permitted to be a passive victim of their genetic inheritance. Just because there might be a genetic vulnerability to the child having ADHD, this is never an excuse to do little about it by ignoring it or throwing your hands up in the air in defeat. Just like the person who has a family history of heart disease, they can respond in a way that limits the impact of the disease by changing their diet, exercising regularly and avoiding high stress situations. Just as with the angry child in the previous story, the fate of a child with ADHD is not determined.

## BRAIN INJURIES

According to one professor of psychiatry, for almost 100 years scientists have noted similar behavioural patterns between children with ADHD and people who have sustained injuries to specific regions of their brain. Since then, an excess of case studies and reports from the medical, neurological and psychological sciences has found that a range of different injuries to the brain were the chief causes of ADHD. Such injuries included trauma to the brain due to a fall or a blow to the head or complications during pregnancy and birth, brain tumours, strokes, diseases or wounds that may have penetrated the brain and infections such as encephalitis and meningitis. However, there is a serious flaw with these findings, as very few children with ADHD have sustained brain injuries. It is estimated that brain injury only accounts for about 5 to 10 per cent of children with ADHD.

# The neuroanatomy of ADHD

Perhaps the greatest argument for ADHD as a legitimate disorder comes from research conducted on various regions of the brain, the observed and measured deficits a person may exhibit after sustaining damage to those regions of the brain and, of course, the noticeable differences in a child's behaviour and attention while on medication for ADHD. Because a number of different regions of the brain have been implicated in ADHD, it is often referred to as a neurological disorder. One prominent investigator of ADHD stated in his address to the Centre for ADHD Awareness, Canada (CADDAC):

> *Understanding the neuroanatomy of ADHD will help us to understand the nature of ADHD, the complexity of ADHD, the seriousness of ADHD, and why ADHD is the most impairing outpatient disorder seen in psychiatric clinics ... ADHD is currently among the top three psychiatric disorders.*

Our cognitive abilities are the product of a very complex system resulting from an integration of many brain functions. In fact, at the present moment, there are five known interconnected structures of the brain that have been implicated in ADHD:

- the frontal lobe
- basal ganglia
- cerebellum
- anterior cingulate cortex, and
- corpus callosum.

Each of these structures will be discussed in more detail below, but before that can happen we need to develop a basic understanding of the brain. As you will soon realise the brain is extremely complex and often you will find that multiple areas of the brain play an important role for a single function, such as concentration.

## THE BRAIN AS OUR 'CONTROL CENTRE'

The brain is the organ in the human body that determines who we are as individuals and how we might experience the world around us. It has been estimated that the brain contains about ten billion (that's 10,000,000,000) nerve cells, or neurons, and weighs just over 1 kilogram (or approximately 3 pounds in the old scale). Neurons are tiny cells that are the building blocks of the brain and are about one-millionth of an inch in length. Each neuron will have many thousands of connections to other neurons which enable them to communicate with one another (actually each neuron could have 10,000 connections and the human brain is estimated to have about 100 trillion connections). The communication between neurons in the brain is made possible by neurotransmitters — chemicals released by one neuron and received by another to relay signals or information throughout the brain and on to the central nervous system (CNS) and other parts the body. For example, neurotransmitters tell your heart to beat and your stomach to digest food. Medications and drugs are designed to affect the way in which the chemical messages or signals are transmitted to our brain.

Our brain has often been referred to as our 'control centre'. Among its many other 'jobs', the brain registers feelings, impressions and perceptions, and links them with one another and with other information that has already been stored. The brain also makes decisions and helps us to take the appropriate action, and it is the centre for our intellect, emotions and memory. The brain truly is an amazing organ. However, the function of the brain isn't just limited to these jobs, as it is also responsible for the body's physiological responses and for controlling our behaviour. Impressive as it is, the brain cannot accomplish all of this on its own and requires the help of the body's sense receptors, which requires the brain to be connected to our muscles and glands if it is to accomplish its 'job'.

The brain and the spinal cord make up the central nervous system, which processes many different kinds of information from the rest of the body by communicating with the body through the nerves or neurons. The spinal cord is long and thin and is attached to the base of the brain. It runs the full length of the spinal column and is made up of about 100 million nerve cells. The spinal cord contains circuits of nerve cells that control some of our most simple reflexes, such as pulling our hand away from a hot surface, and provide signals that control our body movements and regulate the operations of our internal organs. The nervous system also allows us to sense various smells, tastes and textures, produce speech and remember past events.

Basically, the nervous system has three primary functions including the sensory function (taking in information), the integrative function (processing the information that has been taken in), and the motor function (producing an action or response). The sensory function senses internal stimuli such as an increase in blood pressure and it also detects external stimuli such as a spider crawling across your hand. This sensory information is carried back to the brain and to the spinal cord through a complex system discussed below. The integrative function

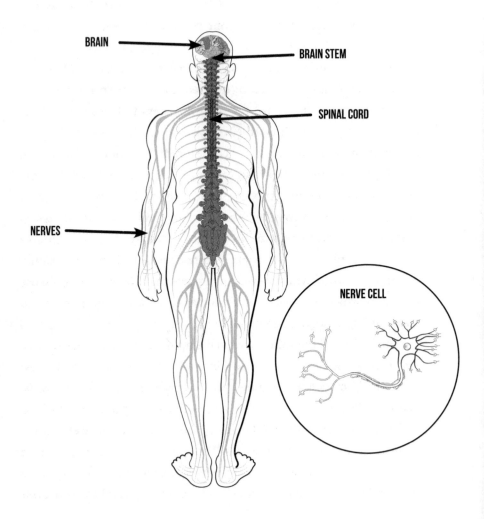

BRAIN

BRAIN STEM

SPINAL CORD

NERVES

NERVE CELL

processes that sensory information by analysing it and making the most appropriate decision for a response. Then once that information has been integrated, the nervous system produces the most appropriate motor response. For instance, the most appropriate motor response for many people when a spider crawls across their hand is to frantically shake their hand about, and jump around the room in a manner resembling some kind of an ancient tribal dance all while screaming hysterically. All of this can only be accomplished by the activation of muscles and glands through both the cranial and spinal nerves. When the muscles are activated, they contract and perform a desired task.

## REGIONS OF THE BRAIN IMPLICATED IN ADHD

Basically our brain is divided into two 'parts' — the left hemisphere and the right hemisphere. The left hemisphere is on the left side of the brain and the right hemisphere is on the right side of the brain. While the left and right hemispheres might appear to be a mirror image of each other, they are not exactly the same size nor do they perform the same functions. Some of the brain's functions are specific to one hemisphere.

For most people, the left hemisphere is the dominant 'side' of the brain and is important for maths, science, reasoning, spoken and written language, and the ability to understand and use sign language. The left hemisphere enables meaning to take place. It categorises and analyses information and solves problems, it organises information and puts events in order, and then places those events in time. The left hemisphere also forms symbols such as maths and language, and it facilitates memory and a non-verbal emotional reaction of the right-sided structures. Given that the left hemisphere is the side of the brain where verbal work such as talking and being able to understand what other people are saying takes place, damage to the left hemisphere can result in signs of aphasia, which literally means there is a disturbance in the person's language and their verbal communication.

Conversely, the right hemisphere is the expert in music and art, spatial and pattern perception, it's a specialist in recognising the emotional content of language, it can discriminate between different smells, and it can produce mental images of our senses such as sights, sounds, touch, taste and smell and then compare relationships among them. The right hemisphere, then, is the side of the brain that specialises in non-verbal recognition and emotional memory. For example, the right hemisphere is really good at recognising faces, reading or recognising an emotional state in other people, and assessing and understanding the emotional significance of an event. The right hemisphere is involved in creativity and non-verbal problem-solving, it generates new and unique, even sophisticated responses to practical and emotional situations, and it generates mental images to help us understand three-dimensional

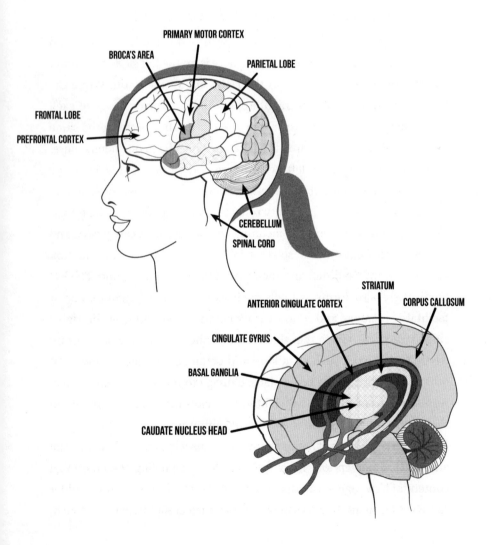

relationships such as drawings, sketches and reading maps. It enables rhythm in speech, music and movement and regulates the nervous system and hormonal responses from the senses.

Even though the two hemispheres have different operations and perceive the world somewhat differently, we are not aware of this fact. This is because even though the right and left hemispheres perform different functions, our perceptions and our memories are unified. This is all made possible because of the corpus callosum.

## THE CORPUS CALLOSUM

The two hemispheres of the brain need to cooperate with each other and this is achieved by connecting the right and left hemispheres and the corresponding parts together by a large cluster of nerves (estimated to be some 50 million nerves) known as the corpus callosum. Because of the corpus callosum, each region of the brain knows what the corresponding side is doing. In other words, the corpus callosum connects the two parts of the brain together and allows an interchange of information between them. The corpus callosum also integrates thoughts, feelings and actions and temperamental reactions.

## THE FRONTAL LOBE

The surface of the left and right hemispheres is covered by the cerebral cortex, the wrinkly tissue of the forebrain or the outer part of the brain that we see. The cerebral cortex contains billions of nerve cells. There are large folds in the cerebral cortex that are called gyri, which in Greek means 'circle', and the small creases in the cortex are called fissures meaning 'trench'. The cortex can be 'divided' into four regions known as the frontal lobe, the parietal lobe, the temporal lobe and the occipital lobe. The front part of the cerebral cortex is known as the frontal lobe (located in the region of your forehead), and it is this area which has been implicated in ADHD.

The frontal lobe, or the front part of the brain, is the largest part of the cortex and plays a role in many processes such as motor control, cognition, planning, organising, problem-solving, selective attention, behaviour and emotions, memory and impulse control, language and decision-making. Speaking and understanding language are also located in the frontal lobe. The frontal lobe also has 'substructures' including the prefrontal cortex, the orbital-frontal cortex, the motor and premotor cortices and Broca's area. Broca's area is primarily concerned with spoken and written language as well as language processing and comprehension. Some sources have suggested that the language areas are located in the left hemisphere of the frontal lobe in up to 97 per cent of the population. What that means is that the planning and production of speech occurs in the left side of the brain for most of the population. Damage to Broca's area can lead to a failure to express language, including stopping or pausing when speaking, repetitive speech, problematic syntax and grammar and problematic structure of individual words.

The front section of the frontal lobe is called the prefrontal cortex and it is reported to be one of the most 'complex and interconnected regions of the human brain'. The prefrontal cortex takes up about one-third of the brain's total volume and is referred to as the 'central management system' because it is connected directly with every functional unit of the brain that:

- receives sensory input
- controls movement
- manages memory
- deals with emotion
- makes decisions
- controls activation, and
- maintains stability of vital bodily functions.

The prefrontal cortex has numerous connections to other areas of the brain and is involved in regulating all aspects of human behaviour and is important for the higher cognitive functions (for example, working memory, mental imagery and willed action). The prefrontal cortex is critical for regulating our attention as it screens out distractions, and while sustaining our attention it can shift, divide or coordinate attention over a period of time in a manner that is appropriate for the task at hand. It accomplishes this by delaying a response in the presence of a distraction that protects the individual's performance from interference. The right side of the prefrontal cortex is crucial for regulating our behaviour and emotional responses and especially in regulating or inhibiting inappropriate emotions, impulses and habits. The prefrontal cortex also regulates moral reasoning and a sense of self, and we need it for allocating and planning for the future so we can achieve goals and organise our thoughts and behaviours and for suppressing irrelevant thoughts. Given the function of the prefrontal cortex, what would happen if this area of the brain was damaged somehow or wasn't working properly? To answer that question we again need to look at the research.

The kind of research that is used to study the brain often involves neurobiologic, neuroimaging and neuropsychologic studies. These studies are revealing some notable patterns of deficits in the brains of individuals with ADHD, showing strong support for deficits in the frontal lobe and the connections between the frontal lobe and other key areas of the brain. Studies using neuroimaging provide direct assessments of brain structure and function and with computerised tomography or magnetic resonance imaging (MRI) have found evidence of structural brain irregularities in people with ADHD.

Neuropsychological and medical imaging studies have demonstrated that the prefrontal cortex in people with ADHD is underactive with weakened connections to other parts of the brain, and this is said to contribute significantly to ADHD symptoms. Other research has found that the prefrontal cortex in people with ADHD has a smaller volume, particularly on the right side. Damage to the prefrontal cortex often causes symptoms similar to ADHD such as impaired working memory and forgetfulness. Lesions to the prefrontal cortex often means the individual is easily distracted as they experience enormous difficulty blocking out irrelevant stimuli. They experience poor concentration and organisational skills, they are more vulnerable to competing distractions, and they can be impulsive and experience difficulty controlling their behaviour, especially if the damage is to the right side of the prefrontal cortex. Damage to the prefrontal cortex can also bring on problems with sustaining attention, particularly for any period of time, and it impairs divided and focused attention. Lesions to a specific area of the prefrontal cortex can impair the person's ability to regulate their emotions and often as a result we see inappropriate social behaviours such as aggression.

## THE CEREBELLUM

The cerebellum, which is often referred to as the 'little brain' and looks a bit like a cauliflower, is situated towards the back of the brain. The cerebellum is a section of the brain that has traditionally been credited with the roles of controlling and coordinating movements at a subconscious level. In size, the cerebellum is about one-tenth the volume of your brain, yet it has been estimated that it contains almost half of the neurons in the brain. While its role in the coordination of voluntary movement is well understood, increasing evidence suggests the cerebellum is also involved in:

- attention
- verbal fluency and reasoning
- emotion
- balance
- posture
- walking, and
- integrating memory and dreaming.

Its role in movement-related functions is what is most understood at this stage. Our movement does not originate with the cerebellum itself, but rather it contributes to our coordination, allowing movement with precision and accurate timing. Because it 'fine-tunes' movement, damage to the cerebellum does not cause a person to become paralysed as such, but the person will have problems with their fine motor skills (small movements of the hands, wrists, fingers, feet and toes), steadiness or balance, posture, and sequence learning. Injury to this region may also impair the ability to judge distances and when to stop, it can affect rapid alternating movements, and it can cause movement tremors, staggering, wide-based walking and (possibly) slurred speech. Without getting too technical, particular problems can occur if a specific area of the cerebellum is damaged and, of course, this would also depend on how much damage occurred in that region.

## THE BASAL GANGLIA

The basal ganglia are a group of nuclei found deep within the cerebral cortex, which are closely connected to the frontal lobe and are essential for automatic movements and postures. The basal ganglia have many connections to other brain structures and their major role is helping to control the starting and stopping of movements as well as in planning. The basal ganglia also control muscle contractions of the skeletal muscles at a subconscious level so we don't make any unwanted and possibly embarrassing movements. Finally, the basal ganglia also help with some cognitive processes such as attention, memory and planning, and they also appear to interact with the limbic system that helps us to regulate our emotional behaviours.

The basal ganglia include the caudate nucleus, which has a large head and a body connected to a smaller tail. The caudate nucleus is connected to several other areas of the brain including the temporal lobe and receives input from these regions including the frontal lobe and is believed to be involved in a number of motor and cognitive tasks. Finally, the basal ganglia also include the striatum, which controls or inhibits behaviour and helps with sustaining attention. One investigator has suggested that the striatum is where your thoughts will guide your actions or behaviour. But it has the more important role of keeping a private thought just that — private. What is important to note here is that several studies have shown that the basal ganglia are smaller in people with ADHD.

## Executive functions

Now with an understanding of the brain and the role each structure plays in human functioning, we can see how they work together in creating and controlling human behaviour. Executive functions (EFs) is a term used to describe the higher order of the human brain. It seems that certain parts of the human brain, such as the frontal lobe (for example, the prefrontal cortex), are like a central management system that works to coordinate all the various functions of the brain. Some authors have described EFs as being just like a CEO who coordinates all of the company's activities, while others have described them as a conductor of an orchestra who enables the orchestra to produce complex music by uniting the sounds of all the different instruments and controlling the musicians' timing throughout the entire concert. Executive functions organise the brain to perform both routine and creative or complex tasks. In fact, EFs are considered critical for complex human behaviour and include:

- the ability to organise (both physical and mental)
- being able to prioritise
- the ability to integrate information
- being able to formulate and implement problem-solving strategies and have a back-up plan in case the first plan fails
- being efficient
- being able to self-regulate thoughts, actions and emotions (self-regulation means any self-directed action used to change your own behaviour so that you alter the chance of some consequence in the future)
- mental flexibility
- certain components of attention
- reasoning abilities
- being able to make plans
- being able to inhibit impulsive responses and actions
- being able to shift one's attention
- being able to control interference, and
- working memory.

So it would seem there are four common factors in the definition of EFs including:

1. formulating goals
2. planning
3. executing plans to reach our goals, and
4. effective performance.

This means that EFs are involved in:

- identifying what we want and how to achieve our goals
- planning how to achieve our objectives

- arranging our objectives into a sequence of actions according to the plan, and
- monitoring our performance, correcting mistakes or changing plans when our initial plan is not working.

Because the human brain continues to develop until we are about 25 years of age, and the prefrontal cortex is the last area to reach maturity (what implications does this have for the over-representation of motor vehicle accidents among young drivers!), this may also explain why we don't see the same extreme symptoms in the adult with ADHD because as they have matured they have also developed an increase in their ability to be self-controlled, independent and responsible. Given the frontal lobe is the last area of the brain to develop it might also explain why deficits in young children are extremely hard to recognise until the young child is required to use them — say, at school. There is now an abundance of evidence suggesting that children with ADHD exhibit marked deficits in executive functions.

## An integrated theory of ADHD

With a better understanding of both the brain's regions that are implicated in ADHD and executive functions, we can turn now to one of the most influential theories regarding ADHD that integrates all of the information above — that ADHD is not a disorder of attention, but a disorder of working memory and the executive functions.

Dr Russell Barkley, a psychologist and an expert on ADHD, proposed that the biological inability to regulate inhibition has quite a detrimental effect on the executive functions, which then results in poor self-guidance and self-regulation. Executive functions help us to 'switch off' impulsive behaviour and inappropriate actions or prevent us from seeking immediate gratification and instead enable us to think out an appropriate response based on what the future might hold for us. In other words, EFs allow the person to work out the long-term results over the short-term consequences. It is important to know, however, that Dr Barkley has been very clear that his theory can only be applied to the

ADHD Combined Type, that is a person who displays both inattention and hyperactivity–impulsivity.

According to Barkley, the right frontal area of the brain (for example, the frontal lobe containing the prefrontal cortex) is where inhibition takes place — the 'inhibitory centre'. This is where the ability to control behaviour seems to stem from. This then allows the rest of the frontal area, which is where thinking takes place, to take control over our behaviour. But if this inhibitory centre is not functioning properly, the chances are that whatever you are thinking has very little consequence and you will act impulsively.

As we know, the basal ganglia seem to be smaller in people with ADHD. You will remember the striatum is one of the structures of the basal ganglia and is considered to be a 'switching system' that determines whether our thoughts become something we act on or whether they remain just thoughts without being acted on. According to Barkley, the striatum is the switch that determines the private self (our thoughts) from the public self (our actions) and in ADHD that switch (being the striatum) is broken. This essentially means that the thoughts of people with ADHD could very well be expressed publically, meaning that people with ADHD are thinking out loud and before they know it their thoughts are an action.

Barkley has suggested that ADHD can be defined as a 'disorder of persistence toward the future', which is significantly influenced by the person's inability to resist distraction. People with ADHD just cannot help themselves, they will get distracted by almost anything, and once they have been distracted it is nearly impossible for them to get back to the task at hand because all the goal-oriented planning (for example, 'I'll aim to finish this chapter by lunchtime') cannot be held in mind any longer. Furthermore, once the individual has been distracted it seems that working memory is so severely affected that the person's goal is gone — they are off with the fairies and the distraction will now have more importance. It doesn't matter what else happens, that distraction will be more gripping than any goal they may have previously had. People without ADHD might experience a distraction, but they can get back to the task at hand and finish it off. This is all part of working memory. When this is taken into account it suggests that ADHD is not a disorder of attention but of working memory. Remember that working memory is part of the executive functions and since ADHD may be a disorder of working memory this might also have serious implications for the other executive functions. It effectively suggests that ADHD may well be a disorder of executive functions, particularly in adults.

The anterior cingulate cortex (the front part of the cingulate gyrus) has two separate functional zones with the upper region being involved in decision-making in social conflict situations that may have immediate and future consequences depending on your chosen responses to that situation. So the anterior cingulate cortex helps you negotiate the best outcome when you are faced with a conflict between what is happening now and what might happen in the future if you act on your private thoughts. It gives you the time needed to think about the situation and your desired action and then it helps you to behave in a way that is beneficial to both your immediate and long-term welfare. The lower region of the anterior cingulate cortex has been identified as being involved in emotional conflict. So whenever a situation causes you to want to express an emotion that might be harmful to your long-term welfare, this lower region 'lights up' because the frontal lobe is going to help you suppress that emotion.

The anterior cingulate cortex has been found to be smaller in people with ADHD and it doesn't seem to turn on in adults with ADHD. Unfortunately, this means that the limbic system, which is involved in creating emotions such as compliance and anger and has a role in motivation, will not be regulated and the individual will be rather emotionally impulsive. The person could be described as having a low frustration tolerance, as being impatient, becomes angry quite quickly, displays a hatred of having to wait, and shows their raw and unrestrained emotions more quickly than individuals without ADHD. Now this is not necessarily a mood disorder, in fact the moods might be quite normal, rather the individual is failing to *suppress* their emotion. An individual without ADHD would inhibit their emotions and use self-calming and self-soothing techniques. They contemplate what they are feeling (and thinking) and then moderate how they express their emotions to best suit their long-term welfare. A person with ADHD finds it very difficult to do this. So ADHD then is a failure to *regulate* emotion. Barkley provides the following example of how this might look:

> So if you are an adult with ADHD and in a business meeting where you have just been insulted by your supervisor, you are much more likely to leap across the table and throttle your supervisor and you will be fired. Everybody else felt as you felt, thought what you thought, and summarily suppressed it; in their mind they throttle the supervisor, but it is not released to be expressed through the spinal cord into real behaviour and action. The mood is the same; the expression of the mood is not.

This shows us then that this failure to regulate emotion is just as much a part of the anterior cingulate cortex as inattention, poor working memory, poor time management, and impulsive decision-making. It is the inability of the anterior cingulate cortex to manage the limbic system; so that once emotions are provoked they are not expressed in a manner that is detrimental for our social goals. Barkley also suggests that these parts of the brain are typically two to three years behind in their development.

An area of the brain that hasn't been discussed yet is the primary motor cortex. According to Barkley this part of the brain matures far too quickly in people with ADHD and is where small and discrete behaviours take place. This would, of course, explain the restlessness and hyperactive movements seen in people with ADHD. This early-matured part of the brain is not controlled by the immature frontal region of the brain and it is this that causes hyperactivity. This would explain why adults may experience a sense of restlessness but don't exhibit hyperactive behaviour.

Then there is the frontal-striatal circuit that is the connection between the frontal lobe and the basal ganglia. The basal ganglia are associated with cognitive and emotional functions and influence which one of several possible actions a person chooses to carry out at a given time. This is also where our working memory is located. Working memory has a limited capacity to temporarily store, process and manipulate information and is where we hold plans and take the necessary steps to accomplish those plans. There is also a second system that connects from the frontal lobe back into the cerebellum which is also part of the 'cool executive network' and determines when we will attempt to accomplish our plans and the timing of them, which is so important to completing our goals. A third network connects from the frontal lobe through the anterior cingulate cortex into the limbic system. This is an emotion network and is known as the 'hot executive system' and is where we moderate our emotions so they are consistent with achieving our goals. Those of you reading this who have children with ADHD would know they have real problems in this area.

Barkley further suggested that an emotion is actually a motivational state that can be described as arousal, approach or withdrawal, and reward or punishment. In this instance, it is important to understand the motivational aspect because if emotions are in fact motivations, and the frontal lobe is regulating those emotions, you should be able to self-regulate your motivation. The frontal limbic circuit is where we are able to motivate ourselves when there is no reward or punishment. This is where thinking about our goals actually becomes our motivator — you have a goal, you want to reach that goal and that motivation will keep you going almost regardless of how long it takes even when there are no rewards. The limbic system can motivate behaviour and this is where persistence, willpower and the ability to map out a course of action and stick to it comes from. Many people with ADHD simply are not self-disciplined enough to reach their goals and need immediate rewards and consequences to help them persist with a task. They are literally dependant on external forms of motivation.

It might come as a bit of a surprise to some of you, but according to this theory ADHD *is not* an attentional disorder but rather a short-sightedness to the future and to impending future events. This means that people with ADHD don't really think about or plan for the future, they simply wait until the future is at their doorstep and then they try to deal with it. ADHD, as a disorder, prevents the person from being able to prepare and organise for the distant future so there's no point in telling little Johnny that if he is good for the whole year he will get a special reward at the end of it. This means that everything has the potential to become a crisis. Most of you parents out there will know that homework is put off until the very last minute (if the child remembers at all) and then there is a major crisis the night before (or in the morning) trying to get it completed in time. This is frustrating for parents because they know the crisis could have been avoided if their child had just put in the effort and organised themselves a little better and wasn't so 'damned lazy'. But now you know this carefree, lazy attitude may very well be an executive failure. Because future-directed behaviour or planning for the future is intentional, this means then that ADHD is actually a disorder of intention.

The executive system is the place where we take our knowledge and apply it to our everyday life. The back part of our brain is the area that gains knowledge and the front part of the brain uses it. However, ADHD has separated these two so it really makes no difference what knowledge the person may have, they simply cannot use it as successfully as people without ADHD. This suggests to us then that ADHD is a performance disorder and not a knowledge disorder. Most people with ADHD have just about the same amount of knowledge as most other people in their communities with the same level of education but they are not able to use that knowledge as well as people without ADHD. Barkley suggests, 'people with ADHD know what to do, but they can't do what they know'.

## How is the brain studied?

How do we really know there are any brain regions implicated in ADHD? The answer lies in brain studies. There are many ways in which the brain is studied but for the purposes of this book, we are only going to focus briefly on a few of these. Currently there are about five main ways to study the brain and this is through imaging techniques. Such techniques typically fall into the two categories of magnetic imaging and nuclear imaging, however, many of the studies in ADHD only use the magnetic imaging technique in an effort to avoid using the radioactive substances required in nuclear imaging. There are three main variations of magnetic imaging:

- Magnetic Resonance Imaging (MRI)
- Functional Magnetic Resonance Imaging (fMRI), and
- Magnetic Resonance Spectroscopy (MRS).

Each one of these techniques has a role to play and can tell us something very important about the different regions of the brain. For instance, the MRI permits a structural analysis of the brain such as the location, shape and size of different subregions and is thus used in studies of ADHD to determine the size of different brain regions. Functional Magnetic Resonance Imaging (fMRI) is a little bit like MRI but when a region of the brain is busy it has an increase in oxygen levels containing haemoglobin in the red blood cells. The fMRI is able to detect differences in oxygen levels and this means it can identify the activity level of the brain in a given region. The MRS has some very real limitations to it and for that reason alone it is limited in its use in studies. Essentially, MRS looks at different chemicals in the body such as dopamine, the main chemical implicated in ADHD. The problem is that dopamine cannot be isolated and directly measured.

## WHAT DOES THE RESEARCH SAY?

One might reasonably ask if there is any evidence that might support all this theorising? The answer is a decisive yes. In fact, we could dedicate an entire book to just looking at the different studies on the brain that consistently demonstrate differences in brain regions of people with ADHD. The results of these studies demonstrate:

- FMRI and single photon emission computed tomography (SPECT) have revealed less activity in the cingulate gyrus of children with ADHD.
- FMRI studies have also demonstrated that the cingulate gyrus is dysfunctional during certain activities.
- SPECT has been used to examine cerebral blood flow in children with ADHD. The results have consistently shown

a decrease in blood flow to the right prefrontal regions of the brain and the pathways that connect them to the limbic system via the striatum (specifically the caudate nucleus) and the cerebellum.

- MRI studies have found differences in the size of certain brain regions in children with ADHD. The studies have shown significantly smaller right frontal regions, and a smaller caudate nucleus.
- Other studies have shown that the size of the basal ganglia and the frontal lobe correlate with the degree of problems with inhibition and attention.
- Still other studies have found smaller cerebellar volume.
- Increasing evidence from the different imaging techniques has found that children with ADHD have anatomical differences in the prefrontal cortex, basal ganglia and the corpus callosum.
- Other areas of the brain, such as the parietal lobe and cerebellum, have also been shown to have anatomical differences in people with ADHD.
- Studies comparing brain activity between people with and without ADHD have constantly shown there is less striatal activation and less prefrontal activation in those with ADHD.
- Functional imaging has found lower levels of activity in the striatum.
- One of the most important neuroimaging studies of ADHD found smaller total cerebral brain volumes from childhood through to adolescence.

What a chapter to work through with so much technical information! While this evidence may seem impressive, we do have to be mindful that with all studies on the human brain there are definite limitations and because of these limitations we cannot generalise the findings to the entire population of people with ADHD. Furthermore, we must be very careful that the results of such studies don't infer that the anatomical differences *cause* the disorder but rather indicate the disorder is very real and not a figment of the imagination. We know that not only are there neurological implications to ADHD, but we have seen there are other causes to ADHD such as smoking and alcohol consumption during pregnancy and exposure to toxins. The question is, do we have to go to the extent of having the brain examined to determine whether or not a child might have ADHD? Well, not really. There are a number of recognised and reliable assessments that professionals use to assess people of all ages for ADHD.

# CHAPTER 5

## Diagnosing ADHD

The website of the Australian Psychological Society had an article about ADHD that read:

> *A US study has recently found the use of drugs to treat ADHD had more than tripled worldwide since 1993 and Australia was among the heaviest users of these drugs. It was reported that about 30 per cent of Australian children diagnosed with ADHD were misdiagnosed and one in 100 children were medicated for it. The reason ADHD was often misdiagnosed was through a misunderstanding of the disorder.*

If this report is correct, it is alarming that 30 per cent of children diagnosed with ADHD are actually incorrectly diagnosed. The personal, social, emotional and academic fallout from such a misdiagnosis could be huge — and it often is. Essentially, this report is stating that one in three children is misdiagnosed with ADHD and one in every 100 children is medicated for this disorder. Such a report is disturbing for a number of reasons and ought to generate some very serious questions such as, 'How is it possible that so many children are being misdiagnosed with ADHD?' This naturally generates more questions of equal importance such as, 'Who is doing the diagnosing and how is it possible that these individuals can be so wrong?' But the report above gives us the answer: *The reason ADHD was often misdiagnosed was through a misunderstanding of the disorder.* The most obvious questions remaining then are, 'How is ADHD assessed and who should be performing assessments to make a diagnosis for ADHD?'

A couple of years ago I was somewhat disturbed at the sudden increase in parents attending my clinic claiming their child had just received a diagnosis of ADHD. Each of the parents reported they had taken their child to individuals who had apparently not only claimed they were professionals but who were also qualified to diagnose ADHD. Unfortunately, the so-called professionals only spent about 10 to 15 minutes with the parents before they reached a diagnosis of ADHD. As I spent time with each family a disturbing trend in the diagnostic procedure began to emerge. Each of these professionals did not refer to the diagnostic criteria once in the process of diagnosing the children, but made a diagnosis based purely on what they considered to be a child's hyperactive behaviour. An extremely detailed clinical developmental interview with the children's parents and subsequent assessments revealed that not one of the children who had been diagnosed with ADHD in a 10-minute session actually had the disorder. In fact, the poor children were found to have other disorders such as autism spectrum disorder, auditory processing disorder, and learning disorders. Try to imagine for a moment how difficult that whole process must have been for the parents and the child. They first had to come to terms with receiving a diagnosis of ADHD from someone using their *authority* to make the diagnosis. Then, when the parents who were still coming to terms with the implications of that diagnosis sought further help, they were informed that the diagnosis they had originally received was wrong, that, in fact, it was suspected the child was autistic and in order to know for sure the child would need to undergo a number of other assessments. Imagine how the parents felt when the results came back and for the second time they found themselves on the receiving end of bad news.

Throughout this book you will notice I have stated again and again the need for a qualified professional to be involved in the assessment and treatment of your child for ADHD, and not just anyone claiming to be a professional, but one who is appropriately trained and experienced to make such a diagnosis and offer appropriate treatment. During my career as a psychologist I have seen firsthand the emotional distress, anxiety, fear, anger and uncertainty placed on entire families when their child is diagnosed with a disorder such as ADHD. Unfortunately, there have also been a number of times where for such a family their emotional distress has just begun. Too many times families have been sitting in my clinic seeking help to learn how to cope with and manage this disorder, only to be informed that the ADHD diagnosis is most likely incorrect and that their child will need to undergo further assessments to determine the true nature of the problem or cause of concern. It is frustrating when you see the parents' immediate joy, elation and sigh of relief at being told their child does not have ADHD turn to confusion, sadness, frustration and anger at having to deal with a completely new diagnosis. Consider the following account of a family that sought my assistance for their son.

John and Mary were seeking a new school for their son — we'll call him Dylan. They had heard about a local school that was well regarded not only for its academic excellence but also for the way the teachers were dedicated to their job and to the emotional and social wellbeing of their students. So, after attending an open day, John and Mary decided they would enrol Dylan in the school, even though he was halfway through grade two. Dylan had only been at the new school for six weeks when his mother was confronted by his schoolteacher, who requested a meeting with her to discuss Dylan's progress. According to the teacher, the transition to a new school had been a bit of a struggle for Dylan. The day of the scheduled meeting arrived and for the parents their assumption was that they would only be meeting with Dylan's classroom teacher. However, when they arrived for the meeting they were somewhat surprised to see that the educational support coordinator (Jan) and the primary school coordinator were also present for the meeting. As the meeting progressed (or intervention, as it later became known), Mary began to notice it was not the kind of meeting she thought it would be and told me she felt:

> ... quite ganged up on and intimidated especially as the un-introduced educational support coordinator bombarded me with questions regarding Dylan, including our parenting and disciplining and his early development ... I was asked to reveal quite personal information to individuals who had done little to gain my trust.

The 'meeting' had gone on for about 40 minutes when Jan confidently announced her diagnosis to John and Mary that their son had Asperger's syndrome (Asperger's syndrome is high-functioning autism). Imagine how difficult this situation must have been for the parents. Even more disturbing is what happened next. When the parents questioned this 'diagnosis', Jan quickly replied, 'Many parents initially deny the diagnosis and many prefer to live in denial than to understand a different kind of normal'. Mary continued to question Jan's diagnosis and contacted a friend of hers who had not only known the family since Dylan was a toddler, but who was also at the time a teacher at a specialist school for children with autism. This woman was also quite surprised at the diagnosis and believed it was incorrect. Mary then contacted an early learning centre for further information and they informed her that the school had no right to make such a diagnosis. And the early learning centre was right: a diagnosis for autism spectrum disorder can only be made when a paediatrician, a psychologist and a speech pathologist are involved. Notice this list does not include an educational support coordinator at a local primary school.

For the rest of his first year at school, Dylan's parents heard nothing more from his teachers. However, two months into the second year at the same school, it started all over again when Mary and John were called to an intervention meeting where the same diagnosis of autism was raised. This time it was suggested that Dylan begin to see the school's welfare officer. Mary agreed and Dylan began presenting to the welfare officer. By the end of the first term, however, the welfare officer reported she couldn't offer Dylan any further assistance and that Mary and John should take him to see a psychologist. So, Mary and John found a local psychologist who, during their first meeting, informed them he was familiar with Dylan's school and that he had seen a number of students there. Mary informed the psychologist that in his first year at the new school, Dylan had been diagnosed with Asperger's syndrome by the school's educational support coordinator, and that they disagreed with this diagnosis. They believed the underlying issue for Dylan was anxiety, as he had just started a new school and was not getting along with his teacher. So it was agreed the psychologist would assess Dylan in an effort to find out what was going on. As part of the assessment phase, Dylan completed an IQ assessment and his teacher was sent a behavioural questionnaire to fill out. The psychologist also mentioned that he would be able to conduct a behavioural observation of Dylan during school hours.

What seems to be somewhat astounding here is that by Mary's reports the psychologist failed to appropriately assess Dylan for autism spectrum disorder (a psychologist, paediatrician and speech pathologist must all be involved in the assessment for autism). Dylan was not referred to a paediatrican or a speech pathologist and as such this failed to rule out autism as a potential cause for his behaviour. Instead, this psychologist concluded Dylan was not depressed or psychotic, and noted in his written report that he felt there were:

> *Attention Deficit Hyperactivity Problems ... Oppositional Defiant Problems ... and Anxiety Problems ... In all settings Dylan has consistently displayed high levels of poor impulse control and constant, restless movement. This is consistent with his teacher's observations ... In my opinion [this] indicates Dylan has ADHD ... I'm not convinced that he has an Autistic Spectrum Disorder.*

Why is it such a big deal to not rule out one problem from another? Well, it's quite a significant issue because as mentioned in earlier chapters there are a number of childhood disorders with overlapping symptoms and many times children have been misdiagnosed because of the similarities of symptoms between two or more childhood disorders. Furthermore, that Dylan was not observed in different settings is also significant. A developmental disorder does not just show up at school — it must be evident across a number of different settings. Mary further reported that once the assessment was completed, the schoolteacher, the educational support coordinator, the primary school coordinator, the psychologist and both parents had a follow-up meeting at the school. According to Mary all the 'professionals' at this meeting were surprised to find out that Dylan did not display any of the behaviours associated with autism or ADHD in a number of different settings including at home and while attending church services that would often last for up to two hours. No one had bothered to check. The psychologist only observed Dylan *once* on the school property and failed to establish any significant impairment in any other environment.

Following the meeting John and Mary received a copy of the meeting's minutes and noted that the educational support coordinator had made an addition to the minutes that the parents would follow up with a paediatrician regarding possible treatment and medication for ADHD. As it turns out the issue of consulting with a paediatrician to have their son medicated was never discussed in the meeting with the parents. Some months later Dylan was sent home for 'inappropriate internet usage' (remember we are talking about an eight-year-old child, so the application of 'inappropriate internet usage' is unknown and could simply mean the boy was playing games). According to Mary, she had to speak with Jan as part of the process of Dylan returning to the school. During this meeting Jan wanted to know about Dylan's medication for ADHD. Apparently she was not very happy when Mary informed her that, as they did not agree the diagnosis was correct in the first place, they were not having their son medicated. Jan simply replied that if the parents did not medicate their son they 'might need to re-visit their relationship with the school'. Eventually Dylan was referred to a specialist ADHD clinic where it was found that he was an intelligent boy who was articulate and very sensitive to others' feelings with no signs of oppositional defiant disorder and that he did not have ADHD or autism spectrum disorder, but that it was more likely anxiety.

The teachers in the above examples are highly trained individuals in their field and as part of their job they are exposed to a lot of mental health disorders in children. Schoolteachers have a very clear part to play when it comes to children's mental and emotional health and should not be mistrusted or ignored because of the examples above that demonstrated some unfortunate outcomes. Teachers do have your child in their care anywhere from six to eight hours per day and believe me they get to see both the best and the worst in a lot of children. Because of their training and experience, teachers will often be aware that something is not right with a child and, as has been pointed out, 'the vast majority of recommendations for psychiatric evaluation of our nation's children continue to come from the school system'. If your child's schoolteacher raises concerns about your child, it would be wise to follow up those concerns with an appropriate professional. The point of such an example is not to undermine the professionalism of such highly trained individuals, but rather to provide you with a deeper understanding and knowledge of how problems can occur in the diagnosis process, what to expect if you have to go through this process and what questions to ask the professional to ensure you get the right person with the right training to help you and your child.

Professional organisations around the world recognise the complexity of diagnosing ADHD, such as community sentiment, the fears and concerns around what appears to be such a common diagnosis, and the medicating of children for a disorder that may be considered a hoax in the first place. Such organisations are also aware of the way the media presents their reports about the professional community and ADHD (more about this later), the dilemma professionals face when assessing for such a disorder, and the problems often associated with the assessment phase. Because of the concerns many people might have, professional organisations around the world have developed standards or positions on the assessment, diagnosis and treatment of ADHD which their members are expected to follow.

The Australian Psychological Society (APS) is the professional association with which many thousands of psychologists around Australia hold membership. Among the many roles the APS performs, it offers members of the public information on quite a lot of common mental health issues they might be facing, including ADHD. With their opening statement, 'There is much debate over the most appropriate ways to measure ADHD', the APS readily recognises the complexity of diagnosing ADHD and the importance of seeking the right person to provide the diagnosis. The APS recognises the need and the right of the involvement of the medical profession in the process of diagnosing ADHD when they state, 'Assessment or diagnosis of ADHD is often undertaken in the first instance by a medical professional such as a paediatrician or child psychiatrist ...'. When a psychologist is involved in the process of diagnosing ADHD, the APS has released a position paper informing the psychologist of what is expected of them in order to make a reliable diagnosis. Consider the following:

> *It is strongly recommended that psychologists use rating scales, questionnaires and other measures with known, or well-established, psychometric properties [in other words highly reliable tests] ... and other tests that have different versions for collecting information from the child, their parents/caregivers and their teachers ... Measures of intellectual capacity and potential, as well as attentional tests, adjustment tests and behavioural assessment scales should all be completed. Observation of the child's behaviour is usually undertaken to supplement the tests. Cognitive tests of attention and its impact on memory and learning can be helpful in establishing and analysing the attentional disorder. Other measures used by psychologists include IQ tests; tests of learning, reading and mathematics; scales that assess behaviour and social interactions; as well as information about the child's birth and early developmental milestones, including any significant life events such as injuries and hospitalisation ... Assessment of the child's behaviour at home and in school must also be undertaken.*

Also in their position paper, the APS covers the issue of comorbidity. Comorbidity is simply a term that means two or more disorders can co-exist. As you will learn in Chapter 6, ADHD is often comorbid with a number of other disorders such as depression, learning disorders and other behavioural disorders. The APS position paper reads that psychologists must also possess *the necessary skills and understanding to look for co-morbidity.* This is one reason why such a comprehensive assessment phase is critical before a diagnosis can be made.

The Royal Australasian College of Physicians was funded by the Australian Government's National Health and Medical Research Centre (NHMRC) to draw up a draft edition of guidelines for assessing

ADHD to update the old guidelines that were withdrawn in 2005. The end result was quite an exhaustive approach for the assessment, diagnosis and subsequent treatment of ADHD. The guidelines state that doctors should use the DSM-5 criteria as the absolute minimum to make a diagnosis of ADHD. But the diagnosis can only be made 'after a comprehensive assessment. This includes medical, developmental and psychosocial assessment and elicitation of evidence of impairment in multiple settings, via gathering information from multiple informants'. So for doctors, they are also expected to complete a comprehensive assessment phase that would normally include a psychologist, child psychiatrist or paediatrician.

The guidelines painstakingly describe each phase of the assessment, including what assessments ought to be used and how and what to do when assessing children, adolescents and adults. For instance, when assessing children and adolescents, the guidelines recommend the use of the Conners Rating Scales (CRS) for children, and for adults the recommended assessment is either the Conners Adult ADHD Rating Scales (CAARS) or Barkley's Adult ADHD Quick Screen as the initial assessment. Furthermore, the guidelines also suggest that a full assessment for ADHD requires a comprehensive medical assessment, and a developmental and psychosocial assessment by an individual such as a paediatrician or a child and adolescent psychiatrist as, according to the Royal Australasian College of Physicians, they are considered to be 'the best qualified clinicians with the training and skills required to assess and treat ADHD'.

Interestingly, there are a number of similarities between the APS recommendations and the Royal Australasian College of Physicians guidelines for diagnosing ADHD. For example, the Royal Australasian College of Physicians also recommends that information about the child is collected from multiple informants, including the child, the parents or caregivers, teachers and other health professionals to determine just how long and how bad the behaviours are before a GP can diagnose ADHD. Furthermore, doctors are advised that in order to avoid an over diagnosis of the disorder, they should not solely rely on the use of parent or teacher information in isolation, but rather information from *both* parents and teachers. As in accordance with the DSM-5, doctors are also directed to seek evidence of 'moderate to severe impairment across settings, including home and school', and are therefore advised to seek evidence of ADHD symptoms by having a detailed discussion with the family members. Then doctors are encouraged to assess for comorbidities such as learning disorders, anxiety disorders, depression and other behavioural disorders and they need to conduct a *psycho-educational* assessment to determine whether there may be other problems such as cognitive deficits, learning difficulties and social adaptive problems.

The American Academy of Paediatrics Clinical Practise Guidelines for the assessment of ADHD also recommend a comprehensive evaluation of a child take place, particularly if the child is between the ages of six and twelve and is unusually:

> ... *inattentive, hyperactive, impulsive, underachieving at school; or having behavior problems. If the parent/caregiver or teachers note these issues it is recommended that a paediatrician evaluates the child to determine if ADHD is present.*

Paediatricians are then informed that the child must meet the criteria as set out in the DSM-5, and they must also have direct evidence from parents or caregivers that the symptoms are present across a number of different settings, including how long the symptoms have been present and how the symptoms impair the child's performance or ability to function in various settings. The paediatrician must also gather information from the child's schoolteacher to determine whether ADHD symptoms are evident in the classroom and how much they might interfere with the child's learning or whether the child may have a learning disorder or behavioural disorder. Further informants include the child, kindergarten or preschool teachers, and childcare staff. The paediatrician must then make sure there are no comorbidity concerns and make a thorough medical examination of the child in question before reaching a diagnosis of ADHD. This process is not going to happen in a 10-minute session with your local doctor or in a meeting with your child's schoolteacher. Also, you will note that only paediatricians, child psychiatrists, psychologists and some family doctors are in a position to make a diagnosis of ADHD. We could go on and on reviewing the position papers from professional health organisations from countries all over the world, but the point has been made! It's time now to look at the way critics refute the existence of ADHD by contesting the validity and reliability of assessments used to diagnose the disorder.

## Criticisms of assessments used to diagnose ADHD

The way in which ADHD is diagnosed has not escaped the critics. At first glance such arguments appear to be substantiated and can appear to be quite convincing, and then there are those arguments that really don't deserve to be mentioned at all! One of the claims against the existence of ADHD refers directly to the lack of any one single diagnostic tool. According to this position, ADHD simply cannot exist because diagnosing the disorder requires the use of a number of different assessments. Consider for a moment what you have just read in the above section and what is involved in order to reach a correct diagnosis of ADHD:

- The parents are given questionnaires to complete about the child.
- The parents are also interviewed to provide a comprehensive developmental history of child.
- The child is directly assessed.
- Teachers are given questionnaires to complete about the child's behaviours and academic performance.
- Parents, teachers and the individual concerned can all be interviewed independently.
- A full medical check-up is expected and the child must be observed in multiple settings.
- The child is also assessed for disorders that might account for the problems, such as another behavioural disorder that might be confused with ADHD.
- The child is also assessed for comorbid conditions such as depression, anxiety and learning disorders.

This comprehensive process must take place because ADHD is an incredibly complex disorder that affects the individual in so many different ways, from concentration to behaviour to their social skills (or lack thereof), to their relationships with others, to school performance and academic success, to employment options and opportunities, right through to affecting different parts of the brain. Because of this, numerous assessments are required to provide a reliable diagnosis of ADHD.

There have also been criticisms about the status of the rater, which is the person who completes the questionnaires. The objections include the tolerance level of the rater, the rater's understanding of normal childhood development, the gender of the rater, the age of the rater, their personality type and so on. Such objections suggest that the frazzled schoolteacher at the end of a long day will most likely be intolerant of the child's behaviour and that this intolerance would be reflected in the answers the teacher provides in a questionnaire about the child's behaviour. Thus the teacher would more be likely to indicate the child's behaviour is worse than it really is. Again it sounds like a feasible argument on the surface and in some circumstances this might be a valid concern, as it is true that there can be rater bias. However, as already noted the parent/teacher rater forms are only ONE part of the diagnostic procedure. The objection about the gender of the rater is a very real cause for concern. There appears to be a particular uneasiness about the gender of teachers. According to this objection just about all schoolteachers are female and are practising feminists. Because most of them are feminists they most likely will not tolerate 'normal' overt male behaviour. This intolerance would then be reflected in a questionnaire about the child's behaviour and thus give a false positive of ADHD.

However, critics don't stop there; they also believe the actual questions or statements in questionnaires used to help determine ADHD are too abstract and generally wrong. For example, the statement concerning the child 'often fidgets with hands or feet' doesn't make sense to the critics, as they demand a working definition of the word 'fidgets'. Likewise the statement, 'often has difficulty playing quietly' also presents a problem as they argue, 'What culture expects that children will play quietly?' It seems these individuals can't understand who would want a child to play quietly or in what circumstances it might be appropriate for a child to play quietly. I can think of a few cultures that might object to a noisy child playing cops and robbers at a funeral. The statement, 'often fails to give close attention to details or makes mistakes in schoolwork' also seems to be problematic for these individuals as they argue, 'children are notorious for paying close attention to that which interests them'. You know, it almost seems as if these individuals really don't know what ADHD looks like in the classroom, at church, at a funeral, at school, or even at the shopping centre, and it's amazing how they keep forgetting the behaviours far exceed those of other children without the disorder.

Often questionnaires will have from four to five options to answer the questions or statements, such as Never, Rarely, Sometimes, Often and Always. One individual raised an objection that these terms are far too abstract for people to really make an informed decision and therefore this undermines the reliability and validity of the results. The argument generally sounds something like this: 'The answers contained in the ADHD assessment questionnaires are also highly subjective'. Such an argument suggests that you and I would have very different interpretations of 'Never' or 'Always' and on the surface this sounds like a plausible argument. Consider the following example. A schoolteacher is provided a questionnaire about one of her students as part of the assessment phase for ADHD. One of the questions she has to answer is '[the child] often fails to give close attention to details or makes mistakes in schoolwork'. The possible answers she can choose from are: Never, Rarely, Sometimes, Often and Always. As she reads this question and looks up at the child she is assessing to compare his classroom behaviour against that of the other twenty students sitting in front of her, do you really think that teacher is going to struggle trying to understand the definition of 'Rarely' as she notes that the child is out of his chair for the hundredth time that day and is talking loudly to the children sitting next him trying to convince them it's time to go outside and play? Likewise, supposing the parents are given a similar questionnaire that asks, 'Does your child constantly get down from the dinner table each evening for the duration of the evening meal?' Do you think the parents are going to have a philosophical dilemma trying to determine if 'Often' or 'Always' for the father means exactly the same as 'Often' or 'Always' for the mother? I don't think so. If your child gets down from the dinner table every 30 seconds every single night of the week, I think both parents might know exactly what they are talking about!

Consider the following account that took place in my clinic. A boy was referred to me because his schoolteacher was concerned that he might have ADHD. On meeting the boy for the first time, I noticed he could not sit in his chair for more than 15 seconds at a time without jumping up and investigating every book in my office, every pencil and every pen on my desk, and the computer and printer in the office. Each new find was followed with questions such as, 'What's this?', 'What do you use this for?', and 'How come you have so many pencils?'. Grabbing the cord to the telephone he asked, 'Why is this connected to the telephone?' and before I could answer him he dropped the cord and ran to the other side of the office to the window, where with unmeasured enthusiasm he grabbed the venetian blinds and pushed them apart with such force that they were permanently bent, just so he could look out of the window to see what fun he was missing out on and then demand to go outside and play. While he was looking out of the window he saw a pushbike leaning against a tree and wanted to know to whom it belonged; again, before I could answer him he began demanding to ride it. His behaviour in the office reminded me of a blowfly that had just been hit with a burst of fly spray — he was buzzing around everywhere. When he did sit on the chair he swung his legs back and forth constantly. He fidgeted about in the chair picking at the material and investigating its frame. Then it was back to roaming about the office. All of this took place in roughly the first 10 minutes of our meeting. Such a description would to most reasonable people suggest that this boy's behaviour does not necessarily fit 'normal' childhood behaviour. Now place this boy's behaviour in the classroom and ask yourself if you were the teacher of this boy and he behaved like this every single day from beginning to end and you were asked the question, 'often fails to give close attention to details or makes mistakes in schoolwork', how do you think you might answer? I suspect most people might know what they mean by 'Often' or 'Always'.

If the parent/teacher rater questionnaires were the only means of diagnosing ADHD, one might raise concerns that such an assessment procedure could very well be inadequate, but not for the reasons noted above. Proponents of the theory that ADHD is a disorder dreamed up by drug companies conveniently forget that the questionnaires that parents, teachers and other carers, as well as the child, complete are but one part of the whole assessment phase. To take one part of the whole assessment procedure and argue it is worthless is a preposterous argument as it ignores the whole process. Once each of the raters has completed and returned their questionnaires, the results from all of the different questionnaires are collected, calculated and compared to each other. One would expect that any significant variation between the raters' answers would be evident and accounted for by the professional when they are analysing the data. If there were significant variations between the raters, the professional would be ethically obliged to investigate this further before making a diagnosis. This is a sore point for the critics, as it seems they really don't want you to trust that the professional actually knows what they are doing.

## How do we know assessments are reliable?

We've been discussing some of the more common criticisms around a number of the assessments used to determine a diagnosis of ADHD, but how do we know if the tests are reliable in the first place? The full account of the way in which the reliability and validity of psychological assessments are determined is beyond the scope of this book, so without getting caught up in the complexity of statistical analysis and how an assessment is subjected to rigorous and unforgiving analysis, a reliable assessment is one that shows consistency. A valid and reliable assessment must be proven to measure what it was designed to measure.

This means that a reliable and valid assessment is not just a bunch of random questions someone slaps together in a haphazard way in the hope of getting some positive response to support their suspicion the individual has ADHD, or any other mental health disorder for that matter. An assessment will undergo rigorous scrutiny and will also be subjected to peer revision *before* it is used with members of the general public and *before* a professional will take it seriously. It is during this process that researchers will find out if any of the questions they intended to use are inaccurate. If a question or series of questions is found to be inaccurate and cannot be altered so it is accurate, the question will be dropped from the questionnaire. We cannot use a questionnaire that does not accurately gauge what it was designed to measure. Once an assessment has undergone this process and all necessary changes are made to ensure it is valid and reliable, the researchers will then use that assessment with volunteer families to confirm the test's reliability and validity and to begin developing norms. That is, the researchers will often gather hundreds or even thousands of volunteers and develop what is considered to be 'normal' behaviour in that age group, that gender, that culture and that disorder and so forth and then compare the results to groups of people without the disorder. For example, this process was done with the most widely used and accepted intelligence test, the Wechsler Adult Intelligence Scale (WAIS). By establishing norms of functioning and intelligence we are now able to determine if someone has an intellectual disability or if the person may experience problems in particular areas such as processing verbal instructions, or even if they are intellectually gifted. In other words, any assessment must consistently yield very similar results each time under the same or similar conditions before it can be considered reliable and valid and be used with members of the public.

## What assessments are used to diagnose ADHD?

There are typically a number of assessments that a professional will use for the diagnosis of ADHD. This information is essential for the reader to be aware of for a number of reasons. First of all, if you are about to have your child tested for ADHD, the information below will give you some idea of what to expect during the assessment phase. Also some of the assessments discussed below are only available to registered psychologists. This is an important point to note because it means that some charlatan cannot try to take advantage of you by telling you they have all the right assessments they need to make a diagnosis of ADHD. It also means that if a professional has these instruments, you will know that they are more likely to be well trained and experienced in diagnosing ADHD.

## DIAGNOSTIC AND STATISTICAL MANUAL OF MENTAL DISORDERS, 5TH EDITION (DSM-5)

The *Diagnostic and Statistical Manual of Mental Disorders*, 5th edition, (DSM-5), is the leading diagnostic tool used by professionals. The DSM covers a gamut of mental health disorders from childhood through to adulthood, and where possible, records the symptoms of the disorder, the usual comorbid conditions of the disorder, the aetiology of a disorder (or the known causes of the disorder) and other important information such as differences in the rates of the disorder between the genders, and the typical age at which the disorder is likely to develop. Because the DSM provides such a clear understanding of a particular mental health disorder, it also aids in the preparation of the most appropriate treatment options for the individual. The American Psychiatric Association writes the DSM 'is a categorical classification that divides mental disorders into types based on criterion sets with defining features'. However, the DSM is not just for diagnosing mental illnesses as it is also used to help professionals identify many childhood problems including behavioural problems and behavioural disorders such as ADHD. It is important to remember that childhood conditions such as ADHD are way outside what is considered to be 'normal' childhood behaviour. It has been stated of the DSM that:

> ... *researchers and clinicians ... diagnose and conceptualize the conditions presented (symptoms of a disorder) [in DSM] as disorders that are qualitatively distinct from normal functioning and from one another.*

The DSM classifies attention deficit hyperactivity disorder (ADHD) as a neurodevelopmental disorder that is first seen in childhood and persists into adulthood. Simply, neurodevelopmental disorders are problems that come into being during a child's developmental period. The DSM states that:

*... neurodevelopmental disorders are a group of conditions with onset in the developmental period. The disorders typically manifest early in development often before the child enters grade school, and are characterized by developmental deficits that produce impairments of personal, social, academic, or occupational functioning ... ADHD [is] defined by impairing levels of inattention, disorganization, and/or hyperactivity–impulsivity ... symptoms that are excessive for age or developmental level.*

According to the DSM, ADHD has three core symptoms including inattention, hyperactivity and impulsivity. Each of these 'core' symptoms has associated problems that are typically evident across the child's different environments. The DSM lists the associated problems to each of the three core symptoms, and in order to receive a successful diagnosis of ADHD, each of the three core symptoms must be accompanied by a set number of different problems. Also, the associated problems must be well outside normal childhood developmental stages, have been present for at least six months and be considered maladaptive. The DSM criteria are listed in the table below.

| Inattention | | |
|---|---|---|
| The problem of inattention must have six or more of the following associated problems: | | |
| The child often struggles paying close attention to details and often makes careless or silly mistakes in schoolwork, work, or other activities. | Children with ADHD often lose things that they need to complete a task such as pens, pencils, school assignments and even their toys or for the adult his tools. | They dislike and will often avoid homework or schoolwork and are reluctant to undertake almost any task that requires sustained mental effort. |

| | | |
|---|---|---|
| Parents and teachers often complain the child does not follow through with instructions, nor do they finish schoolwork or chores, or duties in the workplace. These problems are not due to oppositional behaviour or the child failing to understand the instructions. | Often parents and teachers complain the child appears as though they are not listening when spoken to directly. | Even in playtime or other tasks the child often has difficulty with their attention. |
| Children with ADHD have real problems organising tasks and activities. | Children are often easily distracted by almost anything. | They are forgetful in their daily activities. |

### Hyperactivity

The problem of hyperactivity must have six or more associated problems that have also persisted for at least six months. For hyperactivity these include:

| | | |
|---|---|---|
| The child will almost constantly fidget with their hands or tap their feet and squirms about in their seat. | The child constantly runs about or climbs excessively in places where it is inappropriate to do so. In teenagers or adults this may be seen or experienced as constant feelings of restlessness. | Children with ADHD find it very difficult to play or engage in relaxing or restful activities quietly. |
| The child is constantly out of their seat in the classroom or in pretty much any other situation that demands they remain seated. | Children with ADHD are often 'on the go' or act as if 'driven by a motor'. | Children with ADHD often talk excessively. |

### Impulsivity

For impulsivity the associated problems include:

| | | |
|---|---|---|
| Children can't seem to wait their turn and they will often blurt out an answer even before the question has been completed. | Children often interrupt or intrude on others (for example, butt into conversations or games). | Some of the hyperactive–impulsive or inattentive symptoms that cause impairment must have been present before the child was seven years old. |
| Several inattentive or hyperactive–impulsive symptoms were present prior to the age of twelve years. | The child must experience some impairment from the symptoms in two or more different settings like school, home or work. | There has to be very clear evidence that the symptoms have caused significant problems for the person in social, academic, or employment situations; and |

| Are not the result of another disorder like schizophrenia, pervasive developmental disorder, mood disorder, anxiety disorder, dissociative disorder, or a personality disorder. | (*Source*: American Psychiatric Association, 2013, *Diagnostic and Statistical Manual of Mental Disorders* (5th edition).) |
|---|---|

Why would the DSM stipulate the symptoms of ADHD had to be present before the child was seven years old? Well, the simplest answer is that many childhood disorders have similar or overlapping features and symptoms to ADHD. For instance, depression, bipolar disorder and various anxiety disorders share many of the same characteristics as the three core features of ADHD. The DSM is aware that an incorrect diagnosis could be made by ill-qualified individuals and for that reason has provided a number of qualifiers such as age of onset, duration of the symptoms, and the pervasive or impairing nature of the symptoms. The age of onset is given as seven because symptoms occurring after this age may be indicating something very different such as an anxiety disorder, or major changes in the family such as parental divorce. You might remember the DSM states that any impairment from the symptoms of ADHD must also occur across *at least* two different places such as school, the child's home, church, a friend's place, or for the adolescent or adult, the workplace. This is because if the behaviours were to occur in only one setting such as school, it might be indicating the child has a learning disorder. It must also be very clear that the impairments interfere with normal developmentally appropriate social, academic or occupational performance and a clinician must also seek verifiable evidence that there is, in fact, significant interference in these settings. These additional criteria help the professional make a correct diagnosis.

Even if the child displays these symptoms, a diagnosis of ADHD still cannot be made until further information has been collected. Usually this information must be gathered from several key sources and includes interviewing the child's parents and schoolteacher as well as observing the child in their natural environments such as the school classroom or playground or at home. As such, when a psychologist is interviewing teachers and parents and observing the child, they are in fact gaining vital information from multiple sources and are building a case formulation. So while a cluster of symptoms like fidgeting, restlessness, forgetfulness or being terribly disorganised may suggest ADHD, the professional will need to rule out whether there is another disorder such as an anxiety disorder, post-traumatic stress disorder, depression, child abuse, learning problems or any one of a number of other potential problems that share similar features. In addition to this, some disorders also occur together or co-exist more frequently. This will be discussed at length in Chapter 6.

Given the DSM clearly defines the symptoms of ADHD and the typical behaviours associated with the disorder, assessments then primarily focus on the child's behaviours. The various assessments are designed to determine whether or not the child's behaviours are typical for children of that age or way outside 'normal' childhood behaviour and typical for a child with ADHD. That being the case, these assessments serve a second function: if ADHD has been ruled out, these assessments also help to point out what the problem could be.

## ACHENBACH CHILD BEHAVIOR CHECKLIST (CBCL)

The Achenbach Child Behavior Checklist (CBCL) is one of the most broadly used assessments to describe a child's behavioural and emotional problems using forms that are completed by parents, teachers and the older child. Forming part of the assessment procedure, the CBCL is considered to be highly reliable and dependable for gathering relevant information regarding the child and providing important information about how the child functions in a number of different environments. The CBCL was designed to be used by registered mental health professionals and suitably experienced medical doctors. The CBCL has two versions: one for children between eighteen months and five years of age, and another for children between six and eighteen years of age. These two questionnaires are each four pages long and are for obtaining reports from parents about their child's competencies and problems. They typically take about 20 minutes to complete. The CBCL six to eighteen questionnaire is subdivided into seven sections. The Competence or Social Competence section focus on the child's activities, social relationships and competence at school, while the Problem Behaviours section focuses on 118 specific behaviours with a further two sections for parents to record any other problem behaviours they might be aware of. The remaining sections of the CBCL include the Teacher Report Form (TRF), the Caregivers-Teacher Report Form and the Youth Self-Report (YSR 11–18). The Caregivers-Teacher Report Form will not be discussed here.

The first four subdivisions of the Social Competence section require parents to write in what sports their child likes to do, their child's favourite hobbies, activities and games, along with any clubs or teams the child might belong to and what jobs or chores the child does. The 118 items in the Problem Behaviours section are rated by the parent with three available answer options ranging from 0 if the item is not true of their child, 1 if the item is somewhat or sometimes true, and 2 if the item is very true or often true. The 118 items are designed to assess problem behaviours across a wide range of behaviours that include being withdrawn, somatic complaints (headaches, nausea and vomiting that may be the result of intense emotional stress), anxiety and/or depression, social problems, problem thoughts, problems with attention, delinquency and aggressive behaviour.

Equally, the child's schoolteacher is also provided a form to complete called the Teacher Report Form (TRF), and for concurrence of problem behaviour, it is recommended that more than one teacher be given the form to complete. The TRF is a 112-item report which measures internalising and externalising problems covers has many of the same items as the forms completed by the parents. The Attention Problems subscale measures symptoms of inattention, impulsivity and hyperactivity. Having two or more teachers complete the TRF will allow the clinician to compare the teachers' responses to the parents' responses. Finally, where a child is between the ages of eleven and eighteen, they can also be asked to complete the Youth Self-Report (YSR 11–18) containing 113 items to describe their own behavioural and emotional problems and competence.

Once each of the forms is completed and returned, the clinician will analyse and score the data and then make comparisons between each of the reports. Comparing the parents' reports with the reports from teachers and adolescents is especially important for identifying the consistency of behavioural problems reported across a variety of situations and with people the child may interact with as well as anxiety, depression, somatic complaints and attention problems. If there are discrepancies between a parent's response and a schoolteacher's response, the clinician will seek to understand this because such an inconsistency could be revealing something else. If, for instance, a child is aggressive at school yet these behaviours are not evidenced elsewhere, the clinician would need to determine the reason behind this inconsistency. Remember, though, that just because one teacher might report aggressive behaviour it does not automatically mean the teacher got it wrong or that the teacher is the cause of the child's problems. There are many reasons why a child's behaviour might be especially noticeable in one setting or with one person and not another. For instance, it might be that the child and that one teacher do clash or it might be that the child has a learning disorder, or it could be that the child is bullied at school and is fighting back. Once the clinician is satisfied there are no discrepancies, the results would then be compared to the child's age and gender norms to provide a measure of the severity of the behaviour or how deviant the child may be in comparison to children of the same age and sex.

## CONNERS RATING SCALES (CRS)

Another common form used by professionals to measure children's problem behaviour is known as the Conners Rating Scales (CRS). The individual who designed the CBCL has stated that the Conners Rating Scales are 'among the best known … for obtaining parent and teacher ratings of attention problems and hyperactivity'. Where it is suspected a child has ADHD, these rating scales are frequently used in conjunction with the CBCL. The CBCL is a good tool for assessing the degree of a child's problems across a number of different settings, while the CRS mainly focuses on attention problems and hyperactivity.

Dr Conners began developing the rating scales in the 1960s while he was completing his training at the Johns Hopkins Hospital, USA. At the time, Dr Conners was studying what effects stimulant medication had on young delinquents when he realised that parents and teachers were very good informants about the behavioural changes in the child. He ended up developing a list of problem behaviours that he found to be common in this group of children and provided the list to parents and teachers so that he could measure the changes in the child's behaviour. Eventually this list of problem behaviours was shared with colleagues who also gathered further information about how parents and teachers rated a child's behaviour at different ages. However, it wasn't until 1989 that the first copyrighted version of the Conners Rating Scales was published. Soon after publication, the CRS very quickly became a global success and is today considered to be the gold standard for assessing ADHD. In fact, this rating scale is arguably one of the most reliable, dependable and comprehensive assessments used in the diagnostic and identification process of ADHD. The CRS is also an important tool for the clinician to begin monitoring the progress of the child once therapy has begun.

The Conners Rating Scales is now in its third edition (the Conners 3, published in 2008), and is used not only for assessing ADHD but also common comorbid conditions such as conduct disorder and oppositional defiant disorder. As with the CBCL, the scale also includes a parent report form that assesses behaviours and other issues in children between the ages of six and eighteen, a teacher report form that also assesses behaviours and other issues of concern in children of the same age, and a self-report form that can be completed by children aged between eight and eighteen. As with the CBCL, both the parent form and the teacher form are used in conjunction to determine if there are any apparent differences between home and school. Again, if there are discrepancies between a parent's response and a schoolteacher's response, the clinician will seek to understand this because such an inconsistency could be revealing something else. The Conners 3 has four different form lengths that include the full-length version for parents, teachers and the child, a short version for parents, teachers and the child, and an ADHD Index Form (3AI) and a Global Index Form (3GI). The full-length version contains 110 items on the parent form, 115 items on the teacher form, and 99 items for the child to complete on the self-report form. The short version of the Conners 3 has 45 items for the parent to complete, 41 items for the teacher to complete and 41 items on the self-report form for the child to complete. The full-length version obviously yields quite a lot more detailed information and is typically used in the initial evaluation of the child, whereas the shorter version is used when there is limited time. The shorter version provides an assessment of the key areas of inattention, hyperactivity–impulsivity, learning problems, executive functioning, aggression, and peer relations. The full-length Conners 3 is subdivided into eight sections comprising the Content Scales, DSM symptom scales, Validity Scales, Screener Scales, Critical Scales, Index Scales, Impairment and Additional Questions, while the short version contains only the Content Scales, Validity Scales and the Additional Questions. The full-length version takes an average of 20–25 minutes to complete, while the shorter version takes about 10–15 minutes. The parent and child would normally be expected to complete their report forms in the clinician's office. There are four available optional answers ranging from 0 if the item was not true at all about the child, or it never (or seldom) happened, 1 if the item was just a little true about the child, or it happened occasionally, 2 if the item was pretty much true about the child, or it happened often (or quite a bit), to 3 if the item was very much true about this child, or it happened very often (frequently).

The Content Scales focus on the key aspects of ADHD and conduct disorder and oppositional defiant disorder and are further divided. The primary key points of ADHD such as inattention and hyperactivity–impulsivity are captured by this scale. Problems in executive functioning (for further information on executive functioning refer to Chapter 4 on the causes of ADHD), learning problems/disorders and family and peer relationships issues that are very often associated with ADHD are also measured by this scale. Finally, the primary behaviours that are key to behavioural disorders are also identified in the scale. The DSM symptom scales provide identification of three behavioural disorders based on the DSM classification. This allows the clinician to make a diagnosis of ADHD by subtype (for example, Inattentive, Hyperactive–Impulsive, Combined), conduct disorder and oppositional defiant disorder, as necessary. It is also worth noting that the Conners manual also points out that symptoms alone are not enough to make a diagnosis. There are other very important criteria that are required before a diagnosis can be made. The Screener Items are seeking evidence of possible anxiety and depression. If there are any positive responses to the items in this scale the clinician would need to investigate this further. Having such a screener is important as mood disorders such as depression often co-exist with ADHD, and if left unchecked, can literally put a child's life at risk. The Critical Scales represent concerns about pretty severe misconduct such as future violence or harm to others. This being the case, such behaviours would require immediate further investigation by the clinician as they may need urgent intervention. The Conners 3 ADHD Index Form is based on the rater's responses and informs the clinician if the child is more similar to children diagnosed with ADHD or more similar to children in the general population. The Conners 3 Global Index Form is generally considered to be a very good indicator of a child's general functioning while the Impairment items take into account school, home and social settings and ask the rater how much the symptoms might be impacting the child's functioning in each of the three settings. The Additional Questions importantly provide an opportunity to record the child's strengths and allow the parent, teacher or older child to report any additional information that they may feel is important or that was not covered in any other scale.

In summary, the Conners 3 assesses a child for general psychopathology, inattention, hyperactivity–impulsivity, learning problems, executive functioning, aggression, peer relations, family relations, ADHD Inattentive Type, ADHD Hyperactive–Impulsive Type, ADHD Combined Type, oppositional defiant disorder and conduct disorder. Looking at this impressive list you begin to appreciate just how comprehensive an assessment the Conners 3 really is and why clinicians around the globe use it as an integral part of the ADHD assessment phase. As you might imagine this is a fairly complex assessment that requires the involvement of specifically trained individuals such as psychologists, paediatricians and child psychiatrists.

## INTELLIGENCE TESTING

Before we begin this section it is important to draw a distinction between the type of intelligence tests professionals use and other so-called intelligence tests freely available through media outlets and found in an array of magazines. As intelligence is a construct that has many facets rather than being something tangible, an intelligence test is designed to assess a number of different abilities commonly associated with intelligence. The test result yields an intelligence quotient, or IQ as most people would be familiar with. This is a figure that indicates a person's measure of intelligence, which then can be compared to an average. For instance, the average person has an IQ of 100. The higher the IQ score the stronger those particular abilities are, while the lower the score the weaker those abilities are. People with very low scores (for example, 69 or below) are likely to have an intellectual disability, while people with an IQ of 130 or above are said to be 'gifted'. Also, an intelligence test can clearly show that a person may have strengths in one area and weaknesses in another. In reference to people with ADHD, the information yielded from such an assessment will have important implications in revealing the impact of ADHD on the intellectual development of the child, identifying the child's cognitive strengths and weaknesses, and it will help inform the clinician of the best intervention for both the child and the parents, and whether or not the child may require educational support or what specific educational needs the child might have. In other words, the information provided by such an assessment will help provide a profile of ADHD and the child's strengths and weaknesses in different settings. So just remember, authenticated intelligence tests are not found in magazines or at the bottom of a cereal box and only a competent licensed psychologist or psychiatrist can administer such a test.

Because intelligence takes on so many different elements, trying to define just what intelligence is and what it involves is not an easy task. However, today there is a general consensus that the attributes of intelligence generally include the ability to adapt to one's environment, basic mental processes, and higher-order thinking such as reasoning, problem-solving and decision-making. In 1987, just over 1000 experts in the fields of psychology, education, sociology and genetics were all brought together and asked to rate thirteen behavioural descriptors of intelligence. An analysis of their ratings demonstrated a clear agreement of what they considered represented intelligence and, importantly, the experts concurred that intelligence was multifaceted. For example, there was just over 99 per cent agreement between the experts that abstract thinking or reasoning was an important element of intelligence, while there was almost 98 per cent agreement that problem-solving ability was important, with 96 per cent agreement that the capacity to acquire knowledge was an element of intelligence. There was an 80 per cent agreement that memory was also an element of intelligence, with a 77 per cent understanding that adaptation was considered an element of intelligence, while almost 72 per cent agreed mental speed and 71 per cent agreed linguistic competence were also important elements of intelligence. So when we think about the term IQ we really need to be aware that intelligence is made up of a number of different abilities.

## WHY WOULD A CLINICIAN USE AN INTELLIGENCE TEST AS PART OF THE ADHD ASSESSMENT?

Intelligence tests generally do not and were never designed to diagnose ADHD on their own, but they do form a very significant part of the assessment phase of children with ADHD. Even just knowing the overall cognitive abilities of a child with ADHD is extremely important for planning the most appropriate therapy and educational support. The clinical features and cognitive deficits or problems associated with ADHD are not only identified but the extent of the problem can be measured with intelligence tests. A number of investigators have addressed the question of why a clinician would need to use an IQ assessment as part of the diagnosis of ADHD. Apparently intelligence and achievement results can help the clinician establish whether a child has ADHD in direct and indirect ways. For instance, we know that children with ADHD fail to develop age-appropriate cognitive skills. Failure in these particular areas would likely show up in the results of the intelligence test. Thus indirectly the IQ assessment can uncover particular weaknesses commonly associated with ADHD along with helping to determine the severity of the child's impairment. Intelligence testing can also help the clinician clearly identify if there is any other disorder that may explain the child's behaviour or poor performance at school as well as identifying any co-existing disorders. Remember, when it comes to childhood disorders, there are a number of disorders with overlapping symptoms so an IQ assessment is critical in reaching the right diagnosis. Furthermore, an IQ assessment is also used to help determine whether or not the child has a learning disorder that may co-exist with ADHD, or whether or not the learning disorder in itself might explain the child's poor attention. For example, an eight-year-old child was referred to my clinic because of poor performance at school and inappropriate social skills for her age. A typical clinical interview with the mother over several sessions revealed the child may have had a learning disorder. The child was referred to a specialist where she was tested with the Wechsler Intelligence Scale for Children (WISC-IV). The results of the assessment revealed the child had a non-verbal learning disorder. A non-verbal learning disorder often remains undiagnosed as it is relatively unknown. The results gained from particular tasks within an intelligence test may identify certain weaknesses that in combination with the other assessment findings reveal ADHD symptoms.

Wechsler's intelligence scales were first developed around 1939 with the Wechsler-Bellevue Intelligence Scale. Since then the Wechsler intelligence scales have developed into the most universally used tests of intelligence for both children and adults alike. Today, the most commonly used Wechsler scales include the Wechsler Adult Intelligence Scale (WAIS), the Wechsler Intelligence Scale for Children (WISC: for ages six to sixteen and eleven months), and the Wechsler Preschool and Primary Scale of Intelligence (WPPSI: for ages four to six-and-a-half years). To discuss each of these scales is well beyond the scope of this book and as such there will only be a brief discussion about the intelligence test that would be used during the diagnostic process for ADHD in children: the Wechsler Intelligence Scale for Children (WISC-IV). Such an intelligence test is used because the deficits that arise as a result of ADHD tend to be clearly identified in the results.

The Wechsler Intelligence Scale for Children — Fourth Edition (WISC-IV) has four separate domains including:

- the Verbal Comprehension Index (VCI)
- the Perceptual Reasoning Index (PRI)
- the Working Memory Index (WMI), and
- the Processing Speed Index (PSI).

Each domain or index has either two or three subtests totalling ten primary subtests in all. Each of the four domains yields a score along with a Full Scale IQ score (FSIQ). The FSIQ score is considered to provide the best measurement of a child's general intellectual ability and is therefore a representation of the child's overall level of intellectual functioning. The FSIQ scores range from 40 to 160, while the four separate indexes provide information about and estimates of specific cognitive abilities. Each of the indexes contains a number of subtests to help evaluate the intelligence of the child.

The Verbal Comprehension Index contains:

1. Similarities.
2. Vocabulary.
3. Comprehension.
4. Information and Word Reasoning as two supplemental subtests.

The Perceptual Reasoning Index features:

1. Block Design.
2. Picture Concepts.
3. Matrix Reasoning.
4. Picture Completion as the supplemental subtest.

The Working Memory Index features:

1. Digit Span.
2. Letter–Number Sequencing.
3. Arithmetic as the supplemental subtest.

The Processing Speed Index contains:

1. Coding.
2. Symbol Search as the two subtests.
3. Cancellation as the supplemental subtest.

The supplemental subtests are only administered under special circumstances where it may substitute for a core subtest but only in strict accordance to the instructions provided in the WISC-IV Administration and Scoring Manual. For instance, if a core subtest is spoiled or not administered for any reason, a supplemental subtest could be used in its place.

## THE FOUR INDEXES OF THE WISC FURTHER EXPLAINED

The Verbal Comprehension Index (VCI) is essentially drawing on the child's knowledge base as it assesses a child's ability to first recall a certain word and then apply reason to that word, to know the meaning of the word, and to express that word appropriately. Thus the VCI measures a child's knowledge gained through formal schooling and through other forms of learning or informal learning and reflects how the child applies their verbal skills to new situations. The VCI also measures verbal comprehension and how well a child applies their verbal skills and information to problem-solving, as well as how the child processes verbal information, their ability to think with words, and their mental flexibility that also includes being able to shift mental operations, along with their ability to self-monitor.

The Perceptual Reasoning Index (PRI) is a measure of performance-related ability and the child's ability to interpret visually perceived material, organise that material and to further develop and test assumptions related to problem-solving. The PRI also assesses a child's ability to interpret or organise the visual material within a time limit. The PRI measures perceptual reasoning, which is a child's ability to think in terms of visual images and manipulate those images with ease and speed, and their mental flexibility, which also includes being able to shift mental operations, and the ability to self-monitor. Finally the PRI also measures relative mental speed, a child's non-verbal ability, and their ability to form abstract ideas and relationships without the use of words, and fluid reasoning.

Remember the different parts of the brain that are affected by ADHD? Well working memory is considered to be a core deficit in ADHD. Consider for a moment what role our working memory plays in our day-to-day lives. Working memory includes those processes needed to construct, maintain and manipulate incoming information. Working memory is needed for problem-solving and for the execution of an organised plan of action or behavioural sequence. Working memory refers to the ability to temporarily store and manipulate information and to be able to hold a number of facts or thoughts in our mind for a short period of time while we are trying to solve a problem or perform a task. A major factor of working memory is being able to control our attention and inhibit outside or irrelevant information from distracting us. In other words, our working memory is the ability to sustain attention, concentration, and exert mental control by not being distracted. This is something a child with ADHD finds incredibly challenging. The Working Memory Index (WMI) measures the child's short-term memory, their ability to maintain attention, their numerical skills, encoding ability, their auditory processing skills, and their ability to shift mental operations, and self-monitor.

The Processing Speed Index (PSI) is a test of speed and accuracy and assesses whether a child can process simple or everyday information without making mistakes. Concentration and good eye–hand coordination are important components in this part of the assessment as the PSI measures a child's speed of processing information, speed of test taking, their ability to discriminate between symbols, speed of mental operation, their attention, their short-term visual memory, visual–motor coordination, numerical ability, and the ability to shift mental operations, and to self-monitor.

Under normal conditions, it usually takes about 1 to 1½ hours for the child to complete the WISC-IV. However, under certain circumstances an examiner may suggest it would be beneficial for the child if they were to complete the test over two sittings rather than one prolonged sitting.

The best way to conceptualise an IQ test is to imagine the test has been divided into four separate parts (domains or indexes). Each of the four domains has been designed to measure something different. Each of the four domains is further divided into two or three subtests, which are added up to produce a total score for that domain. Then the scores from each of the subtests are also added together to produce a full score (Full Scale Score).

Now that you have this information, if you ever find yourself in a position where it is recommended you have your child assessed for ADHD, you are in a position to start asking appropriate questions that just might save you the heartache Dylan's parents went through. You are also now aware that most of the assessments discussed in this chapter can only be used by psychologists (or child psychiatrists) and paediatricians who are specially trained. Furthermore, if you are seeking an appropriately trained and experienced psychologist to assess your child, you are now in a better position to test their experience and expertise in this area. For instance, you can begin with a sampler question like, 'Will my child have an IQ assessment?'. As this is considered an integral part of the diagnostic phase, any psychologist who answers 'no' might not be the right person for you (there is a clause to this though: if your child has been previously assessed with a Wechsler Intelligence Scale for Children (WISC), you would need to discuss this with the psychologist as it is recommended a certain amount of time elapses before a person is retested). Equally, if the answer is 'yes', you can then ask the psychologist, 'How many times have you administered the WISC to children?' or 'How many times have you used the WISC as part of the diagnostic phase for ADHD in children?'. When you ask these questions don't accept an answer where the individual may have used the WISC just once about ten years ago. You want to know the professional has used the tests frequently and is experienced with them and you also want to know the other assessments the psychologist intends to use and whether or not the psychologist will observe your child and how many observations will be made and where the observations will take place. Remember, ADHD must be evident in two or more settings so a single observation of your child at school arguing with a teacher they do not like may not be appropriate.

# CHAPTER 6

## Co-existing conditions with ADHD

Before discussing common co-existing, or comorbid, conditions associated with ADHD, there are a few things you first need to know. When a doctor, psychiatrist or psychologist talks about comorbid conditions, or comorbidity, they mean that a number of different, independently diagnosable conditions can co-exist, or occur, at the same time. For example, it isn't uncommon for someone with depression to also have an anxiety disorder, or for someone with post-traumatic stress disorder (PTSD) to also have another anxiety disorder such as generalised anxiety disorder or agoraphobia. In these examples, the primary condition (depression or PTSD) is said to be comorbid with another disorder such as generalised anxiety or agoraphobia. Second, when I talk about ADHD being comorbid with another disorder I mean that ADHD is the primary disorder, as there are a number of different comorbid conditions commonly associated with ADHD.

There is considerable comorbidity with childhood ADHD, including oppositional defiant disorder (ODD), conduct disorder (CD), depression and anxiety disorders, pervasive developmental disorder (PDD), Tourette syndrome (TS), and substance use. Language delays, learning disabilities and motor delays are also found to be commonly associated with ADHD. For example, one large research design used 449 children between the ages of six and eighteen with ADHD. The results of the research demonstrated that only 145 children of the 449 *did not* have a comorbid condition. This means that just over 67 per cent of those children in this survey had a comorbid condition including oppositional defiant disorder, conduct disorder, generalised anxiety disorder, obsessive compulsive disorder, separation anxiety disorder, social phobic disorder and simple phobia.

The prevalence rate of comorbidity with ADHD is really quite disturbing. In fact, after viewing the following section you will begin to realise why professionals all over the world have suggested that ADHD without a comorbid condition or *pure* ADHD is highly unusual. Research has found that ADHD often has a comorbidity rate of between 13 to 51 per cent with internalising disorders (such as anxiety and depression) and a comorbidity rate of between 3 to 93 per cent with externalising disorders (behavioural disorders, such as conduct disorder). It's also important to remember that each of the following disorders has its own diagnostic category in the DSM and, as with ADHD, must meet a set number of symptoms from a list of criteria and cause significant impairment in social, occupational, academic or other areas of life.

## Oppositional defiant disorder (ODD)

The presence of comorbid behavioural disorders such as oppositional defiant disorder or conduct disorder within children and adolescents with ADHD has been a well-known fact for a number of decades. Oppositional defiant disorder (ODD) is a behavioural disorder usually first diagnosed in childhood. It is typically noticeable before the child turns eight years of age and does not normally develop later than early adolescence. Oppositional defiant disorder is characterised by negative interactions with other people, defiance and being oppositional, disobedience, and hostility toward those in authority. Children with ODD are stubborn, resist instructions and orders, they are unwilling to compromise and will not give in, they constantly test the boundaries (actually it's more like push the boundaries), and they have a tendency to blame others rather than accept responsibility for their own actions. Other symptoms of ODD might also include:

- Unrelenting temper tantrums.
- Arguing with adults, especially those in authority.
- Refusing to comply with reasonable adult demands.

- Annoying others.
- Vindictiveness and nastiness.

The comorbidity rate for ADHD occurring with ODD has been reported to be around 50 per cent. Unfortunately, ODD is often a precursor to a second behavioural disorder that is typically much worse — conduct disorder.

## Conduct disorder (CD)

Conduct disorder (CD) is also classified as a behavioural disorder and is said to be one of the most widely studied disorders today, primarily because both ADHD and CD develop in childhood. Conduct disorder is characterised by repetitive and persistent behaviour in which the basic rights of others, or major age-appropriate societal norms, are violated. Conduct disorder is further characterised by physical aggression towards other people or animals, destruction of property, lying and stealing, and violating the rules of different social groups. Clinical descriptions of CD add to this list and include impulsive behaviour, reckless and destructive behaviour, a marked lack of empathy for others, and negative feelings and moods.

While the DSM does not appear to have listed a typical age of onset for CD, the general consensus is that the disorder is progressive throughout childhood with the symptoms or behaviours becoming more noticeable around thirteen to fifteen years of age. However, some of the behaviours of CD can be present before this age. For instance, one study found that boys between the ages of eight and ten were fighting, lying and bullying before they were diagnosed with CD. There were noted differences between males and females with CD that indicate girls between the ages of thirteen and fifteen were less likely to be involved in setting fires, burglary, and cruelty to animals compared to males of the same age. However, according to these researchers, that's where the differences stop as they further found males and females were similar across all other symptoms. Conduct disorder is prevalent in 6 to 16 per cent of adolescent males and between 2 to 9 per cent of adolescent females with

ADHD. While other research has indicated that CD has a prevalence rate of about 30 per cent in children and adolescents with ADHD.

Delinquent behaviour and the progression of more serious criminal behaviours are also of major concern. Delinquent behaviour associated with CD usually involves an illegal act, such as theft, burglary, robbery, violence, vandalism and drug use. At present, the professional world agrees that the progression to serious delinquency typically begins in childhood; commonly the child experiences difficulties at school, problems at home and problems with making and sustaining friendships. Furthermore, it has been argued that the pathway to criminal behaviour has its foundations in impulsivity, ADHD, and other factors such as life stressors and poor parenting practices. These various problems are currently thought to be associated with an escalation in antisocial behaviour that will eventually find the individual engaging in more and more criminal activity.

Unfortunately, delinquent behaviour is often a chronic (in this instance chronic means long-term) problem for children with comorbid ADHD and CD. This indicates that those children with ADHD who are at risk of developing CD in adolescence follow a maladaptive pathway leading to serious delinquent behaviour. However, it is also agreed that only those children who go on to develop comorbid CD are more likely to become involved in serious and persistent offending. However, just to confuse the issue a bit, some research has also indicated that children with ADHD who have not been diagnosed with a comorbid condition of ODD or CD are also at risk of becoming involved in later delinquent behaviour.

## Substance abuse

Substance use and abuse is a problem area that has attracted a lot of attention and subsequent investigation by professionals all over the world. As a result of such comprehensive and consistent research findings, it has been firmly established that substance abuse is of major concern for children of the ADHD Hyperactive Type or for those children who have also developed conduct disorder by adolescence. However, the relationship between ADHD and substance use is really quite complicated. ADHD has been associated with both an increased risk of developing a substance use problem, but it is also linked with behaviours that are suggestive of more severe substance use. This means there is a risk of the child using drugs at an earlier age, using drugs for longer periods of time, and if they seek professional assistance they are unlikely to stay long enough to get the total benefits and they experience high relapse rates. Now while we might be aware that adolescence can be associated with drug experimentation, the association between ADHD and substance use is not by chance.

Many reasons for substance use in the ADHD population have been postulated over the years with some having more weight than others. For instance, it is argued that hyperactivity plays a significant role in substance use as people who are impulsive don't always stop to consider the risks involved and because they prefer smaller, immediate rewards rather than having to wait for a larger reward. However, borderline personality disorder, ADHD and CD are very common among people who use illicit drugs. Because of this and the fact that ADHD is often comorbid with other behavioural disorders, it is difficult to determine what effect pure ADHD might have on the severity of substance use. For instance, when it comes to ADHD, it is often difficult to determine whether it was the ADHD that influenced the substance use or the comorbid condition. Some research has found that pure ADHD is not really a significant influencing factor when it comes to substance use. However, when ADHD is comorbid with CD, there is a greater likelihood that substance use will occur. Research has indicated then that CD and not ADHD is an influencing factor.

## Depression

Depression is one of those mood disorders that is said to affect one in every two people in the general population at some point in their lifetime. The typical symptoms of depression include moodiness, irritability and frustration, taking minor criticism personally and finding it difficult to manage, isolating yourself from friends and family, a sense of helplessness and hopelessness, a general lack of motivation, lethargy, loss of interest in hobbies and pleasurable activities, sleeping difficulties, feelings of worthlessness and suicidal ideation (thoughts of death and killing yourself). The development of depression in children with ADHD is thought to have a number of potential 'causes' that include the child believing they are incompetent and having little control, negative life events, and environmental stressors such as a disrupted parent–child relationship. Negative family relationships that are often present in the homes of ADHD children are also considered to be a precursor to developing depression, and again parenting behaviours such as control (being overly controlling, dominating), intrusiveness and inconsistency are also associated with childhood depression.

Children and adolescents with ADHD are at a greater risk of developing depression compared to children without ADHD. In fact, the risk of suffering depression in children and adolescents with ADHD is five-and-a-half times more than children without ADHD. Unfortunately, comorbid depression also appears to place the child at an elevated risk of added impairment and can significantly increase the amount of time the child might suffer from the disorder.

## Anxiety disorders

Looking at the incidence of anxiety co-occurring with ADHD in children, one researcher reported comorbidity rates were as high as 30 per cent. Somewhat disturbingly, research has found that children with ADHD are three times more likely to have anxiety as compared to children without ADHD. Other researchers have reported on the effects comorbid ADHD and anxiety have on the child. For instance, children with ADHD and anxiety had more problems with maintaining attention, experienced more school fears, had a higher prevalence of mood disorders and fewer social skills compared to children with just ADHD or just anxiety. Other researchers have found children with comorbid anxiety will more likely show worse school functioning, appear sluggish and slow moving, and exhibit working memory deficits compared to children without ADHD or children with pure ADHD.

# Pervasive developmental disorder (PDD)

Pervasive developmental disorder (PDD) is an umbrella term referring to a number of developmental disorders. Pervasive developmental disorder is characterised by severe and pervasive impairment in several areas of development and is typically evident in early childhood. The word 'pervasive' means that these disorders are not minor problems, but have a significant impact on the person throughout their life. The areas of development include severe impairment in the skills required for give-and-take in common social interactions and, as such, children with PDD do not develop social relationships that would be expected for their age. There are also severe impairments in communication skills, or the presence of restricted patterns of behaviour (like licking the back of their hand), as well as limited interests and activities. Pervasive developmental disorder includes autism spectrum disorder, Rett syndrome, childhood disintegration disorder, Asperger's syndrome, and pervasive developmental disorder not otherwise specified (PDD-NOS).

# Tourette syndrome (TS)

Tourette syndrome (TS) is characterised by sudden, brief and repetitive movements that are involuntary and that involve only a limited number of muscle groups. Tourette syndrome will also include one or more involuntary vocalisations. These involuntary movements and vocalisations are referred to as 'tics'. The diagnostic criteria for Tourette syndrome requires evidence of multiple motor tics and at least one vocal tic that occurs many times throughout the day almost every day for more than one year. However, this does not have to be continuous for both types of tics.

There are typically a number of different muscle (motor) tics that can occur simultaneously or at different periods during the disorder. Tics are classified as either simple or complex, with simple motor tics including eye blinking, head jerking, shrugging of the shoulders, facial grimacing and nose twitching. Simple vocalisations might include repetitively clearing the throat, sniffing or grunting. Complex muscle tics include touching objects, hopping, jumping, squatting, retracing steps, and twirling when walking. The complex vocal tics include various words or sounds such as grunting, yelping, barking, sniffing, snorting and coughing. Finally, the disorder must have developed before the child reaches eighteen years of age and it cannot be caused by a medical condition, medication or illicit drugs. Tic disorders are consistently found to be linked to ADHD and the combination of the two disorders tends to find children more prone to angry outbursts, disruptive behaviours and social problems.

I remember quite a few years ago watching a media report on television about a phenomenon where an individual had no control over shouting out obscenities. This urge to swear could and often did occur anywhere and at any time. Of course, this report focused on an incident where the mother was lining up in a checkout line at a supermarket and was extremely embarrassed to find her young child screaming obscenities at the cashier. This report was about a rare version of the vocal tics, or complex vocal tics. Complex vocal tics include uttering swear words and are evident in only a small percentage of cases. In fact, coprolalia (uttering obscenities) only occurs in about 10 per cent of cases. Echolalia, or repeating the words or phrases of other people, is also a complex vocal tic of Tourette syndrome.

## Language problems (or communication disorder)

Language problems or communication disorder is one those disorders that is found in ADHD at an alarming rate, with most estimates suggesting comorbidity between 40 to 45 per cent. The term 'language problems' is an umbrella term that typically means the child is experiencing problems or delays in the development of normal speech and/or language. These developmental problems or delays may not be attributed to ADHD if the delays can be better explained by an intellectual handicap, or a physical handicap, hearing loss and blocked or partially blocked Eustachian tubes in the ears, or emotional disorders.

Language impairment can represent a problem with pragmatics where the child tends to talk too much during a spontaneous conversation. In other words, they tend to talk excessively. But there can also be delayed development of first words. Children with ADHD also experience problems when they are making a transition from one task to another, and in play settings. They can also experience problems with their timing, such as knowing when to start a conversation, or when to take turns in a conversation. They tend to blurt out answers, frequently interrupt the conversations of others or can experience problems with maintaining or changing topics during a conversation. There is also a greater tendency to be disfluent (impairment in being able to produce smooth, fluent speech), and a tendency for poor performance on school tests or standardised tests.

## Learning disorders

Learning disorders are again among those disorders that have a high comorbidity rate with ADHD. In fact, some authors have suggested the comorbidity rate between ADHD and learning disorders is as high as 25 to 40 per cent, while others have put the comorbidity rate at 30 per cent. The US Centers for Disease Control and Prevention found boys were twice as likely as girls to have both ADHD and a learning disorder. The presentation of ADHD and learning disorders is a similarity between the symptoms of both disorders. For example, in both disorders the child struggles to achieve, they typically struggle academically, and display both social and behavioural difficulties and deficits. Unfortunately, it appears the child often experiences the difficulties of each of these disorders along with a markedly greater expression of academic, attentional and behavioural problems.

## Motor delays

While a child with ADHD may experience problems with motor skills, it should be remembered that such problems, as with all disorders, must be clinically significant and interfering with and interrupting a child's normal daily activities. Keeping this in mind, we are then able to differentiate motor delays or problems from 'normal' childhood clumsiness, for instance. Motor delays or problems can range from gross motor difficulties (such as coordinating the large muscle groups in the arms and legs), to fine motor difficulties (such as coordinating the small groups of muscles in the hand). Parents may view their child with gross motor problems as clumsy as the child stumbles, falls and bumps their way through life. The child may also experience problems with running, climbing, jumping and so on. While the gross motor difficulties may become fairly evident as the child becomes more and more mobile, how do you spot problems with fine motor skills? Unfortunately, problems with fine motor skills are not as evident and may not show up until the child begins writing. The problem lies in getting all those small muscles in the hand to work together. Unfortunately, in most cases, this type of problem is only evident when the child begins school.

Having this information dumped on you all at once can be really scary for parents. It's bad enough that you have just found out your child has ADHD, but then to be told your child may have a comorbid condition can be very confusing, very confronting and difficult to manage. But as difficult as this information may have been, there is some good news. It is important to remember that not every child with ADHD will have a comorbid condition, nor will your child have *all* of the above conditions. Even if a comorbid condition does exist, the degree of that disorder may not be in the severe range or even in the clinical range. This simply means that there may be some behaviours or characteristics of a disorder present but it is not the full-blown disorder. You must also remember that ADHD and the comorbid conditions do not spell the end of all hope, as most of these conditions respond very well to the various treatments that are currently available. Finally, if you find yourself in this position, it is important for you to talk to your practitioner about how you feel, tell them your hurts, your disappointments and your fears, and let them support you through this difficult time.

# CHAPTER 7

# Medicating ADHD

The decision to medicate a child can be painfully difficult for many parents, as the use of stimulant medication in children and adolescents with ADHD has been at the centre of some pretty intense criticisms over the years and to this day remains controversial. Now while we might already have dealt with one or two popular myths about medications, there are understandable concerns around the issue of side effects and whether or not a child might experience complications from long-term use. The decision to medicate a child can be all the more difficult for parents, given the arguments from critics that stimulant medication is also potentially dangerous to a child.

Contrary to popular beliefs and reports, medicating children with ADHD is not a new phenomenon as there is a fairly long history of stimulant use for hyperactive behaviour in children. One of the earliest described uses of a stimulant was back in 1937 when amphetamines were used. Following this were a number of controlled trials of Ritalin in the 1960s that reported quite significant changes to a child's attention and focus with further improvements in schoolwork, grades and behaviour. Furthermore, those same results indicated that there were no serious side effects for the child. The use of stimulant medications, such as methylphenidate, is one of the most extensively researched and successful treatments for children, adolescents and adults alike with ADHD. In fact, when you look at the results of well constructed, competent and independent research, it is hard to ignore the fact that stimulant medication is very effective for improving the core symptoms of ADHD. All these benefits (and more) have been well documented by professionals around the world time after time who have no 'incentive' to support the use of stimulant medication. We have to be very, very careful about how much credibility we give to anyone who suggests or infers that professionals who prescribe medication for ADHD are 'only in it for the money'.

---

There are times when it seems that everybody is arguing that ADHD is on the rise and the critics often turn to statistics in an effort to prove their case. But do statistics really indicate that ADHD is growing at such an alarming rate as some would have us believe? Well, it's not quite as simple as that because the increase in prevalence rates of ADHD and visits for medication can be influenced by a number of factors. For instance, there seems to be a greater awareness of ADHD symptoms among kindergarten staff and schoolteachers, who may suggest taking the child to a specialist. Parents, siblings and even the child are often aware something is not quite right with their behaviour and will seek help from a medical professional who may then refer the family for a formal diagnosis. As we can see, this is not necessarily due to ADHD actually increasing; it simply means that, as the general population becomes more aware of the disorder, they will be more likely to seek professional help. As we have already determined, ADHD has always been around but people may have just assumed the child was being naughty so they were not seeking appropriate help. When looking at statistics we need to keep it in context.

Approximately 2 per cent of Australian children aged six to seventeen are said to be taking ADHD medications. This is apparently one of the highest rates of ADHD prescriptions in the world. Then, of course, there is the rather touchy subject of the apparent exponential annual increases in prescriptions for ADHD medication. According to a study conducted in the Netherlands, children receiving medication for ADHD increased from 30 in every 10,000 to 75 per 10,000 between 2001 and 2007. While there is an increase here, it is important to note that in comparison to other illnesses, medicating for ADHD is relatively low. For example, in Australia:

- Two per cent of the population are said to be affected by ADHD compared to 32 per cent affected with heart disease.
- Currently there are 420,000 prescriptions per year for ADHD medications as compared to more than 51 million prescriptions for heart disease back in 2000.
- The US Centers for Disease Control and Prevention found ADHD was increasing about 4 per cent per year among children aged twelve to seventeen years, while in Australia there was a 16 per cent increase in heart disease in just one year.
- Between 2008 and 2009 there were over 12 million prescriptions written for antidepressants.

A student of psychology or medicine can well testify that the rule of informed consent is hammered into them from very early on in their learning. Informed consent literally means that patients have a right to receive all the necessary information they need in order to make a sound decision about treatment options. This means knowing both the good and bad of any treatment, including medication. The following information on pharmacotherapy for ADHD is intended to provide parents and caregivers with the necessary information about the different kinds of medications used to treat ADHD and the potential risks and benefits of each one. Having a firm understanding of each medication will allow you to be acutely aware of the side effects that may require a follow-up visit to your health professional. Finally, when parents are provided with such information, they are in a better position to make sound decisions regarding their child's treatment options and not be unduly influenced by media reports or critics of medication.

This chapter will look at the different medications available for treating ADHD. You will read about the side effects of each medication and, while this is important to know, it is a 'general' list of every side effect ever reported. As with any medication, it is important to keep watch and if your child is experiencing side effects that you are worried about or you have any other concerns about the medication, go back to your medical specialist and talk it through. While medication plays an incredibly important role in the overall treatment of ADHD, we must also remember that is not the only treatment. As you will learn in Chapter 8, there are a number of successful alternative therapies for ADHD, including parent management training, cognitive behavioural therapy and social skills training, to help the child with ADHD develop appropriate social skills and behaviours for school and at home.

## Stimulant medications used for ADHD

Virtually every professional article on the efficacy of medication for ADHD plainly states that stimulant medication has proven to be the singular most effective treatment in reducing the core symptoms of ADHD — hyperactivity, impulsivity, and inattention — because of the way it works. Stimulant medication increases the arousal level of the central nervous system, and for many people with a hyperactive child, this seems to be an absurd approach. We know that the central nervous system of people with ADHD is actually underaroused and not hyperaroused, as some might think. Stimulants work by increasing the levels of neurotransmitters, such as dopamine and norepinephrine, and by enhancing transmission of these neurotransmitters in the brain. These neurotransmitters are found throughout the brain but are concentrated in regions that are involved in arousal, attention, concentration, motor planning, motor control and self-regulation — the very behaviours that are impaired in people with ADHD. Research suggests that where the individual has been administered ADHD stimulant medication, there is activity in the brain in those particular regions. Once the drug begins to work, the affected regions of the brain return to 'normal' functioning and we see a reduction in hyperactive, inattentive and impulsive behaviours. The problem is that when the medication begins to wear off, the symptoms return.

One of the largest studies ever conducted on the treatment of ADHD is most likely the Multimodal Treatment of Children with Attention Deficit Hyperactivity Disorder (1999) or the MTA. This study included almost 800 children who had been diagnosed with ADHD and ranged from seven to ten years of age. The study followed the children for fourteen months and produced extensive information about medication and alternative treatments. Overall, the results showed that medication significantly reduced ADHD symptoms compared to all the other types of treatments that were offered. Obviously with such a large study, results like these have been very influential in the conclusion that medication really is a sensible option for treating ADHD.

The most commonly prescribed stimulant medication for ADHD is methylphenidate. Methylphenidate is available as either short acting or long lasting. The short-acting methylphenidate includes:

- Ritalin
- Attenta
- Gen Rx Methylphenidate.

It is short acting because the effects of the tablet usually last for about four hours. Thus a child typically requires two (or more) dosages during the day. The long-acting methylphenidate includes:

- Ritalin LA
- Concerta (extended release tablets).

The long-acting methylphenidate lasts up to twelve hours and has made the dosing process much easier for parents, schoolteachers and the child as there is only one dose required per day. It would seem fairly obvious that most families would prefer the long-lasting medication given the benefits it offers. For instance, a child prescribed short-acting Ritalin would typically need to take between two to four tablets every day. This means that parents, school staff and the child may all be involved in the medication process. There are a number of potential problems with this method as the child could forget to request the medication from the teacher, or the teacher could just as easily forget to give the medication to the child. Also, long-acting methylphenidate, such as Concerta or Ritalin LA, could very well be more suited to those children who would not adhere to dosing instructions or even because of the stigma so often attached to ADHD. As dosing is required just once daily, the child or adolescent could take the medication in the morning before heading off to school, thus reducing a number of potential problems and allowing the child to maintain a level of privacy and confidentiality about the issue.

Short-acting Ritalin typically comes in a 5, 10, or 20 mg capsule, and is a fast-releasing medication that begins to work within 35 to 45 minutes of administration. Ritalin reaches its single peak performance in about one to two hours and lasts for about three to four hours, whereas Ritalin LA (the long-acting one) typically comes in 10, 20, 30 and 40 mg capsules and is biphasic, which means the tablet has two peak performances, the first being in one to three hours of consumption and reaching the second peak in five to eight hours. Ritalin LA also begins to work in about 35 to 45 minutes. According to the manufacturer, Novartis Pharmaceuticals Australia, the biphasic action is made possible by the contents of each capsule. Apparently the Ritalin LA capsule contains a mixture of 50 per cent immediate release granules or beads and 50 per cent extended release granules or beads. The immediate release beads are just that, they begin acting 'immediately', whereas the extended release beads are covered with a special coating that takes up to four hours for stomach fluids to begin breaking down by creating small pores through the coating. As the stomach fluid enters the pores it dissolves the Ritalin, thus releasing a second dose equivalent to the first release granule. Concerta is based on a similar principle using stomach fluid to 'push' the methylphenidate through a hole in the capsule over the course of the day.

## Response rates or problems to stimulant medications

The administration of stimulant medication to those with ADHD has an impressively high response rate, usually around 80 per cent or higher. Simply, this means that 80 per cent or more of people on methylphenidate will experience some positive changes to the core symptoms of ADHD. Furthermore, it appears those most responsive to methylphenidate are children who are the most active, most impulsive, and most distractible. One way of determining the overall effectiveness of the stimulant medication on ADHD symptoms is to observe the child during the day. Such observations would include how effective medication has been, how long the effects have lasted, and whether or not the child was able to tolerate the medication. Even though methylphenidate has such a high positive response, not all people respond so positively to stimulant medication. For instance, some children cannot tolerate the side effects of stimulant medication.

## KNOWN SIDE EFFECTS OF METHYLPHENIDATE

Determining whether a person will have side effects to any medication is impossible. Potential side effects are a reality for all medications — controlled or not. The side effects listed for any medication do not mean the person *will* experience any or all of the known side effects. It is law that the production companies list any known side effects during their human trials, even if one side effect was a rare occurrence. Furthermore, it appears that some side effects may depend on the dosage rate. For example, while insomnia is a common side effect of methylphenidate, it seems the severity of insomnia could depend on whether the child is taking 10 mg or 40 mg daily and also at what time of day the child is given the medication.

We cannot ignore the side effects, however, as managing them can become a significant challenge for everyone involved. The most commonly reported side effects include loss of appetite and insomnia; such side effects can possibly be managed by changing to a short-acting medication. Other common side effects can include:

- emotional flattening
- changes in mood (irritability, depressive symptoms, mania/ hypomania)
- sleep difficulties
- headaches
- stomach aches
- lack of motivation and tiredness
- mild increases in pulse and blood pressure (also dependant on the cardiovascular history of the child and their family)
- nervousness
- loss of appetite
- nausea

- dizziness
- heart palpitations
- tics
- anorexia
- rash
- growth concerns (discussed in more detail below)
- 'rebound' effects where certain behaviours may occur between doses as the effects of the medication begin to wear off, or if the medication is abruptly stopped.

Other side effects such as appetite suppression, dull/listless appearance, and tearfulness were also found to be common but the severity rate also depended on higher methylphenidate doses.

## SLOWED GROWTH RATE

Slowed growth rate in children is a possible side effect of taking methylphenidate and has been one of those issues that tends to be sensationalised in the media. In my experience, this issue does cause a lot of fear and concern for parents considering medicating their child. Because of the apparent confusion around the issue, sensationalist media reporting and the possible lack of available information, it is worth taking a moment to look at this concern in more detail.

Consider the following warning from the Brown University Psychopharmacology Update (a forum about the use of psychotropic medications):

> ... *height and weight should be followed in children and adolescents taking methylphenidate, as there is some evidence that consistently medicated children (i.e., treatment for 7 days per week throughout the year) has a temporary slowing in growth rate without evidence of growth rebound during this period of development.*

The issue of a slowed growth rate has received quite a lot of negative attention over the years and has consequently been the subject of intense research. No one denies that there is *some* slowed growth in *some* children who have been prescribed stimulants. However, we are not talking about the significant stunting of growth but rather that the differences in height have been found to be minimal when compared to peers of the same age. Furthermore, these slight differences tend to diminish in time with most children anyway, simply meaning that most children are expected to eventually catch up in height with their peers.

## How safe are stimulant medications?

In light of the side effects listed above, asking how safe ADHD stimulant medications might be sounds like a strange question to ask. It might surprise you to know that stimulant medications used as a treatment for ADHD have been found to be very safe. At the right dosages, stimulant medication, as prescribed by a medical practitioner, has few side effects and most of the time children develop a tolerance for the side effects. If the child is unable to tolerate the side effects, the medical practitioner will reduce the medication while still maintaining a positive effect on the core symptoms of ADHD. If for any reason the side effects still remain intolerable for the child, the medical practitioner will change to a different stimulant or a non-stimulant medication. The risk of negative side effects increases significantly if the medication is taken at *higher doses* than prescribed by the paediatrician. Actually, the evidence would suggest that high doses are quite unusual as children and adolescents with ADHD tend to miss their doses or just stop taking the medication all together. One very large study found side effects, such as emotionality and irritability, were only evident after the children withdrew from the study, presumably because they stopped taking the medication.

Before we move on it is very important that you seek medical advice from your medical specialist (for example, paediatrician, doctor or child psychiatrist) if your child is experiencing side effects from the medication (or any medication for that matter!) as soon as possible. Once medication has been prescribed, the medical practitioner will typically want follow-up sessions with the parents and the child to ensure the medication is set at the right dose, to ensure the child's safety, and to check whether or not the child is experiencing any side effects. Obviously this is your opportunity to raise any concerns you may have. Paediatrician Dr Julian Haber, from the Cook Children's Physician Network in Texas, advises that when a child begins medication for ADHD, they should be seen by the treating medical practitioner, such as a paediatrician, every four to six weeks until a stable dose has been achieved, at which point the time between visits could be pushed out to three to four months. However, you need not wait for a session with your specialist if you are concerned. Be proactive and call the specialist to make an appointment. When you are with your medical specialist you might consider asking questions such as:

- What is the medication you are thinking of prescribing (stimulant or non-stimulant)?
- Why that medication?
- What other medications are available?
- What are the common side effects of that medication for children this age?
- Are there any particular side effects I should watch for?
- What is the dosage you are thinking of prescribing?
- Why that dosage?
- Will you prescribe a long-acting or short-acting medication (tell the specialist your preference)?

Don't be afraid to ask any other question you think of.

## The good and bad of methylphenidate

### THE PROS OF METHYLPHENIDATE

When children have been taking methylphenidate, many long-term and short-term benefits often occur in a fairly short period of time and across a wide range of settings. The most noted positive effects of stimulant medications are on the core symptoms of hyperactivity and inattention. Other benefits include:

- Academic improvements in accuracy, productivity, performance and the amount of written-language output, and homework completion.

- Measured improvements in attention and behaviour.
- Noticeable changes in focused behaviour.
- Less distractibility, longer attention spans and less active and impulsive behaviour.
- Less fidgetiness.
- Better social interaction with parents, peers and teachers.
- Demonstrated differences in a child's or adolescent's self-esteem and improvements in family relationships.
- Demonstrated differences in the child's social functioning and friendships.

One study looked at children who had been on stimulant medication for an extended period of time without comorbid learning disorders and whether or not the changes these children experienced would be sustained if the children stopped taking medication. It should be clearly understood that the children were off the medication for only a short period of time when this study was conducted. Remember though, that even 24 hours without medication can often see a return of the core symptoms of ADHD. Impressively, however, the children performed in the average range for all tasks involving attention, response inhibition, writing and verbal working memory (keeping information in mind while solving a problem). The results demonstrated their performance was significantly better than the group of children who had never been on medication. The authors concluded:

> *The improved performance on measures that require attention to detail as well as the ability to plan and organize even when off medication suggest that these children are able to sustain neuropsychological gains made on medication even when the medication has been discontinued.*

Children in this study who had never taken stimulant medication tended to display significant difficulty with the same tasks. Unfortunately, the un-medicated children were also found to be experiencing non-clinical yet 'significant emotional distress as rated by their parent'.

This distress included non-clinical depression, aggression and conduct problems as compared to the children on medication. The authors suggested that methylphenidate may in fact 'be in their best interest for their emotional wellbeing'.

Any parent who has a child with ADHD will testify to the fact that their children can be quite aggressive. In fact, children with ADHD are aggressive even when they don't have a co-occurring behavioural disorder. It would seem a reasonable expectation that a goal of ANY therapy claiming to be effective for ADHD would also focus on reducing aggression. Methylphenidate is one such treatment that has proven to significantly reduce both the rate and intensity of aggressive behaviour in children with ADHD.

In an effort to understand the causes, nature and the most adequate therapy for aggression, aggressive behaviour has become one of the most widely studied issues across a number of different professions including psychology, sociology and criminology. A result of all this work has shown that there are a number of different 'types' of aggression with different causes or triggers. Two such types of aggression are proactive aggression and reactive aggression. Proactive aggression is defined as non-impulsive, non-angry, 'cool', goal-oriented aggression that happens without prior incitement, baiting or being hassled. Whereas reactive aggression has been defined as impulsive, angry, 'hot' aggression that is a result of either real or perceived incitement, baiting or being hassled.

A number of researchers have measured proactive aggression by examining a child's behaviour and emotions during certain trials that included being at the receiving end of low through to high provocation in a type of game situation. The results of the study indicated that children with ADHD had marginally higher levels of proactive aggression compared to children without ADHD. The results also found that children with ADHD were twice as likely to approach the task with higher rates of aggression compared to children without ADHD. Also children with ADHD had higher levels of reactive aggression compared to children without ADHD. Interestingly, ADHD children on medication were found to be *no more* aggressive when compared to the children without ADHD. And finally, ADHD children without medication recognised themselves to be angrier than ADHD children on medication during the provocation trials. The end results showed that un-medicated ADHD children were typically more aggressive than medicated ADHD children and children without ADHD. Because methylphenidate is known to increase inhibition and decrease many of the behavioural problems associated with ADHD, the researchers concluded, 'It is possible that children in the medication group were able to inhibit their impulses to react aggressively to provocation' and 'reducing anger may be one key impact of MPH' (methylphenidate).

Another study followed 594 children with ADHD from kindergarten through to fifth grade, evaluating their academic performance when they were on medication and when they were off medication. During those five years the children underwent five maths and reading tests. The children on medication performed significantly better on the maths test compared to the un-medicated children but there were no real differences on the reading tests. However, for those children who had been on medication for a longer period of time their performance was much better on the reading tests compared to the un-medicated children.

## THE CONS OF METHYLPHENIDATE

While it appears stimulant medication offers some pretty amazing benefits, there are also a number of noteworthy limitations. For instance, the abovementioned study noted some astonishing changes for the children on medication; however, even though the children were performing much better in the trial on maths and English, they still needed a 60 per cent gain in the trial test scores just for them to receive the same scores as children without ADHD. This suggests that while medication may provide opportunities for children to manage educational demands a little better, on its own it will not necessarily help the child with every educational demand or challenge. The authors of this study recommended a multi-modal approach (see Chapter 8).

Sadly, at this point in time there is no known cure for ADHD. This also means that any type of medication (or psychotherapy for that matter) is not a cure but rather the symptoms are only under control while the child is taking the medication. This is one of the most readily recognised limitations of methylphenidate, for once the individual stops taking the medication the symptoms of ADHD reappear quite rapidly. Other limitations include:

- Twenty per cent or more of children are unable to tolerate stimulant medication.
- There is concern about the possible long-term side effects of the stimulant.
- Infrequent use of the medication.
- The side effects might outweigh the benefits.

It's no secret that children with ADHD really aren't equipped with the greatest of social skills, and while it has been noted that stimulant medication can help to improve the child's social functioning, it doesn't change the child's behaviour so that it resembles that of children without ADHD. In other words, children with ADHD on medication will still struggle with social deficits, therefore requiring some kind of social skills training. Furthermore, most parents (and siblings) are well aware of how long the positive effects of the medication typically last. Unless the individual is taking long-acting stimulants, the effects of the medication may only last for four to eight hours. This means that if a child is medicated in the morning before school the effects of the drug have all but worn off by the time they arrive home from school. This leaves a number of hours each evening when the child is not medicated, leaving the parents or caregivers to deal with the child's behaviour. Parents can really struggle trying to manage the child's impulsive, oppositional and generally disruptive behaviour that occurs at the end of the day and thus the parents may require support in the form of a parent management course.

While methylphenidate is highly successful in treating ADHD in children and adults, it is not the only medication available for treating ADHD. Thankfully, there is recognition that some people just cannot take stimulant medication for any number of reasons. This problem pushed the professional world to search for a non-stimulant medication that would treat ADHD just as effectively as the stimulant medication. Atomoxetine (or Strattera) is one such medication.

# Non-stimulant medications used for ADHD

Even though stimulant medications are the first-choice treatment for ADHD in children, not all children (up to 30 per cent) can tolerate them nor do a number of children respond adequately to the medication. In Australia, the most noted non-stimulant medication is atomoxetine (AT-oh-mox-e-teen), or Strattera as it is commonly known. As a non-stimulant, atomoxetine is a highly selective inhibitor of norepinephrine uptake, that is, the drug slows down the rate at which this neurotransmitter is taken back into the cell or broken down, which in essence makes norepinephrine more available to those areas of the brain affected by ADHD. Once again, as the drug begins working, we see a reduction in the core symptoms of ADHD.

There are a number of reasons why atomoxetine may be used as a preference to stimulant medication. Typically, atomoxetine is an appropriate alternative for children who fail to show an adequate response to stimulant medication, such as Concerta or Ritalin LA. In fact, some estimates suggest that between 10 to 30 per cent of children are unable to take stimulant medication. Also, the medication might be prescribed if children are unable to tolerate the noted side effects of stimulant medication or simply because the parents may have a preference for non-stimulant medication. Effectively, atomoxetine is a second line choice of treatment for ADHD.

Interestingly, this medication was originally designed to be used as an anti-depressant but was approved for use in America in 2002 by the Food and Drug Administration (FDA) for treating ADHD in both children and adults. However, it took Australia a little longer to catch up as the Therapeutic Goods Administration (TGA) did not approve the use of atomoxetine for treating ADHD until 2004.

Atomoxetine is manufactured by Eli Lilly Australia and comes in doses of 5, 10, 18, 25, 40 and 60 mg capsules and it has been shown to be very effective in managing ADHD symptoms. It has been subjected to a lot of trials over the last few years with some pretty impressive results. For example, one very large study of 3264 children and adolescents and 471 adults, with all types of ADHD, demonstrated that atomoxetine reduced the inattentive and hyperactive–impulsive symptoms of ADHD in over 70 per cent of the people taking part in the trials.

Atomoxetine usually reaches its peak performance about one to two hours after taking the medication with the effects lasting for about six to ten hours. Because of this, the medication can be given either once or twice a day, although it is recommended the medication be taken twice daily as it provides greater coverage from ADHD symptoms compared to stimulant medication.

## KNOWN SIDE EFFECTS FOR ATOMOXETINE (STRATTERA)

Being a non-stimulant medication does not exclude some individuals from experiencing side effects with atomoxetine. The US Food and Drug Administration (FDA) requires any labelling of atomoxetine to include warnings for potentially severe liver injury. It appears there were further revisions to include warning statements regarding an increased risk of suicidal ideation in children and adolescents taking this medication. The recommendation came after a number of trials in the US that included 2200 patients and 1357 patients respectively, who were taking Strattera, showed an increased risk of suicidal ideation for the first few months of treatment. What this means is that in the trials about four people in every 1000 had a greater risk of suicidal ideation than the patients who were given a placebo. However, the FDA also reported that similar analysis of adult patients taking Strattera found no increased risk of suicidal ideation. As with stimulant medication, the side effects appear to be separated according to how serious they are. The side effects of atomoxetine are well documented and generally benign and include:

- anxiety
- agitation
- panic attacks
- trouble sleeping
- irritability
- hostility
- aggressiveness
- impulsivity

- restlessness
- mania, and
- depression.

Parents are advised to watch for 'common side effects in children and adolescents' that include:
- upset stomach
- decreased appetite
- nausea or vomiting
- dizziness
- tiredness
- mood swings
- minor weight loss over the first two to four months (however, typically this will not last for more than twelve months)
- slight increases in blood pressure and heart rate (if concerned seek medical advice).

There are also common side effects for adults that include:
- constipation
- dry mouth
- nausea
- decreased appetite
- dizziness
- trouble sleeping
- sexual side effects
- menstrual cramps, and
- problems passing urine.

The FDA now has an updated label warning of potential liver injury after a teenager and an adult developed liver problems. Apparently they had been taking atomoxetine for several months when the problems developed. While it sounds pretty awful, the pair recovered after they stopped taking the medication. Apparently a further three children developed hepatitis after taking the medication.

## THE PROS OF ATOMOXETINE

After reading this book the one thing that should be evident to all is just how difficult ADHD is for everyone involved in the child's life, especially for the child's family members. The stress within these families can be significant and often their quality of life really takes a battering. Quality of life is something that every parent wants for their ADHD child and according to some studies atomoxetine may just offer that opportunity as it:

- Often results in significant improvements in parent–child relations, peer relations, school behaviour and academic performance as rated by parents and teachers.
- Reduces the symptoms of ADHD.
- Reduces the symptoms of oppositional defiant disorder (ODD).
- Reduces the symptoms of comorbid ADHD and ODD.
- Doesn't appear to be harmful to the cardiovascular system.

As mentioned earlier, atomoxetine can be considered either a first or second choice of treatment for ADHD, particularly where certain comorbid conditions exist. For instance, where children might have comorbid ADHD and generalised anxiety, obsessive compulsive disorder, or tic disorders (for example, Tourette syndrome), atomoxetine could be used as a first-line treatment, as stimulants are known to actually exacerbate the comorbid conditions. There are added benefits of atomoxetine:

- Because it is not a stimulant, it really doesn't have an abuse potential.
- It is safer to use with children or adolescents who have a history of substance abuse, or if the child is living with a person who abuses drugs.
- It normally doesn't interrupt the child's sleeping patterns.
- Parents who might be concerned about stimulant medication in light of the negative media attention it attracts can use atomoxetine as an alternative to put their concerns at ease.

But if the child is at risk due to problematic behaviours (for example, suspended from school, being harmed by others, aggressive behaviour), it may be necessary to begin the treatment with stimulant medication, particularly if the comorbid conditions as listed above are not so much of a problem. Stimulant medication is pretty quick at reducing the core symptoms of ADHD.

## THE CONS OF ATOMOXETINE

While there appears to be quite a number of positive aspects of atomoxetine, there are also some limitations associated with this medication. For instance, some research has indicated that atomoxetine may not work as well in reducing the symptoms of anxiety when ADHD is comorbid with generalised anxiety disorder. Also where children have been previously taking a stimulant medication and then swap over to atomoxetine, the effects of the drug on the symptoms of ADHD aren't always as good as the stimulant. While stimulant medication is considered to be fast-acting in reducing the symptoms of ADHD, atomoxetine appears to be somewhat slower in stabilising ADHD. Finally, it is not considered a safe alternative if there are pre-existing medical conditions such as high blood pressure, heart disease, glaucoma or liver dysfunction.

## CLONIDINE

Clonidine is another non-stimulant medication that was approved for the treatment of ADHD in Australia in 2010 for children and adolescents aged six to seventeen years. In its immediate release (IR) form, clonidine has been available as an antihypertensive medication for 30-odd years and some of you might know it as Catapres. As an immediate release, clonidine showed promise for managing ADHD and conduct disorder, but there were a number of problems with the drug, not least of all the need for frequent administration. As a result, clonidine extended-release (XR) was developed as a slow release medication lasting for up to twelve hours. This answered part of the problem with immediate release as administration can be just once or twice a day. Clonidine has also been used to treat tics, insomnia and explosive behaviour in children and adolescents.

Clonidine has been approved in the US as a monotherapy — or for use on its own in treating ADHD — and as an adjunctive or add-on medication to stimulants for the treatment of ADHD. While it might sound a little odd to *add* more medication to treat ADHD, especially given how effective stimulants have proven to be, the combination of the two medications has some impressive results. In fact, it is generally considered that adding clonidine to a stimulant produces better results in reducing the symptoms of ADHD in children where stimulants have not been overly effective. One study of 198 children aged six to seventeen years who weren't doing so well on stimulant medication alone, demonstrated that adding clonidine to the stimulant resulted in significant improvements in hyperactivity and inattention symptoms for the child (it has also been used in combination with stimulant medication to combat sleeplessness). What's more, the study also found that the combination of the medications was safe and well tolerated by the children with some mild side effects including sleepiness, headaches, nasal congestion and fatigue being the most commonly reported.

## KNOWN SIDE EFFECTS FOR CLONIDINE

The side effects of clonidine XR as listed below are those that appear to be the most common in clinical trials. Some of the side effects were primarily noted when clonidine was used as a monotherapy and were found to be mostly mild to moderate in intensity in the group receiving 0.2 mg doses:

- somnolence or sleepiness
- fatigue
- irritability
- pain in the pharynx and larynx.

In this group of side effects, fatigue was found to be the most severe but still only occurred in 1 per cent of the people taking part in the trial. The more serious side effects appeared restricted to the group who were taking the highest dose of clonidine at 0.4 mg daily and included:

- Six per cent of the participants experienced somnolence.
- Five per cent experienced infection.
- One per cent noticed feelings of aggression.

- One per cent experienced fatigue.
- One per cent experienced quite severe constipation.

Again, if you feel for any reason your child is not tolerating the medication, it is strongly recommended that you do not abruptly stop the medication but seek medical advice as the drug should be slowly tapered out. In addition, there are also a number of health cautions that come with using this medication, particularly for those at risk of:

- low blood pressure
- bradycardia (abnormally slow heart rate)
- heart block (abnormal heart rhythm).

It is further recommended that prior to using clonidine the patient has their blood pressure checked and recorded and if or when the dosage must be increased and at what intervals. People using clonidine should avoid becoming dehydrated or too hot and anyone with vascular disease, cardiac conduction disease (a serious heart disease) and kidney disease or failure should inform their doctor, as you will need to be monitored very closely if you are taking clonidine.

## What do the kids say?

Being a psychologist in private practice I learned a very important lesson early on in my career. It's a lesson that I believe has enabled me to go on and help many, many children and their families. While I might complete a comprehensive interview with the parents for vital information, it is equally important to spend time with the child to get their perspective on things. Children at any age have lots to say and can offer some very important insights. And this is certainly the case when it comes to medication. While we adults can generate intellectual, emotional and theoretical arguments about medicating children, very few people seem to stop and actually ask the child how they feel about it. Fortunately, there has been some research on children's experiences with medication. The children were quite frank and provided some very interesting responses.

One study questioned children between the ages of nine and seventeen about the positive and negative effects of taking stimulant medication. The questionnaire asked the children to rate the positive effects of taking medication in four different areas: ADHD symptoms (for example, 'I feel like I can concentrate better when I take my medication'); academics ('I can more easily do my homework when I take my medication'); aggression and defiance ('I get angry less often when I take my medication'); and social relations ('I think that it is easier to play with friends when I take my medication'). The children were also asked to rate the negative effects of the medication, such as experiencing physical complaints (headaches, stomach aches, loss of appetite, and difficulty falling asleep). In order to answer these questions, the children could choose from one of four possible answers ranging from 'not at all' through to 'very much'. Finally, the researchers wanted to know if there was ever a time the children wanted to stop taking their medication and if they knew when the medication was leaving their body. Again they had a choice of four possible answers ranging from 'no, not at all' through to 'yes I really do'.

The results of this study were pretty amazing really. For instance:

- Eighty-three per cent of the children reported they experienced large effects in their ability to concentrate.
- Over 70 per cent reported they were able to sit still and complete their homework.
- A further 60 per cent of the children reported positive changes in their social interactions.

Interestingly, the negative side effects were not as frequently reported by the children. For instance, only 27 per cent of the children mentioned loss of appetite and only 19 per cent reported problems falling asleep.

Remember the four options the children had to answer the questions about the negative effects of taking medication? When the researchers only paid attention to the highest answers — which would indicate they felt the negative effects very much — they found 43 per cent of the children experienced just one or two negative side effects and 45 per cent said they had never experienced a negative side effect.

When it came to the questions about the children wanting to stay on their medication, 43 per cent said they had never wanted to stop taking their medication. Interestingly, none of the children reported that the side effects were a reason to stop taking their medication. Instead the biggest reasons for staying on the medication included:

- The children were having much more fun at school.
- They were finding it easier to make friends.
- They were nicer to their family members.
- They didn't feel as angry.
- They were able to notice when the medicine was leaving their body.

Finally, another study asked children between the ages of nine and fourteen their views about receiving a diagnosis of ADHD and if medication helped their social behaviours and schoolwork. Generally speaking, children with aggression problems reported a number of positive effects of medication including:

- It helped them to calm down.
- They were able to think first rather than acting out.
- And they felt less angry.

There was kind of a snowball effect here because the children were aware that they were able to make and maintain friendships. One of the most important aspects coming out of this research was that the medication was having a positive impact on classroom behaviour, both verbal and physical. Other encouraging results were also found:

- The children felt they could concentrate and focus a lot better.
- There were improvements in their schoolwork, particularly with writing and maths.
- Some of the children received better marks on standardised tests.
- Interestingly the children felt generally positive about their medication and they realised it was necessary for them and was a normal part of their lives.
- They were aware they had become less impulsive and unruly.
- They did not report any concerns about taking the medication.

- The kids knew that if they stopped taking the medication they were more annoying to others and out of control.
- The kids also knew their behaviour was problematic to some degree.
- Some of them admitted to occasionally using the diagnosis as an excuse for their behaviour.
- But they also felt responsible for managing their behaviour and believed the medication helped with this.

The children also reported negative feelings about their medication, mainly that taking medication was annoying.

When we look at the answers these children have provided, it would appear they are very much aware that they are better off on medication for a number of personal, social and academic reasons. It would seem that the benefits of taking medication far outweighed any reported negative effects.

## Other negative factors of taking medication

The abovementioned research also indicated two other areas that were found to influence a child's decision to quit the medication. The researchers noted that if a child didn't really understand the reason why they were on medication, they were more likely to want to stop taking their medication. Also, children appeared to be influenced by their parents' negative feelings and beliefs about medication.

The importance of the family context cannot be over-emphasised when it comes to medicating children for ADHD. Parental attitudes toward ADHD medication and the frequency with which it is taken have been well documented. I have met parents who absolutely refuse to even allow me to discuss the various types of medications available to treat ADHD. Furthermore, parental mental health problems have also been implicated in compromising the potential positive outcomes from psychological and behavioural interventions because parental attitudes are not usually directly addressed in therapy. One such example springs to mind where I attempted to inform a single parent of a teenage child with ADHD about treatment options for her child. The single mother had been diagnosed with a personality disorder. She had been battling with this most of her life and also suffered from depression and anxiety. While the mother was doing her best to stay on her medication and raise her child, when I discussed with her the different treatment options available, including a parent management training program, she looked me straight in the eyes and refused. Somewhat surprised I asked her what the reason was behind her decision. The mother told me, 'I'm just hanging on myself. It takes everything I have just to keep going from day to day. I can't take on anything else, I just don't have the energy.' This is not an uncommon response as the person with a mental illness can often feel as though all their energy is spent just trying to face another day.

Given these concerns, medication then is likely to show different outcomes for different children. This is really quite a significant issue as if the parents had been unduly influenced by negative biased reports or didn't really have a solid understanding about the medication, they may, in fact, be making a decision for their child based on ignorance. Finally, for the 12 per cent of children who experienced three or more negative side effects, the researchers rightly suggested that these children would fair better on an alternative treatment.

Many parents agonise over the decision to medicate their child with ADHD and the many unknown factors and sensationalised media stories they face only serve to intensify their fears. This chapter has presented a lot of information on the most commonly prescribed medications for treating ADHD in children, adolescents and adults in order to reduce some of the fear and to help you make an informed decision. The important point to remember is that a specialist does not hand out medication like candy at a lolly store; there are many factors that are considered before anyone is placed on either stimulant or non-stimulant medication for treating ADHD. Such factors include previous and present medical conditions, the age of the child, the child's tolerance of the medication. Even abuse potential by others in the child's life is considered. Once it is established the individual can take the medication, the next step is to determine the right dosage. Your specialist will require a number of follow-up sessions to check that the dosage of the prescribed medication is correct. They may also require you, as the parent or legal guardian, to keep a diary, recording specific information over a period of time to help them determine the right dosages for the child.

While we accept that medication for treating ADHD is generally safe, we cannot ignore there are always risk factors with taking any medication. Given these risks it is *strongly* recommended that you consult with your medical specialist to ensure your child is safe and is able to keep on taking the medication. It is also recommended that all parents/legal guardians carefully read any and all information that may accompany the medication. Typically, an information pamphlet from the pharmaceutical company would be found on the inside of the package. Finally, if for any reason you have any concerns about your child's health, consult your medical specialist without delay.

# CHAPTER 8

## Alternative therapies for ADHD

Before introducing the topic of alternative therapies to medication, I want to bring to your attention the potential problems of seeking help and support or 'counselling' from individuals who offer their services, but who are simply not qualified or experienced to do so. In many countries around the world, including Australia, people wanting to be a counsellor (that is, not a psychologist or psychiatrist) are not required to undertake any formal training. This simply means that anyone, anywhere, and at any time, can register a business and call themselves a counsellor. Obviously, not all ill-qualified or ill-experienced individuals are intentionally acting in a manner that may bring harm to those trusting in them. However, it could also be argued that maintaining no or minimal training is in itself unethical, unprofessional and potentially dangerous, as it can pose a serious risk to those who are often in their most vulnerable state.

Because pharmacotherapy is considered to be the gold standard of treatment for ADHD and is typically the first line of treatment, the phrase 'alternative treatments' could be viewed as any treatment that does not include conventional medication. Certainly, alternative treatments can conjure up an array of mental images as well as varied meanings for different people. Alternative treatments for ADHD can range from the downright ridiculous to an approach that, while not medical, does have credible support in professional literature and practice and is known as an evidenced-based therapy. However, sadly, and at times disturbingly, when it comes to ADHD (and other forms of mental illness) there are many people who are more than happy to have their say and push their special brand of intervention as a 'cure-all'. Over the years there have been some rather fantastic claims of so-called 'cures' for ADHD that range from the mysterious and miraculous healing power of crystals (typically rose quartz) carefully placed in deliberate settings around the home to catch all the bad energy of an individual, to balancing on a board or playing 'catch' (at the friendly sum of thousands of dollars per year), to playing love songs to a child at night while he or she sleeps. Some of these 'treatments' are well packaged and even claim to have *scientific* support; however, what the consumer is not told is that the scientific support they claim to have is that their special brand of therapy worked for their child so, of course, it will work for your child. What these people also fail to tell you is that their child was never formally diagnosed with any behavioural disorder, but rather the diagnosis was based solely on their own opinion or that of their friends. Some of the more 'professionally' packaged programs make similar spectacular claims of a 'cure-all' and may even produce papers written by professionals supporting their claims. Again, what you are not being told is that the 'professional' may have a vested interest in the outcome of the program because they are an employee of that company or they are simply taking little bits and pieces from a collection of scientific journals and repackaging the information so that it supports their claims.

*Any intervention for children and their families living with ADHD should be conducted only by appropriately qualified and experienced professionals.* It is very important to note that any worthwhile therapy should produce positive long-term effects, and have been developed by the professional community and well tested in representative community samples, and independently peer reviewed. Not only that, the individual offering the therapy should be a well-trained and experienced professional. You the consumer have both the right and the responsibility to ask as many questions as you like about the individual's qualifications and experience and how they propose to help you in your unique situation. You have the right to ask the professional:

- If they are a registered practitioner, who they are registered with, and with what professional association they hold membership.
- To cite both their professional and business registration details.
- To tell you their detailed plan of how they intend to help you and your child and how many sessions of therapy are likely to take place.
- How many affected people they have seen and ask for examples of how they helped the person with ADHD and their family.
- You have the right to terminate future sessions if you believe the individual is not helping you.

In Australia all psychologists, psychiatrists, doctors, and paediatricians are subject to a single national registration board known as the Australian Health Practitioner Regulation Agency (AHPRA). Every person registered within these professions is required by law to display their relevant qualifications in a prominent place where any patient or client may sight it with ease (for a complete list of professions that are subject to federal registration visit www.ahpra.gov.au). In order to practise your chosen profession in Australia, you must first successfully complete a university degree and be registered with the AHPRA. The AHPRA ensures a minimal national qualification to practise the chosen profession, demands ongoing professional training, and has the power to investigate incompetent or unethical behaviour of the professional. If found guilty of such behaviour, AHPRA can and will cancel the professional's licence to practise.

Most of these nationally registered professions also have a relevant professional association to which they are a member, for example, a psychological society or a medical association. Such an association will also demand high levels of competency from their members, ongoing training, and will also hold their members accountable for inappropriate conduct. Having such a system offers security and protection to members of the public and ensures the professional remains highly trained in order to offer you the best possible help. Finally, in Australia, any person who works with children under the age of eighteen years must have a Working With Children Check and hold a current identification card. Essentially, this is a national background check of the person to ensure that children will be safe with the individual. Any professional working with children will have this check and identification card. It is scary to think there are people out there who will not have undergone such a check and still offer to help children. Such a system of protection is non-existent with individuals who have not undertaken any formal training.

As a registered psychologist in private practice, I have seen first-hand the dangers members of the public face when seeking help from individuals offering their so-called expertise for matters in which they have had no training. I have had the unfortunate experience of spending many hours with people who have been hurt, let down, misinformed or who have received just plain wrong information from people claiming to be counsellors.

## Alternative treatments for ADHD

Alternative treatments tend to fall outside the mainstream treatments for both children and adults with ADHD and, as such, would normally be seen as unconventional. The biggest problem with alternative treatments is that very few have any long-term positive effect, while the vast majority simply have no successful treatment outcomes at all. While research or empirical support has demonstrated that medications are one of the most effective means of treatment for ADHD, there remains a continued interest in alternative treatment options. People's reasons for seeking alternative treatments for ADHD are wide and varied and range from parents who are concerned about medicating their child or adolescent, to those individuals who do not respond to or only partially respond to the medication, to the people who experience unbearable side effects from the medication, to those who may be responding very nicely to the medication but are seeking a complementary approach to further enhance relief from the severity of ADHD symptoms. Given the chronic (meaning long-term) nature of ADHD in both children and adults, it is not surprising that both the sufferer and the parents would seek alternative or complementary treatment options that all but guarantee relief. Sometimes a parent or adult can feel so desperate to see an end to the symptoms of ADHD that anecdotal evidence presented on the television or some comments from a friend of a friend about some alternative therapy they tried that worked can be enough to send a parent down the road to 'trying anything'.

The following section presents a number of available alternative and non-medical treatments for ADHD. This section covers the traditional treatments that have been well documented in the professional literature and rigorously tested by the professional community and have therefore been validated and supported by independent research. Such therapies include psycho-education, mindfulness, parent management training (PMT), behavioural interventions, cognitive behavioural therapy (CBT), cognitive reframing, social skills training (SST), school interventions, and multiple therapies (multi-modal treatment).

Some of the alternative treatments discussed below, such as mindfulness and biofeedback, are currently being tested and reviewed by the professional community. There are concerns that alternative treatments based on anecdotal evidence ('anecdotal' meaning a treatment that has not been rigorously tested, trialled and repeatedly retested under different circumstances by independent researchers and professionals) may only interfere with the traditional treatment programs that have well-established treatment outcomes. These two therapies have been included because of the growing interest in them as alternative therapies to medication.

## PSYCHO-EDUCATION

Basically, psycho-education is just a fancy way of saying that a psychologist or a clinician would spend time with the child and parents, and provide a lot of detailed information about:

- ADHD as a disorder.
- The causes of ADHD, including the neurobiology.
- How the ADHD is likely to continue into adulthood, as it does in many cases.
- The prognosis or what the expected outcome might be.

- Comorbid conditions.
- How the disorder might impact the child emotionally, behaviourally, cognitively, socially, academically; that is, in peer relationships, social relationships, personal relationships and employment relationships, to name a few.

Psycho-education should also involve the clinician providing a detailed account of:

- Any assessments that might be used.
- The type of psychotherapy they believe would be most suited to the presenting problems.
- How long the child might expect to be in therapy.
- In the case of ADHD, the parents would also be informed about undertaking a parent management program and any further necessary information they would need.

The clinician would also discuss the necessity of having other relevant professionals involved, such as a paediatrician for a full medical check-up, and if ADHD is diagnosed, the clinician would also discuss the potential need for medication. It has always been my practice to walk all my patients through this process, providing as much information as they need. In this way they know what's going on and they can make an informed decision and not be taken by surprise or put off by the possible side effects of medication.

## MINDFULNESS

Mindfulness is a treatment that in recent years has begun to receive ever-increasing attention by medical practitioners and mental health specialists alike and, as such, has been trialled for a number of different medical and psychological disorders with some degree of success. Mindfulness has also been trialled with sufferers of ADHD with mixed results. While the research involving the effectiveness of mindfulness on ADHD symptoms is not vast, it is included in this chapter because of the current attention it is receiving as a possible alternative or complementary treatment to medication.

As you are no doubt aware, some of the more problematic issues of ADHD are the difficulties children (and adults) have in maintaining their attention over a prolonged period of time, the trouble they experience making and holding plans and keeping goals in mind, and the difficulty they experience in restricting impulsive responses. Mindfulness is a relatively new adaptation to therapy in Western culture, but as its origins are steeped in Buddhist meditation and Eastern mysticism, mindfulness has a rather long history of some 2500 years.

Mindfulness has been used with adults suffering from depression, pain, anxiety disorders and eating disorders. It has also been claimed that the practice of mindfulness can reduce aggression. Mindfulness is about paying close attention to the present or the in-the-moment experience to increase awareness of the present moment, enhance non-judgmental observation, and to reduce automatic responding. Mindfulness is a type of meditation with an emphasis on observation rather than a reaction to your thoughts, emotions or body states. Mindfulness, it is argued, teaches the individual to become less reactive to what is happening to them in the present moment. So, whether the situation you find yourself in is a positive one or a negative one or even neutral, you can be less reactive to that situation. Another way of describing mindfulness is that you are taking no steps to change the current situation; you are simply observing it. This observational response then enables the person to reduce their general level of suffering (be it physical or emotional pain) and increase a general sense of wellbeing.

## THE PROCESS OF MINDFULNESS

Mindfulness is designed to develop the skills in an individual to reduce personal suffering and to therefore facilitate and enhance positive personal growth and development. Mindfulness involves practical learning by sitting for periods of time in silent meditation or slow walking while maintaining purposeful attention to daily activities and automatic tasks, such as walking and eating. While the person may begin to feel relaxed, this is actually not the reason for practising mindfulness meditation. Instead, the main purpose appears to be focusing your attention on any one particular task.

According to some of the teachings on mindfulness, each person has the capacity and the potential to heal themselves. This is referred to as 'healing from within'. Apparently, when the individual develops the capacity for self-healing they are at a point where they:

> ... may pass from a state of imbalance and distress to a state of greater harmony and serenity with respect to themselves with a consequent enhanced subjective perception of wellbeing. (Germer et al., 2005)

Mindfulness is said to teach the individual to be aware of themselves and to physically, emotionally or mentally alter distressed states by devoting full attention to or refocusing on their breathing or some other activity to develop a sense of peace within their self. There are no thoughts of the past or future, just of the present moment. There is to be no judgment or evaluation or a reaction to the moment. Without all these competing and distracting thoughts the individual is said to be mindful.

It is claimed that mindfulness meditation, being a self-regulating practice, may improve a person's ability to self-regulate attention and their emotions. When it comes to the child with ADHD, this can be achieved by completing three steps:

1. Sitting or walking to bring to the child's (or adolescent's or adult's) attention an automatic action such as breathing. This focusing on an automatic action is said to be an attentional anchor.
2. Teaching the child that they will have competing and distracting thoughts, but it's okay to have distracting thoughts, so just let go of it all.
3. Have the child refocus their attention back to the automatic task, such as their breathing.

These three steps would be repeated over and over during the practice of mindfulness meditation. In between formal sessions or classes of meditation, the individual is instructed to constantly turn their attention to the present moment throughout the day.

## WHAT DOES THE RESEARCH SAY?

Research has put mindfulness to the test to determine whether it might have a positive effect on reducing ADHD symptoms in children. One particular research design developed an extensive manual to provide the children and parents in their program comprehensive training in mindfulness. In their extensive training component the children were taught how to focus and enhance their attention, they were taught to develop an awareness of self and self-control by practising the mindfulness exercises during the program and as homework. The children were also taught how to apply mindfulness strategies or techniques during difficult situations, such as being distracted in the classroom. At the end of each session the children were given homework that was checked each week by the trainers. If the children completed their homework they would receive a reward. The parents on the other hand were taught to deliberately be in the present moment with their child without being judgmental, they were taught self-care strategies, to accept the difficulties of their child, to change the way in which they reacted to their child's difficult behaviour, how to reduce parental stress (as this also influences the way in which parents approach their child), and how to keep their child committed to doing the homework every night. The parents also had to practise mindfulness each night as homework.

The therapists were experienced in delivering cognitive behavioural therapy (CBT) and they had extensive mindfulness experience. They had received mindfulness training from internationally recognised experts in the field and they were experienced psychotherapists who also specialised in delivering group psychotherapy. The therapists met weekly for supervision to discuss the group process, individual participants, and to ensure treatment integrity.

As you can see, this was a fairly comprehensive program and it is important to note the strict conditions with which this study was conducted and the level of training and expertise the therapists had before commencing this program. At the end of the eight weeks of training in mindfulness the parents reported their children's ADHD symptoms had been reduced and that their own levels of stress had reduced and there had also been a noticeable reduction of over-reactive parenting. However, when the schoolteachers were asked to rate the children's ADHD symptoms after the program, they reported very little difference. The authors concluded that because the parents were involved in their own treatment and that of their child's and the teachers were not, the teachers were, in fact, the 'more independent raters of the child's behaviour than the parents', and that they could not 'ascertain that the observed improvements could be attributed to the specific treatment procedures ...' Finally, the authors commented on an important outcome of the program they had not originally intended to measure — that of the parent–child relationship. Given that the parent and child were now spending a great deal of quality time together, the authors could not conclusively rule out the influence this had on both parental stress and the child's behaviour.

In a separate study of mindfulness, another researcher was more interested in teaching mothers mindfulness first before teaching mindfulness to their ADHD child. The emphasis of this mindfulness training was to refocus the mother's attention away from the child's behaviour associated with ADHD, such as impulsivity or inattention, and on to the child's compliant behaviour when their mother made a request. They also wanted to determine whether teaching both the mother and the child mindfulness would increase the child's compliance to the mother's requests. Essentially, the mindfulness program was customised for the participants and included no parenting skills training or self-management training to the children.

The study comprised two mothers with one son each who had been diagnosed with ADHD and were taking methylphenidate. An experienced mindfulness trainer met with each mother and child and told the mother she would be trained in mindfulness for twelve weeks after which her son would undertake twelve weeks of mindfulness training. For the two children the mindfulness instruction was 'customised', and was interactive whereby the children could ask questions with the trainer who would alter or adapt the training for each boy. Each mother was encouraged to practise mindfulness with the family during and after completing the mindfulness training and to also practise with her son daily. While the mindfulness training lasted twelve weeks, the mothers were asked to maintain a record of their sons' compliant behaviour for a total of 24 weeks.

The results of this study found the mothers reporting that the practise of mindfulness was initially difficult for them and that they would have dropped out if they had not asked to be included in the study. However, after persisting for some time, the mothers found they were beginning to enjoy the meditation and were reporting experiencing a sense of calmness and that they were eager to continue the training. The mothers further reported the mindfulness training 'taught' them to listen to their children more and that the family had commented that they also appeared to be quite calm. The two boys reported they liked the teacher and his teaching methods and they also felt they were able to concentrate better at school (though the mindfulness teachers were not asked to give a rating of any differences in ADHD behaviours). However, what seemed to be most important to the boys was the fact that their mothers weren't yelling at them. Both mothers noted changes in their interactions with their boys and an increased sense of happiness with their child.

The authors concluded that while they believed training the mothers in mindfulness may have increased their child's compliance in the short term, it was not enough to 'make a substantial difference in the mother–child relationship'. There was further acknowledgement that training the children in customised mindfulness found greater child compliance to a mother's request. Also, it was noted that after the children had been trained in mindfulness, the mother–child relationship did appear to be more positive. While the results may, in fact, be encouraging in terms of mindfulness training decreasing a child's non-compliance, keep in mind this study had only four people in it or two children with ADHD. Also, the authors included in the mindfulness training teachings on loving kindness, compassion and generosity and 'encouraged' the family and the mother and son to practise mindfulness together. Again, there is a strong component of the family spending quality time together and, in conjunction with the training in loving kindness, compassion and generosity, it is hard to determine if mindfulness had any influence on the child's non-compliant behaviour and if it did, how much. The authors reported that the positive effects they noted did not include measuring any differences in the core symptoms of ADHD such as inattention, impulsivity and hyperactivity, and thus perhaps why the child's teachers were not asked to note any positive changes in the child's behaviour after the mindfulness training. Finally, the authors noted that both the mother and the child agreed the child would comply with the mother's request within a given timeframe. This on its own could be considered an intervention as it could be argued the mere fact that mother and son sat down and talked about the child's problematic behaviour and what mum's expectations would be for that non-compliant behaviour may have significantly contributed to the child's compliance to the mother's request. Finally, one interesting note, the authors of this research suggested that while they were aware the two boys were on medication that targeted ADHD symptoms, this was not the focus of their study. However, the physician of one of the boys began reducing his ADHD medication in the seventh week of the mindfulness training and discontinued the medication three weeks later. The other child's medication was reduced in the thirteenth week of the program and discontinued six weeks later. Apparently there were no adverse changes to the cessation of medication noted for the duration of the study.

As noted earlier, mindfulness training has been used with certain populations for some time and in certain circumstances does appear to have some support for positive effects. However, successfully using mindfulness meditation for reducing the core symptoms of ADHD has a long way to go. In fact, a reduction in the core symptoms of ADHD to the point where there were observable differences in the child's behaviour by schoolteachers, friends, family and peers was not evident as a result of mindfulness meditation.

## BIOFEEDBACK

Recently a colleague contacted me seeking information about the best way for teachers in a local school to manage the behaviour of a child with ADHD in the classroom. We spoke for some time about all the interventions, as noted in this chapter, before I was asked about the lesser-known therapy of biofeedback.

While doing some research on the internet, I came across a rather interesting website that was advertising a non-medical treatment for ADHD. Somewhat intrigued I opened the page and read the blurb that reported ADHD medications are not a safe option and they don't work for everyone anyway. The blurb indicated that this individual's therapy would fix some of the core deficits of ADHD, including inattention. On top of that, the individual was displaying some very impressive qualifications and had even travelled overseas to 'specialise' in biofeedback.

Biofeedback is a rather complicated therapy and to explain it in any depth is beyond the scope of this book. Essentially, a child is hooked up to a machine that measures their brainwaves (an electroencephalograph). Once the child is hooked up to the electroencephalograph, computers enhance the reading of the person's brainwaves generally while they are completing a given task. Then someone who is trained in biofeedback reviews the results to determine if there is a decrease in the child's beta waves (beta waves correspond to alertness) or an increase in theta waves (corresponding to inattention). By training the child in certain activities, the claim is that the therapy will increase the child's beta waves (alertness) and improve concentration. It all sounds rather impressive because it measures brainwaves and uses some very high-tech medical machinery and terminology.

## WHAT DOES THE RESEARCH SAY?

Because of its fantastic claims and apparent promising outcomes, biofeedback is one of those alternative therapies that has received quite a bit of attention by the professional community. Early research around biofeedback as a therapy for ADHD indicated some encouraging results but as it turns out the results were due to other non-specific effects. Reviewing the literature about biofeedback as a treatment for ADHD revealed there was no clear support for it as a therapy for ADHD. It appears that where biofeedback has been used in trials to treat ADHD, there have been so many problems with the methods used that professionals are saying we cannot rely on the results to inform us of anything. In fact, a consensus report on treatments for ADHD by the US National Institutes of Health reported that the evidence for biofeedback as a verified treatment for ADHD was not empirically supported and recommended biofeedback undergo more controlled studies before it could be endorsed as an effective, reliable treatment. Other professionals who specialise in treating ADHD reviewed the outcome of a number of studies where biofeedback was used as an ADHD treatment and found virtually no improvements at all. In fact, they found that if there was an improvement, it was most likely due to other factors. At the completion of their investigation, the researchers actually advised *against* using biofeedback as an ADHD treatment based on the current lack of empirical support it had received.

## PARENT MANAGEMENT TRAINING (PMT)

At one point in history when a child misbehaved in public or at school, the finger of blame was squarely pointed toward the parents, or more precisely at the child's mother. Beliefs and comments like 'What a horrible job you are doing', or 'What a failure as a mother you are', and 'What kind of mother would let her child act that way?' were fairly common sentiments. Depending on the circumstances and where you may be at the time, these sentiments are not entirely a thing of the past today. For instance, what sort of look did you get from other shoppers when your child was having a full-blown tantrum in the aisle of your local shopping centre because you didn't buy a lolly or a toy? Some people might smile sweetly as they pass you by, remembering the days when it happened to them and silently thanking God they don't have to deal with that issue anymore. On the other hand, there are those who will make it very clear they do not approve of your child's behaviour or the way you are handling it, and will give you that look of disapproval that clearly states you need to be controlling your child's behaviour a lot better. A common scenario is an elderly person approaching a young mother and firmly telling her, 'You need to learn to control your child', while the child is having a tantrum in a shopping centre. More often than not, the elderly person will have no idea why the child is having the tantrum in the first place.

When it comes to behavioural disorders, the problem behaviour displayed by those with ADHD doesn't just happen in one place such as the shopping centre when your child can't have a lolly or because you won't pick her up and carry her. Added to this is the fact that the constant difficult behaviour of children with ADHD has been clearly linked to increasing the risks of fracturing and disrupting the parent–child relationship. Also, there is typically a great deal of stress experienced in the sibling relationships and the marital relationship. To present all the research that supports these findings would take millennia. But in this instance presenting all the facts is not necessary, as any parent of a child with ADHD will tell you there are times when they feel overwhelmed by their child's problematic behaviour and have just wanted to get in their car and drive off into the sunset. Some worn out parents who feel they have tried everything to 'control' their child's behaviour have half seriously, half jokingly, reported there were times when they felt as if they could strangle their little angel. The effort to deal with the constant and relentless core symptoms of ADHD along with all the other problems of comorbidities, social problems, academic problems, fractured family relationships and marital problems can be a source of enormous stress in the parent. In such stressful situations parents can begin to develop negative thoughts and feelings about their child and can begin to see their child as the cause of all these problems. One couple seeking marital counselling plainly told me their problems were because of their child with ADHD. The father reported, 'We wouldn't be in this situation if we didn't have Johnny'. This increase in parental stress can be the turning point for the parent to begin using maladaptive or counterproductive parenting styles, as portrayed by one angry father who stated, 'He's a little shit who just needs a good kick up the arse'.

Certain parenting practices have been shown to either improve problematic behaviour or actually reinforce it. Yep, you read that correctly: some parenting styles can *increase* the aggressive and non-compliant behaviour in children, particularly in children with behavioural disorders. Coercive parenting is an example of a maladaptive parenting style that is often found in families with an ADHD child. Coercive parenting happens when a parent uses aversive behaviour to control the behaviour of their child and generally looks as if the parent is:

- Harsh, unfeeling, tough and cold towards the child.
- Disinterested in the child.
- Insensitive to the child.
- Uncompassionate and unsympathetic towards the child.

Obviously in such a parent–child relationship, parental expressions of love, affection, warmth, patience and encouragement may rarely take place. This, in turn, diminishes the parents' willingness to take the opportunity to help their child develop or even reinforce positive social interactions and behavioural skills. Such parenting has been consistently related to increasing and reinforcing a child's aggressive behaviour. The reason for this is that coercive parenting has been found to directly impact:

- A child's self-identity and self-esteem.
- A child's educational achievements.
- A child's social skills and social competence.
- The likelihood of school truancy and dropping out.
- The likelihood of criminal behaviour.
- The likelihood of substance use and abuse, just to name a few.

Where such parenting practices are taking place, there is the added risk of the parent applying harsh and punitive punishments. Believe it or not, using discipline such as corporal punishment (physical discipline, such as smacking) to alter a child's behaviour is now known to be an ineffective form of discipline. While it may appear that smacking a child may change their behaviour, a smack typically only brings about an immediate change in behaviour; it almost never 'teaches a child a lesson' nor does it typically change their long-term behaviour. This is where very serious problems can begin. An exhausted and angry parent lashes out and smacks their child just for a moment's peace or because they have had enough of the child's aggressive and non-compliant behaviour. A smack may bring about an immediate change in the child's behaviour or at least decrease the behaviour long enough for the parent to feel they have a little bit of breathing space, but the trouble is that the parent will begin to recognise the behaviour hasn't changed over time, and they may find they need to yell more and more or need to smack the child more and more to bring about a change of behaviour. Unfortunately, this can bring about further problems because the more the child is at the receiving end of angry, punitive punishment, the greater the risk of the child becoming more and more aggressive. How do we know this? Because harsh, punitive or coercive parenting has been clearly linked to an increase in childhood aggressive behaviour. The very behaviour this parent is trying to control may very well be the behaviour they are increasing and reinforcing in their child. As you can see, this cycle has the potential to become abusive.

Currently there is continued research on trying to determine the development of and possible causes of serious adult mental health problems. Researchers have been looking at whether or not there is a connection between parenting practices and adult personality disorders. The result of decades of research has clearly established a connection between certain parenting practices and adult personality disorders. Emotional maltreatment (defined as both emotional abuse and emotional neglect) and the sexual or physical abuse of children by adults has received enormous attention by the professional community over the years. More recent studies have found that there were no differences between adults reporting childhood sexual and/ or *physical* abuse at the hands of their parents, and those adults being *emotionally* mistreated by their parents. This same research also found that emotional maltreatment by parents was connected to symptoms of certain personality disorders, such as paranoid, borderline, avoidant, dependent and obsessive compulsive personality disorders. If you revisit the above description on coercive parenting for example, it would seem pretty clear that it could very well be categorised as emotional maltreatment and abuse. It has also been clearly established that dysfunctional parenting practices influence and encourage the development of and support the persistence of problematic behaviour in the ADHD child.

Does coercive parenting **cause** childhood ADHD? Absolutely NOT! Parenting styles do not **cause** ADHD. However, some parenting styles can heighten or exacerbate certain symptoms of ADHD. Parenting styles can also reinforce aggressive behaviour in children and tear apart the parent–child relationship.

Coercive parenting is insidious as it creeps into the parent–child relationship ever so slowly. This simply means that parents are often not even aware they are using detrimental parenting practices. Equally, many, many parents do not develop dysfunctional parenting practices. These parents are conscious of their parenting styles, monitor their responses to their child, keep check of their attitudes and behaviours, and desperately try to help their child develop appropriate social skills by encouraging them to make friends at school or to invite friends for sleepovers, or even have their child join a sports team. At the end of the day, after all the jobs are done, these parents diligently sit by their child of an evening and patiently instruct and help their child with their homework. These parents often advocate for their child with other parents, siblings, grandparents and schoolteachers (even employers), yet the parent–child relationship can still be tense as the constant strain on these parents is ever present as they struggle day in and day out. So what help and support is available for parents of a child with ADHD?

Parent management training (PMT) programs have been developed for the very purpose of supporting parents in their parenting attempts and are considered to be the choice therapy for families with a child suffering from ADHD. It makes sense that working alongside the parents and teaching them effective ways to parent their ADHD child may very well increase the chances of a positive parent–child relationship. Parent management programs attempt to alter the often negative communication patterns between the parent and child, and to teach the parents effective, non-punitive measures of discipline that will bring about changes in their child's behaviour. Parent management training programs also attempt to change dysfunctional parenting practices and, if necessary, focus on modifying the parent's perception of their child's behaviour. This is quite important as it is common for parents to misunderstand the nature of ADHD, believing instead that their child is just being naughty, won't listen, or is deliberately misbehaving to get on their nerves. Parent management training often leads to a decline in parental stress, reduced stress in the marital relationship, and a notable decrease in family distress. Such a reduction in stress levels in itself is known to lead to greater family cohesion. Parent management training programs are known to be very effective, as they tend to help both parents and the child to break out of the negative and coercive cycles that so often accompany such disorders and facilitate the healing of fractured relationships. This, is turn, promotes an opportunity for a supportive and positive parent–child relationship to develop. Often this will reduce the amount of aggressive behaviour displayed in the home by both the parents and the child.

As with all interventions, there are quite a few different parent management training programs available in both private and public mental health care practices for parents with children and adolescents with behavioural disorders. While there are a number of different PMT programs available, all programs will share certain similarities. Most PMT programs run for between ten to twelve weeks with each session lasting from one to two hours of structured lessons. Typically, in the early stages of the intervention, PMT includes:

- Providing extensive education to the parents about their child's behavioural disorder.
- Answering the parents' questions and helping them to understand that a behavioural disorder such as ADHD is not a case of the child just being naughty.
- Reassuring parents that the disorder was not caused by their parenting style.

Such programs also aim to further teach parents:

- Problem-solving skills.
- How to effectively communicate with their child.
- How to model appropriate behaviour to their child.

- How to build their child's self-esteem.
- Skills in conflict resolution.

Those programs that are highly structured will demand that the clinician also be highly trained, will usually involve a number of different assessments to determine such things as how fractured the family might be, and will include homework tasks for the parents to complete for the duration of the program. Such PMT programs are normally very successful in improving family relationships, marital relationships, and decreasing the aggressive behaviour of the child or adolescent in the immediate as well as in the long-term future. Finally, at some point in the program, parents will also be taught effective behavioural management strategies or ways to alter their child's problematic or aggressive behaviour. This is commonly known as behavioural modification.

Parent management training programs focus on teaching well-adjusted and effective parenting skills. According to one researcher, PMT refers to procedures in which parents are trained to alter their child's behaviour in the home. Adaptive parenting or authoritative parenting (which is different to authoritarian) practices have been found to have quite a positive effect on the child's non-compliant behaviour, the parent–child relationship and sibling to sibling relationships. The authoritative parent then:

- Respects their child and loves and expresses warmth towards them.
- Does not treat their child harshly or punitively and is concerned for their child's overall wellbeing and their emotional, physical, psychological, and spiritual development.
- Protects their child, supports their child, and stands in the gap for their child.
- Teaches their child how to be responsible.
- Makes any unpopular decisions for their child because of their developmental immaturity.
- Teaches their child ownership of their behaviours and decisions.
- Sets very clear boundaries for the child's behaviour and

monitors their child's activities.

- Implements fair and just age-appropriate consequences for problematic behaviours.

Adaptive parenting then is known to help the development of the child's self-identity, and aids in developing a healthy self-esteem. It is related to educational achievements, pro-social behaviours and can be a predictor of social competence in children and adolescents with ADHD.

As already noted, PMT programs will also teach parents effective ways of disciplining their children that don't require harsh, punitive punishment. Learning appropriate and effective discipline is a major factor in promoting desirable and acceptable social behaviour while reducing undesirable, problematic and aggressive behaviour in the child. The type of disciplinary strategies parents will learn often depends on the age of the child, and the type of problem behaviour that needs to change. Whatever the disciplinary strategies taught in PMT, there will be the common factor of certainty. That is, a particular behaviour will have a specific consequence each and every time. This helps parents avoid power struggles, breaks the cycle of coercive parenting, and teaches the child that their aggressive and defiant behaviour will get them nowhere. In order to accomplish modifying a child's problematic behaviour, the parents may learn how to use the child's privileges as a form of discipline and may also learn how to use rewards in order to promote desirable behaviour. An example of discipline for a four-year-old may be to place them on a chair facing the wall for one minute per year in age. Thus a four-year-old child will have to sit on the chair for four minutes. If the child were to get off the chair the parent would place the child back on the chair and explain the clock has been reset to four minutes. When the child has sat there for the allotted time the parent would permit the child to leave the chair with an explanation about the undesirable behaviour and the subsequent consequence. If the child is in the middle to late childhood age, or even a teenager, the parent could be instructed on using privileges as a means of discipline. For instance, there is no law that states a parent must drive their rude, abusive and aggressive teenage child all over the countryside to visit their friends on weekends.

Who said the parent of this teenager should have to pay for their mobile phone bills? Why should such a teenager be given a mobile phone in the first place if they insist on being rude, disrespectful or aggressive? In Western societies children have many, many privileges that can be used to modify undesirable behaviour. It's a matter of learning how and when to use the privileges or rewards appropriately without being harsh and punitive.

At this point in time there appears to be two schools of thought in the professional world about using rewards to alter a child's behaviour. One school argues against using rewards as part of the discipline process as it is seen to be a type of bribery for good behaviour. Bribing a child may work in the short term, but induction fails to take place. Induction is like learning the lesson, or learning and understanding why and how the behaviour is wrong and why it should be changed. Those against the reward system argue that the child only alters their problematic behaviour in order to receive a constant and often immediate reward. Thus long-term changes to non-compliant, abusive and aggressive behaviour do not eventuate and, as such, rewarding a child for compliant behaviour achieves very little if anything at all.

However, the proponents of using rewards argue that when a child alters or attempts to alter non-compliant or aggressive behaviour, they should be rewarded. In this instance, rewarding a child for compliant behaviour is used to reinforce that positive, pro-social and desirable behaviour. Even if the child fails to completely alter a targeted behaviour, they would still receive a reward if they had made an earnest attempt to alter their problematic behaviour. Rewards could be given daily or weekly and would not be expensive gifts or monetary in nature. Both schools of thought present very compelling arguments for and against the use of rewards for behavioural modification.

As already mentioned, one of the specific goals of parent management training is to teach parents effective and non-punitive disciplinary strategies. One professional was somewhat straightforward in her description of poor parental disciplinary attempts when she stated, 'Inept disciplinary practices, if not addressed, will continue to negatively reinforce child aggression'. As parents progress through the program and begin developing some confidence in their new skills, the focus of PMT will change towards the child's most severe problematic behaviours with the goal of teaching parents behavioural management strategies. However, before parents can begin learning any new disciplinary strategies or techniques, they must first learn to identify, define and observe the problem behaviours of their child. This is quite important, as defining specific behaviours that will be targeted for change is crucial when the parent must enforce the appropriate consequences. Furthermore, if the parents are able to clearly identify problem behaviours, they are then able to evaluate whether or not those targeted problematic behaviours are changing. Finally, during the course of initially identifying the problem behaviours, many parents tend to use generic labels when describing problematic behaviours. For example, one parent reported, 'I'm really worried about his aggressive behaviour when he doesn't get his own way'. The term 'aggressive' is very generic and can mean different things to different people. For instance, aggression can mean yelling, screaming, swearing, being verbally abusive, pushing, shoving, biting, scratching, kicking, hitting, punching, slapping and so forth. One parent described a certain amount of distress at her son's 'attitudes'. But what exactly does attitude mean? Like aggression, it could have numerous behavioural expressions. By identifying specific behaviours, the parents are in a better position to clearly inform their child of exactly what behaviours are being targeted for change.

Once parents have clearly identified their child's most severe behaviours, they would then begin learning various disciplinary strategies and how to use appropriate consequences for when the 'rules' are broken. Parents would further learn how to enforce the rules across numerous environments, such as in the family home, at school, and when visiting friends or while at the shopping centre. Parents would also learn how to apply a consequence to a particular behaviour and for how long the consequence should be enforced without being harsh or punitive. This learning usually takes place during sessions where the clinician would use role-play, examples and further instructions to show the parents how the discipline program would operate effectively.

The child, adolescent or even young adult can attend the PMT sessions as they also learn appropriate pro-social skills, their rights and responsibilities at home and at school (or work) and in relationships. Children are also exposed to the clinician teaching their parents about effective ways to discipline them and modify their problematic behaviour. This also then begins teaching the child acceptable behaviours. Finally, there is an added bonus for the parent when they are being taught effective ways of disciplining their child. By the time a lot of parents seek help they are at their wits' end with their child and, as stated, this is the time when coercive, harsh and punitive parenting may develop. Parents are tired, stressed out, and constantly on edge and react to their child. When a discipline program has been developed and the parent is taught how to use it effectively, parents find they are able to remove themselves from the often emotionally charged situation because they don't have to keep trying to come up with some kind of punishment that might work and stop their child's problem behaviour. It's all done for them. The problem behaviours have been identified and an appropriate consequence has been decided on, and the parent has been shown how and when to apply the consequence. Finally, their child has also been informed of the targeted behaviours, the desired behaviours, and the subsequent consequences for 'breaking the rules'. This simply means the parent no longer has to argue with their child about their behaviour or the consequences anymore. The bottom line is that such a program has the potential to reduce an awful lot of stress and distress in the family home.

## WHAT DOES THE RESEARCH SAY?

So what does the research say about the overall effectiveness of parent management training programs? Well, it all depends on how you measure the results and how or what you are comparing the results to. As medication is considered to be the first-line intervention for ADHD, some researchers have made a direct comparison between the effects of PMT and medication. When this comparison is made, typically the results are clearly in favour of medication, simply because medication has an almost immediate effect on the child's behaviour. However, other research results have suggested that this is not really a correct way to measure the effects of PMT. This is because the long-term effectiveness of medication is questionable and medication alone is not normally responsible for repairing fractured and diminished parent–child relationships or sibling relationships, and it certainly does not teach parents effective and non-punitive parenting. However, when comparing how effective parent management training programs are against other alternative treatments, there are generally some pretty good results.

One investigator reported on the evidence for the effectiveness of parent management training for the past 35 years. According to this researcher, treatment effects, or the positive outcomes of PMT, can be seen in obvious changes to a child's behaviour over a number of different environments, including the home and at school. The changes are recorded in parent and teacher reports of decreased deviant behaviour, by directly observing the child at home and at school, and in school and police records. The positive effects of PMT have also been shown to reduce the child's problematic behaviour so much so that the behaviour is considered to be within the normal range of children without behavioural problems. The question is how long do the positive effects of such programs last? In most cases, the families reported that the positive effects were often maintained for a period of one to three years after treatment, while some parents reported the positive effects were maintained for between ten to fourteen years. How can there be such a big difference in how long the positive effects might last? Well, as with any intervention, it really does depend on how relevant the program is to the problem, whether or not the family is committed to the program in the first place and, after completing the program, whether or not the family continues to practise the skills and strategies they learned or whether the family allows the old patterns to slowly slip back in.

Another study tested a parent management training program and found that there were significant reductions in the child's undesirable behaviour. The child's schoolteachers were informed of the program and asked to note their observations of the child's behaviours for the period of the PMT. By the end of the PMT, the teachers had noticed a reduction in the child's behavioural problems at school and an improvement in the child's social skills. Family cohesion and closeness were also assessed and after the parents had completed the PMT, all the families in the program were reporting they felt much closer to their other family members. The researchers further pointed out that the schoolteachers reported that family cohesiveness was identified as an important predictor for a child's social competence. Furthermore, family cohesiveness was also a predictor of a decline in a child's problematic behaviour both at home and in the school environment. The researchers concluded that children were developing better social skills in the school environment as a result of the changes taking place in the parent–child relationship in the family home. Finally, the researchers suggested that with the increases in family cohesion and family closeness and the changes taking place in the parent–child relationship, members of the family felt a closer attachment to each other. The changes in the parent–child attachments were said to have made it easier for parents to monitor their child's out-of-the-home activities, while the children were more prepared to inform their parents of their whereabouts and what they were doing. Interestingly, family discussions about problems, concerns and worries were also found to have been a lot easier to conduct. These rather impressive results were taken one year after the parents had completed the PMT.

## LIMITATIONS OF PMT

Research has shown there are a number of factors associated with poorer outcomes of parent management training programs, including parental mental health concerns and parental characteristics and commitment. If a parent is struggling to manage their own mental health problems, undertaking another program, even just accessing another program, can be overwhelming or simply too much for that parent to manage. Unfortunately, where a parent has a mental illness they will be more likely to drop out of a PMT program, or they will only be able to make use of limited strategies and skills. On the other hand, some parents just don't give a damn and attending a PMT program is simply an inconvenience to them. Involuntary clients are also a very difficult population to work with. Simply put, involuntary clients are people who, as the term suggests, are not seeking professional help of their own accord. Instead, they may have received a court order or they may have been directed by the Department of Human Services to attend a parenting program. Involuntary clients tend not to be overly committed and may only half-heartedly apply the parenting skills and strategies offered in a PMT program. Also, there are some parents who just will not take advantage of the new skills they are being taught and will continue to use their own parenting practices regardless of how maladaptive they might be. For any number of reasons, some people are simply unable to commit to a twelve-week program and therefore may only complete a limited number of sessions. Unfortunately, these parents do not learn all the skills and strategies that are available to them and they remove themselves from the constant support and assistance the clinician is able to offer them. Other families complete the PMT and initially experience a lot of positive changes in the home. But as time goes on they begin to slowly slip back into all the old habits and before they know it the old frustrated, angry and stressed patterns have taken over again.

Some criticism has been levelled at those PMT programs that do not teach children self-management strategies, where the child learns to evaluate their own behaviour. It has been noted that where children have not learned self-management strategies they are also not learning self-control or ways to control their behaviour across a wide variety of situations, circumstances or settings. Other problems associated with PMT programs also include parents consistently failing to follow through on behavioural management strategies, such as discipline and consequences. To teach children self-control or to teach that same child there are consequences for their misbehaviour seems like commonsense really, but not for some people. For example, I was asked to help a family with a twelve-year-old boy (we'll call him John) who at the time was becoming ever increasingly aggressive and violent; in a fit of rage he would push his mother or threaten her with bodily harm. He verbally abused his father when he attempted to confront the boy about a packet of cigarettes that fell out of his school bag and if he didn't like a particular rule he would just simply run away from home or wait until his parents were in bed and climb out of his bedroom window and roam the streets all hours of the night. His schoolteachers also noticed his increasing aggression and were quite concerned as he was verbally abusive toward the teachers and his classmates and was known to threaten them with bodily harm. His classmates had had enough of his abuse and as a group they began threatening John that they were going to dish out some payback. In response to these threats, John solicited help from a couple of older boys, who turned up at the school threatening to bash his classmates. The school called the police and the older boys drove off in a hurry. The situation was becoming increasingly dangerous not only for John, but for the other school children as well. It all came to a head one night when John was cornered on his own in an alley by about twenty of his classmates. They were going to 'settle the score' right then and there, when John's father, who had been driving around for hours looking for him, found him and went to rescue his son. As John's father was desperately trying to talk peace into the situation, the two older boys drove up and told John to jump in their car and again they drove off. John's father immediately drove to the local police station to report what had happened. According to the parents, after this event they were assigned a social worker who was their case manager. At this stage, the parents had only attended one or two sessions of a PMT program with me when, in the face of everything that had happened, the social worker told them that it was wrong to try to discipline a child. As you might imagine, this information really upset the parents as they could see they needed help managing their son's behaviour and that he needed to learn self-control before he or anyone else was seriously injured. However, the mother told me they felt pressured to follow the instructions of the social worker, and they consequently withdrew from the PMT program. Several months later, the mother contacted me and said nothing had changed with her son's behaviour.

A final factor to consider is the features of the PMT program offered to parents. It is recommended that for a PMT program to be most successful it should not be 'a one-size-fits-all' type of program. The risk of one-size-fits-all programs is that they tend not to take into account the unique characteristics of the family unit and the child with ADHD.

While such programs may offer valuable advice, the recommendations may not suit the unique needs of a particular family. Unfortunately, the family may begin to feel as though the program is not working for them and dropping out becomes a very real option. Over the years I have met many families who felt disillusioned because they have 'tried every parenting program there is', apparently with little success. Unfortunately, many of these parenting programs may be offered by people or organisations that have minimal, if any, training or the program itself is simply not suited to the unique needs of the family. If you are considering looking for a parenting program, here are some questions you might want to ask the specialist or counsellor:

- Who developed the program?
- Is the program supported by mainstream professional literature and research?
- What behavioural disorders is it used for?
- In what conditions was it trialled?
- Who else or what other organisations use the program apart from yourself?

If you are unsuccessful in your search, call your country's national psychological society and seek their assistance.

## BEHAVIOURAL INTERVENTIONS

Behavioural interventions based on behavioural contingencies (learning new behaviours or alternative responses) are known to have a positive effect on ADHD-related symptoms, as well as some of the other impairments related to the disorder. As we already know, children with ADHD aren't terribly good at following rules, doing as they are told, and very rarely show self-control. Furthermore, they aren't very good at keeping themselves motivated to reach a goal, and they don't tend to cope very well in structured environments like the classroom. It is for all these reasons that behavioural interventions are considered to be the best intervention approach if they build the necessary skills and incorporate behavioural management strategies and aid the child in developing and maintaining self-motivation to reach goals.

Research supports the notion that behavioural interventions are effective in treating ADHD. It seems particularly true of those behavioural interventions that use both positive rewards for appropriate and desired behaviour and aversive consequences for noncompliance. I have heard many, many times parents tell me they have tried everything, including taking things off their kids and even bribery in an effort to promote desired behaviour. Well, let me tell you now it won't work, and most of you who have tried it already know it doesn't work. A behavioural management program would typically require the parents and the child's schoolteacher to consult with a behavioural expert, who can teach them how to measure behaviour, target undesired behaviour, and use rewards and punishments effectively, appropriately and consistently. While this is the best approach, there are many reasons why schoolteachers simply cannot meet with a professional or cannot adapt new classroom strategies for a single child. In such instances, I have first helped the parents identify the problematic target behaviours to be modified and introduced how to use rewards and punishments effectively and appropriately. Then once the parents are familiar with the program and are feeling confident about using the program, I simply request the teacher inform the parents that same day if the child engages in any of those behaviours. The parents then respond to the child with the appropriate reward or discipline. In addition, parents learn that this rule must follow the child across all environments, including when they might be at a friend's home or with their grandparents or even at the shopping centre. The reason for such an approach is to provide the child with a more structured and consistent environment in both the home and at school. Providing such a structure for children with ADHD does tend to have positive gains.

Behavioural interventions use the principles of operant conditioning where behaviours are changed by using different kinds of reinforcements. Desirable behaviour in children can be reinforced or strengthened by using a reward (referred to as a positive reinforcer) at the right time, or by escaping or avoiding something that is unpleasant (referred to as a negative reinforcer). Negative reinforcement is not to be confused with punishment as is often the case. The confusion really comes about because of the word *negative*. Punishment is usually designed to immediately stop a particular behaviour; for example, smacking a child each time they have a tantrum in the shops. The purpose of the smack is to stop the child's undesirable behaviour. Negative reinforcers can be a little confusing so a story might help to clear things up a bit. Quite a number of years ago I was working close to the city and at any given time during the day the traffic conditions were horrendous, or so I thought. But the first time I left the office on a Friday afternoon I soon realised what horrendous really meant. It took me about an hour to drive just 2 kilometres! I could not believe how bad the traffic was. After a few weeks of enduring this nightmare, I had had enough and decided to leave the office ten minutes early one Friday afternoon. To my utter amazement the traffic flow was 'normal' and I drove home in one hour instead of the usual one-and-a-half to two hours. So guess what I did every Friday afternoon — I left the office ten minutes early. This is an example of a negative reinforcement. My behaviour of leaving the office early was strengthened by avoiding a negative situation — congested traffic!

Behavioural interventions have been used with children with ADHD due to their success with other childhood behavioural disorders. Essentially, the thought was that because they had worked so well for other problems, there was no real reason why they shouldn't work for ADHD. This approach to treating ADHD was well before we really understood the neurology of the disorder. However, now with greater understanding of the disorder, behavioural therapies are, in fact, a choice intervention for ADHD. Because children with ADHD struggle to regulate their own behaviour, an intervention that helps prompt and guide the child's behaviour, that helps the child with goal-directed motivation through both positive and negative consequences, and with the immediate handing out of those consequences, should have a positive impact on the child's behaviour in certain situations. Such an approach is typically provided in behaviour therapies.

An intervention such as behavioural therapy would typically find a child involved in the program over an extended period of time ranging from months to years, and it would need to be used across virtually every setting to gain the most benefit from it. This is because it takes time for the child to learn and remember the techniques across so many different settings. If the child were to learn behavioural techniques for a single setting only, say for the classroom, then those techniques would not necessarily work at home. Also, just like medication, if for any reason the therapy is terminated too early, the behavioural 'symptoms' tend to return quite rapidly. Because of the time commitment required and the ongoing costs to gain the most benefit, one can begin to understand there could be a significant problem with parents and children dropping out because both can get sick and tired of doing therapy over extended periods.

While there are a number of successful yet different behavioural programs used in clinical settings and in schools, they tend to have a number of core factors in common:

- Parents and teachers praise appropriate or compliant behaviour while ignoring behaviour that is described as mildly negative.
- Parents and teachers provide very specific and simple instructions (KISS approach — Keep It Simple, Stupid)
- Firm routines and behavioural expectations are set for both the classroom and home.
- Very explicit rules are set about behaviour in the classroom and at home.
- Reprimands and consequences are set for inappropriate behaviour.
- The child is reminded of expected behaviour.
- Compliance and appropriate behaviour is rewarded.

The behavioural therapy might also include support for the child in a number of practical ways including:

- Organising homework or school assignments.
- Dealing with emotionally difficult issues.
- Teaching them to monitor their own behaviour.
- Giving self-praise or rewards for appropriate behaviour.

Behaviour therapy has demonstrated some very positive outcomes in improving symptoms in areas such as increasing the child's social skills, reducing aggressive responses and behaviour, and developing a more positive parent–child relationship. However, as we know, ADHD is a pretty robust disorder and behavioural therapy as a stand-alone treatment will not cure the child and it does not typically result in *normal* behaviour in children with ADHD compared to children of a similar age without ADHD. In addition, once the therapy has come to an end, so do the behavioural changes not long after. In other words, behavioural therapy does not tend to produce long-term changes in the behaviour of a child with ADHD.

## COGNITIVE BEHAVIOURAL THERAPY (CBT)

Cognitive behavioural therapy (CBT) is a well-established therapy that has been used by mental health professionals for quite some time. It has enjoyed enormous success over the years across many mental health disorders including anxiety, phobias, depression, trauma, bipolar disorder, bulimia nervosa, obsessive compulsive disorder (OCD) and many other mental health concerns. Many other forms of therapy used today also employ numerous elements of CBT.

Since the early 1970s, CBT has undergone considerable scientific evaluation and refinement and is referred to as an evidence-based therapy that has also been successfully applied to ADHD. An evidence-based psychotherapy means just that — there is ample independent scientific evidence to suggest the therapy is reliable and successful for use with a wide range of mental health disorders. Cognitive behavioural therapy is used for children, adolescents and adults with ADHD and often aims to help the individual develop a wide range of coping strategies to manage both the symptoms and problems associated with ADHD. Typically, this will involve psycho-education along with the person learning certain cognitive techniques such as cognitive reframing of the past, cognitive restructuring, cognitive reasoning strategies, skills development, rationalisation, development of internal and external compensatory strategies and behavioural techniques, and cognitive remediation strategies. In the case of ADHD, a central goal of CBT is to help the individual develop effective coping strategies to manage the symptoms and the associated problems by targeting the impulsive, disorganised and non-reflective manner in which children with ADHD approach both school and their social interactions.

## COGNITIVE REFRAMING

One of the common problems associated with ADHD is the often distorted and dysfunctional thinking patterns or cognitive distortions the individual develops about themselves and their world, and the subsequent influence this has on one's moods and behaviours. Cognitive distortions refer to persistent errors in reasoning or complete misinterpretation of situations. Simply stated, cognitive distortions are inaccurate and faulty forms of thinking that are so common in ADHD that they are virtually expected to be present. The cognitive component of CBT typically has a strong emphasis on how the individual views and interprets their world and the way they view themselves or think about their future. Cognitive behaviour therapy therefore tends to be based on approaches that help the individual to change negative and often destructive self-talk and beliefs.

Children with ADHD (and adults for that matter) often have very low self-esteem and this is often directly related to the very negative thinking patterns they develop about themselves. Often the individual will:

- Judge themselves negatively and without mercy.
- More often than not they will overgeneralise negative feedback and make an assumption, for example that they fail at everything.
- Dwell on their failures, particularly in areas of great importance.
- Continually blame themselves for mistakes.

Such erroneous thinking can then develop further negative thoughts and beliefs where the individual at their very core believe themselves to be stupid and useless and little more than a failure or totally worthless. Unfortunately, these kinds of established belief systems are all too common in individuals with ADHD. Think about this for a moment — you seem to be the only one in the class who doesn't really understand the school subject like everyone else; you can't concentrate like everyone else; even though you know how important it is, you can't seem to get your homework done; you always seem to lose everything that is important; you're the one who constantly gets into trouble with the teacher; you always get low scores on tests (and that's if you passed the test in the first place) and you have been held down a year; not too many people at school actually like you so you don't have many people to play with, nor do many kids turn up for your birthday party. There are constant arguments with your parents, and you always seem to be getting into trouble with them, and basically everyone you know seems to distance themselves from you. Now imagine for a moment that there is nothing you can do to change this situation, that you have no choice and you must endure this day after day, year after year. How do you think you might feel? How might you see yourself — as though there is something fundamentally wrong with you? Is it any wonder that children with ADHD develop depression or anxiety, and feelings of shame about themselves and core beliefs of being a failure?

Cognitive reframing and restructuring would take place after the therapist has learned about how the child views himself or herself and the kind of negative thoughts about the self that child with ADHD has. The therapist would spend time teaching the child to recognise and evaluate cognitive distortions and misattributions or thinking errors that serve to uphold and reinforce a very negative view of self. This will also include uncovering deep-seated beliefs the person holds about the self, other people and the world. The therapist would be looking at how these thoughts were established and what 'evidence' the child believes proves these negative thoughts. Then the therapist would go about challenging these negative thoughts in a very specific way that ultimately brings about a change in the person's core. While it might sound simple, it is not. Cognitive distortions are built up over time and reinforced to the child through their interactions with loved ones, authority figures and peers. Often the child will hold very strong irrational beliefs about themselves such as 'I'm dumb' and use evidence to 'prove' their belief such as, 'Well, I keep failing at school'.

Cognitive behavioural therapy goes far beyond addressing cognitive distortions however, and addresses a number of the comorbid conditions associated with ADHD. This knowledge comes from both research and clinical experience, as CBT is often the choice therapy for a range of anxiety disorders such as post-traumatic stress disorder, obsessive compulsive disorder and depression. We know that children with ADHD often experience low self-esteem, anxiety and depression whether it is a reaction to, a manifestation of, or a comorbid condition of ADHD. Obviously then, when CBT is used with children, adolescents and adults with ADHD, there is often a marked decrease in a number of the comorbid conditions. Furthermore, CBT programs are a very effective therapy for behavioural problems, and as ADHD is marked with problematic behaviours and is often comorbid with other behavioural disorders, it is a choice therapy. To address the issue of problematic behaviour associated with both ADHD and other childhood behavioural disorders, a number of different CBT-based programs have been developed over the years with varying degrees of success. A major goal of these programs is to teach the individual to recognise the symptoms of ADHD and learn how to manage them. One of the most well-known and often used programs is simply called, 'Stop, Think, Do'.

Stop, Think, Do programs have a number of common goals that teach children problem-solving skills (different to social problem-solving skills) and often make use of rewarding the child for pro-social behaviour. The problem-solving skills can be broken down into a number of steps including:

1. Learning how to define a problem.
2. Setting an appropriate goal.
3. Generating a number of potential answers to the problem.
4. Choosing what appears to be the best solution.
5. Considering other previously used strategies and determining if generalising that strategy would work in the current situation and after acting on the chosen solution.
6. Evaluating the success.

In the United States there are quite a lot of programs available for the individual with ADHD, ranging from individual therapy sessions with a clinician, to group sessions, to summer camps specifically tailored for this group. Most of these programs tend to take a multi-modal treatment approach. One such program is the Young-Bramham Programme that provides psycho-education and uses elements of motivational interviewing techniques (an interviewing technique that motivates the person to change their problematic behaviour), cognitive behavioural therapy, and cognitive remediation techniques (CRT is a cognitive rehabilitation therapy using treatments that target problems with attention, memory and the ability to organise one's actions and speech). The Young-Bramham Programme covers a number of the core issues with sessions on:

1. Coping with inattention and memory problems.
2. Coping with impulsivity.
3. Time management.
4. Problem-solving.
5. Social relationship skills.
6. Coping with feelings of anxiety.
7. Coping with feelings of anger and frustration.
8. Coping with feelings of depression, to name a few.

## WHAT DOES THE RESEARCH SAY?

Some researchers used a cognitive behavioural program for adolescents specifically targeting problem-solving skills, communication training and cognitive restructuring in an effort to reduce parent–child conflict and improve the parent–child relationship. Both parents and teens were trained in the five-step problem-solving approach. The five steps included:

1. Defining problems.
2. Brainstorming of possible solutions.
3. Negotiation.
4. Decision-making about a solution.
5. Implementation of the solution.

The communication training component involved helping the parents and the adolescents develop more successful communication strategies when discussing family conflicts including:

- Speaking in an even tone of voice.
- Paraphrasing the other person's concerns before raising their own.
- Offering approval to the other person when they communicated in a positive manner.
- Avoiding insults, put-downs and ultimatums.

The cognitive restructuring component involved helping parents and the teens identify, confront and restructure the irrational, extreme or rigid belief systems they held about their own conduct or the behaviour of others.

Overall the results of this study demonstrated a decrease in both ADHD and oppositional defiant disorder symptoms in the adolescents. However, as with all the other interventions noted in this book, there are limitations with CBT programs. For instance, one program might see a reduction in some behavioural symptoms but have no effect on the child's academic struggles. Equally, one program might evidence some positive changes in a particular school subject like maths, but not on behavioural problems. Also, where ADHD symptoms didn't quite reach the level for a formal diagnosis, children and adolescents might have a better chance of showing improvements in social skills and anger control.

## SOCIAL SKILLS TRAINING (SST)

We know that children with ADHD struggle with self-control that often leads to violating conventional social rules. Breaking these 'social rules' can be disastrous for the child, as they are often rejected by their peers. In fact, a child with ADHD struggling with poor social relationships is one of the biggest predictors of major problems in adulthood, including mental health problems, criminal activity and arrest, poor academic performance and dropping out of school. Possibly one of the most awful aspects of this disorder is the fact that the child doesn't even recognise how socially inept they are. To be successful in social interactions and peer relationships the child must learn to use the right social behaviours at the right moment in various social interactions and develop adequate skills to solve problems in those same social situations.

When it comes to an intervention, social skills training (SST) is considered to be quite an important form of therapy for the child and adolescent as it tends to specifically target peer relationships. Research and clinical practice have demonstrated that ADHD children who are provided the necessary skills to manage or even overcome their social deficits fare better in the long term compared to children who do not undertake SST. While there might be a number of different programs in use, SST generally involves teaching the child social skills, problem-solving abilities in social situations, appropriate or pro-social behaviour, and how to develop close friendships. Such treatments are especially attractive because while we know medication is very effective in helping the child with improved social functioning, the medication does not 'teach' a child appropriate social behaviour and it does not automatically normalise a child's behaviour to resemble that of their peers. It will also not reverse all the negative peer interactions the ADHD child has experienced nor help to develop friendships.

So the ultimate goal of SST is to promote:

- Cooperation in social situations.
- Learning and practising appropriate social behaviour.
- Rewarding the child's attempts at socially skilled behaviour so as to further encourage that behaviour.
- Communication.
- Participation.
- Validation.

Social skills training often involves the therapist not only teaching but also modelling appropriate behaviour to the child for a number of common situations or circumstances the child would be expected to encounter. For example, the therapist would teach the child and then model to the child the kind of behaviours and responses that are important in developing and maintaining friendships at school. So instead of jumping in, the child would learn to wait for their turn, or instead of just blurting out something in class, the child would learn how to appropriately ask the teacher a question. The therapist would teach the child how to handle teasing in the school ground and then the child would be given as many opportunities as required to practise these skills. The therapist might also make use of role-playing that would involve a number of hypothetical yet common situations to help cement the child's learning of these new skills.

One program worked with a group of children who were deemed to have behavioural problems, a lack of social and problem-solving skills, and who were lonely and didn't really understand a different perspective to their own. The group watched between ten to twelve video vignettes of children applying a variety of coping skills in numerous stressful situations. The children would discuss the vignettes and together they would practise a variety of appropriate responses and coping skills they could use in each of the situations. Apart from any other results, it was noted that for a number of the children the very fact that they discussed their feelings and appropriate responses about various situations in group discussions helped them develop strong bonds with other children in the group. For some of these children, this was the very first time they had developed a friendship. By the time the study was finished the researchers found significant improvements in the children's aggressive behaviour and their problem-solving abilities. These results were corroborated by the parents who noted these changes in the home, by teachers who reported the same changes in the classroom, and by an independent observer. There were a number of other encouraging results from this research including:

- A child's ADHD (remember there are three subtypes) nor the presence of hyperactivity 'had any bearing on children's ability to benefit from the treatment program'.
- Family stress (for example, low-income families, parental depression, or marriage problems) as a risk factor did not affect the child gaining positive outcomes from the program. The children were still experiencing the positive changes in their life a year after the program had finished, even in the face of family stress. This means that children learn and

benefit from SST even when there is significant family stress. This is encouraging for therapists who may feel defeated when parents will not get involved in their child's therapy.

- The researchers suggested that the ages of the children in their study (for example, four to eight years of age) may have been a significant factor in the results. Simply meaning that the social, familial, cognitive and academic problems may not have 'set in' and therefore the treatment program experienced much less resistance than might be otherwise expected with older children.

- Sadly though, negative parenting was a major risk factor for the child successfully completing the program. Children whose parents were critical of the child or used harsh punishments were far less likely to gain any improvement from the program.

One particular program combined social skills training and parent management training. The children completed eight weekly sessions that were each 90 minutes in duration. The psychologists running the program set the goal of improving the child's peer relationships and the parent–child relationship. In order to accomplish this, the psychologists taught the children four things:

1. Behavioural social skills where the clinician provided instructions and discussed certain skills with the child. The clinician modelled those skills or strategies to the child and utilised role-play and behaviour rehearsal. The clinician also used a lot of feedback and encouragement to help the child cement their understanding of the skills and learn how and when to employ them.

2. Social perception skills to correct misinterpretation of social cues. This involved teaching the child to monitor, distinguish and identify their own emotions and feelings, the emotions and feelings of others, and the rules of specific social situations.

3. Social problem-solving skills to develop a number of possible solutions to a problem, learning how to predict the likely

outcome of the solution and finally selecting a solution that would have the highest likelihood of success. Consequent learning determines whether or not the chosen response was successful or whether there could have been a better choice.

4.  Promoting generalisation, that is, learning how to apply problem-solving strategies from one situation to another. For example, children would apply the above approaches to solve a problem in a pro-social manner. If the response has been successful, they would learn how to apply that response in a flexible manner with a different problem, essentially building a repertoire of ways to handle problematic situations.

The designers of the program provide us with some insight into how the program operates and how they teach the children appropriate behaviour and responses across a number of different settings:

> *The group includes a highly structured, high density contingency management program. This reward system serves not only to increase the motivation of the children to participate but creates a more playful, 'game-like' atmosphere for them. Specific skills are selected each day from the current skills module being taught. The session always begins with a clear introduction of the 'skill of the week'. These skills are presented didactically and through modelling (using enthusiasm and humour!), they are then taught to students using prompting, shaping and rehearsal, during 'skills games' and role-plays. Children are actively involved in generating examples, participating in the role-plays, and evaluating, when, where and why to use the skill. To promote generalisation, counsellors prompt or suggest role-plays for three different situations: 1) with peers, 2) in the classroom, and 3) at home with siblings or parents ... Feedback both during training and activities includes attempts to help children self-monitor and self-evaluate their social behaviour (e.g., 'Did you show "accepting"' when you were called "out" in the game? Did you use your ignoring skill to deal with that problem?'). If a child has not grasped a key concept (as revealed through lack of participation*

*or inability to succeed at a task), the concept is reviewed verbally and practised.*

As you can see the skills that are taught to the children (for example, accepting consequences, ignoring being goaded or hassled, and problem-solving) are first discussed and then modelled. The children then practise the new idea and skill through role-play and once they begin to understand the new skill they role-play it again using that skill in a number of different settings (generalising the skill). Then they evaluate their own and each other's performance. At the same time as the children are completing the social skills program, the parents are also meeting as a group to begin the parent management training. The parents are instructed on the skills the children are learning and are taught how to reinforce those new skills in the home.

### WHAT DOES THE RESEARCH SAY?

The literature regarding social skills training (SST) as a stand-alone treatment for ADHD is not overly impressive and in some situations can be rather disheartening. For instance, one study of younger children aged between four to eight years of age with either oppositional defiant disorder (ODD), conduct disorder (CD) or ADHD reported encouraging results as the teachers rated positive gains in the child's behaviour. However, the parents didn't believe there were any notable gains in the child's behaviour at home. Another study found the opposite, where after completing an SST program the parents rated positive changes in the child's behaviour at home, but the teachers didn't notice any differences in the child's behaviour at school!

## SCHOOL INTERVENTIONS

Teachers are often the first to identify problem behaviour with children and are burdened with the task of having to inform parents there might be something wrong with their child. ADHD in the classroom taxes the teacher's energy and their teaching efforts, is disruptive to the teaching program, and unsettling to the other children who are trying to concentrate on their schoolwork. Some of the most successful school-based interventions are behaviourally based, or a type of behavioural modification program. These interventions are empirically sound, meaning that they have strong evidential support for treating children with ADHD. When introducing such interventions into a school, there are a number of steps that must be taken to ensure the program has the greatest chance of success:

1. Typically a clinician would provide psycho-education to both the parents and teachers about the program and ADHD and how to identify specific behaviours that need to be modified in the classroom before such a program could be introduced.

2. Regular meetings between the parents and the teacher would take place to decide on the behavioural modification strategies the teacher will use in class.

3. The clinician would instruct the teacher how to use specific behavioural techniques such as praising the child, when and how to ignore certain behaviour, using effective instructions with the child, and how to use time out.

4. If necessary, the clinician may also provide extensive instruction on contingency management programs.

5. Teachers would also learn how to use a behavioural report card to the benefit of the child and the teacher, to promote the best possible chance of modifying challenging behaviours. Typically, this would mean that specific behaviours that are targeted as requiring modification would be set as a goal for the child who is then rewarded when they realise each individual goal.

6. The behavioural goals must be set so that they pose a bit of a challenge for the child, but are not out of their reach. Setting these behavioural goals requires sensitivity on behalf of the parents and teachers.

7. As time progresses the behavioural goals are made more difficult until the child's behaviour is considered acceptable and appropriate.

There are a lot of potential benefits when using a behavioural report card in this fashion. For instance, parents are kept up to date about their child's behaviour during school hours, which would also allow the parents to support and reinforce the expected classroom behaviour. Perhaps most importantly, the card can be used by the parents and teachers as an encouragement or motivator, as it literally records the changes in the child's behaviour. Using praise in this way is a powerful motivator for the child. But equally powerful is the positive message the child receives about themselves.

There is ample evidence from the use of such programs that they are a very effective means of changing the challenging behaviour of children with ADHD. However, the success of such a program really depends on the cooperation of both the parents and the teacher, and regardless of how good a program might be it is doomed to fail if there is resistance or they are unable to implement it as intended.

The simple fact is that parents, teachers and other professionals in the school system must learn to work together if they are to provide the best learning environment not only for the child with ADHD, but for all children. The sad fact is that this doesn't always happen. Take for instance a mother who presented at my clinic with her ten-year-old son. According to the mother, the school had raised some concerns about her child after an incident that took place in the playground. Apparently some children cornered him, pulled down his pants and ridiculed him. My first question was, 'What did the school do about the other children's behaviour?' Unfortunately nothing. The boy wasn't coping too well at all, but I also had other concerns about the child. It turned out that the boy was a loner at school and really had no friends to play with; he was very immature for his age, was very anxious and had a history of poor academic achievement. I referred him to a trusted colleague of mine and also to a speech pathologist for an assessment. Soon enough my concerns were realised when the results confirmed the boy had autism spectrum disorder and an anxiety disorder. Once this was revealed my colleague wrote a report of the assessment results and sent one to the child's paediatrician, the child's doctor, to the boy's schoolteacher and one to myself. Within a week of receiving the report from my colleague, the school's education coordinator reported back to the mother refusing to believe the assessment results and claimed that my colleague, the paediatrician, the speech pathologist and myself were all wrong. She further informed the mother that the school would not be offering the child any educational support in the form of a teacher's aide and that they would not be applying for government financial assistance in order for the boy to have an education aide for the following year. Given the child was very immature for his age and that he was really beginning to struggle with his schoolwork, the mother requested that her son repeat the same grade level. This decision did not come lightly for the mother, but she knew it would be the best thing for her son, as it would give him an extra year to mature and develop further understanding of the schoolwork. The education coordinator refused the mother's request and told her that nothing could make them hold her son down another year, and that if she wanted her son to repeat a year she would have to withdraw him and place him in another school. The paediatrician and myself offered to meet with the principal and the education coordinator to discuss the assessment and available options; however, our offer was refused. It seemed all the opposition from the education coordinator had been leading to a single outcome — move your child to another school!

Other suggestions of how to help children with ADHD in the classroom have also been put forward:

- Teachers can implement multiple methods of teaching and use an approach that involves the child using a number of their senses. For example, the teacher could use visual aids as she provides verbal instructions to the children.
- Keep the classroom to a routine.
- The afternoon is usually the worst time for children with ADHD, so keep the complex subjects for the mornings.
- Utilise teaching techniques that require active responses from the children.
- Frequently provide encouragement and other feedback to the child.
- Keep instructions short and direct.
- Reduce the length of a challenging assignment or break it up into smaller segments to help the ADHD child maintain focus.

- If there is no reading disorder, permit the child to read aloud. This can really help the child to understand the material.
- Give the child a little more time to complete their homework or assignments.
- Restrict those elements that compete for the child's attention, such as allowing children to talk in class or background noise.
- Use bullet points and encourage the child to take notes in the same fashion.
- Continue to teach and reinforce organisational skills and strategies and make use of a study-skills program that will both teach and support these skills.
- Increase the potential of schoolwork completion by using reinforcement strategies.
- Provide the child with more supervision during those unstructured classroom activities.
- Take advantage of the child's peers doing some tutoring or teaching.
- Be aware that testing conditions are going to be very difficult for the child, so try to accommodate their needs here.
- While the teacher is discussing assignments and homework, instruct the children to organise the material they need in that moment.

In other words mix it up a bit, don't just do the same old same old. Even adults get bored with this. If the classroom environment was more interactive and took advantage of engaging the senses of children, this approach would most likely reduce the problematic classroom behaviour of the child with ADHD.

Others have either added to or created further classroom strategies that will potentially reduce the classroom problems associated with the core symptoms of inattention and impulsivity. Each of the effective approaches appears to have a number of common goals in mind that include enhancing the teacher–child relationship and providing the best environment that enables the child to learn. Take, for instance, the following:

- The classroom ought to be structured and predictable with

consistent rules and all work requirements clearly understood by the child.

- Have the child with ADHD seated close to the teacher.
- Prepare the child for changes or what might be coming up.
- Develop a schedule that includes regular breaks or physically active breaks.
- Again use the KISS approach to instructions — Keep It Simple, Stupid — and repeat the instructions a number of times as necessary.
- Recognise and accept the child will make a mistake. Take that opportunity to encourage the child and provide in-the-moment teaching and instruction.
- Teach the child how to set goals.
- Work with the child's parents, and instruct them how to follow on with these strategies in the home.

Dr Karen Waldron is an Emeritus Professor of Education and was formally the Director of Special Education for a well-known university in Texas, for 28 years. Today, she is a consultant to schools and families with at-risk children and children with special academic needs. Dr Waldron has also designed special education programs for children in Eastern and Western Europe, the Middle East, and Australia. Dr Waldron has put forward a list of potential behaviour management strategies for students with ADHD:

- Explain all necessary rules to the students before they begin their work and stand as close as possible to the child with ADHD.
- Use direct instruction — this is the KISS approach.
- Once the child has completed the class, provide immediate supervised practice and encourage the child to practise independently.
- Use facial expressions to redirect the child.
- Don't call to the child from across the room.
- Take advantage of a 'time-away' table for those days that are particularly bad. This will allow the child to get some work

done and avoid an escalation of problem behaviours.

- A reward system can be a very powerful motivator for children with ADHD (or any child for that matter!). Be warned, however: DON'T prolong that reward.
- Some schools use a behaviour contract where the child signs an agreement to alter certain problem behaviours. While this can be used with the child with ADHD, it is recommended that each goal is clearly within reach of the child. This will avoid reinforcing the child's sense of failure.
- If the school is to adopt such a program then graphing the child's successes so they have a visual aid of how well they are doing encourages the child and acts as a great motivator.

## SMALL CLASS SIZES

While it has been briefly mentioned, a common thread in the professional literature is that class size really does matter. It is important to note that smaller class sizes do tend to be significantly beneficial for children with ADHD. Some research has found that where there is an average class size of 25 to 35 students, this makes it that much harder for the teacher to really affect their students' progress. However, class sizes of eight to fifteen are known to be extremely beneficial for children with special needs. We also know that children with ADHD do a lot better at school with one-on-one instruction; it just makes sense to reduce the class size. In a London study, teachers were reported as believing that class size was a major obstacle to including ADHD students in regular education.

## REDUCING DISTRACTIONS

Noise is one of the greatest distracters for children in the classroom, especially when they are trying to sit a test or complete homework. Research clearly demonstrates that children perform quite poorly in noisy situations when compared to adults. This is because the ability to tune out competing sounds or the ability to listen in noisy environments has not yet fully developed in the child. So for parents out there whose child likes to listen to music while they do their homework, chances are that unless they are in their late teens or young adults, they are being distracted by the music. Classrooms are often noisy environments that present many distractions to children without ADHD, let alone children with ADHD. To help with reducing the competition of distracting noises, classroom interventions often encourage teachers to:

- Speak at a volume that all the students across the class can hear.
- Repeat instructions.
- Make sure the classroom is quiet during tests.
- Provide an area that is free of distraction, if necessary.

Teachers who have been in the game long enough know that simply repeating instructions is not going to increase the attention of a child with ADHD (I think most parents would also agree). This is the very reason why numerous methods of reducing noise and distractions ought to be employed in the classroom.

There is another approach that may very well be an ideal strategy in the classroom for improving the academic performance of children with ADHD. Management strategies such as choice making, peer tutoring, and computer-aided instruction have been demonstrated to encourage appropriate classroom behaviour and prevent undesirable and challenging behaviours. It seems this is primarily because the strategy makes learning more stimulating and provides the child with an opportunity to make their own choices related to schoolwork by allowing:

- Children to choose work from a selection of options that the teacher has developed as part of the curriculum requirements for that subject. Where this approach has been used, researchers have found it to be very effective in the classroom with children who have behavioural difficulties in that it increased their academic performance and decreased their difficult behaviour.
- Peer tutoring, where the child's peers are used in a positive way in the classroom. One of the biggest problems teachers face is class size and dividing up their time among 25 or more students. Peer tutoring can reduce the demands on a teacher

by providing one-on-one teaching and at the same time the child has an opportunity to practise their academic skills. As you might imagine, it may also improve the child's peer interactions and help develop some badly needed self-esteem. Peer tutoring has been found to increase a child's accuracy in their schoolwork, their attention when completing a task, and it has had positive changes on a child's behaviour and academic performance.

CASE STUDY

An adult male came to my clinic struggling with a course he had recently undertaken. He described how most of his life he had battled his way through school and really struggled with some subjects like maths. At that time he was undertaking a course that involved some advanced maths and again he found himself really struggling. The educational institution he was studying at did not offer tutoring for the subject so it was up to him to find someone who could help him. By the time he came to see me he felt he had run out of options and was considering quitting the course. However, the one thing he did not think of was developing a study group with others in the course, or paying someone from the same course who was a year ahead of him to tutor him. He decided on both. The last time I saw him he had organised a study group and had approached a student who was doing very well in the course and offered to pay them an hourly rate for tutoring. He was doing very well in his course.

## GET 'EM UP AND GET 'EM MOVING

Given that children with ADHD really battle with maintaining focus and attention, fidget incessantly and are forever getting out of their chair, introducing activities during their normal classroom breaks that are deliberately designed to increase physical exercise might reduce this overactivity. Research has found that if children with ADHD do not get a recess or lunch break, their inappropriate behaviour during class time is elevated. Some of you might say, 'Well, duh!', but think about the child who might have to stay in class during recess because he has a detention or must complete some work before being allowed to go outside and play. The teacher does not understand they are creating a time bomb that will go off during the next class. It has also been shown that where there is increased physical activity during break time, there is a noticeable reduction in disruptive behaviour in the classroom, particularly with hyperactive children. Here's a thought: I wonder if disruptive behaviour in the classroom would be as evident or as constant if teachers planned a number of 'mini breaks' throughout the day where all the children got up from their desks and stretched and moved around the classroom for five minutes?

Depending on where you live, your local school may already have a successful school intervention program in place for your child. In order to access this program you may simply need to have your child tested and then have a meeting with the teachers to discuss the results and what program they can offer. However, it might be that your child's teacher or school has no real expertise with children with ADHD and therefore may not offer a program for your child. If this is the case, you may need to discuss this issue with your mental health specialist and request they contact the school and offer to instruct the school on how best to support your child's academic needs. In my experience, schoolteachers are often very eager to work with specialists and are generally very grateful for any assistance and support they may receive.

## MULTI-MODAL TREATMENT

Because stimulant medication is considered to be the gold standard in the treatment of ADHD due to the almost immediate effect it has on the core symptoms, many believe that medication really is the *only* viable option for treating ADHD, particularly when compared to psychological interventions such as cognitive behavioural therapy (CBT), social skills training and school interventions. However, most of the alternative treatments noted above have experienced success — albeit limited. It is true that the research in general is seeking effective treatments for the core symptoms of ADHD and the literature reports on how successful that treatment might be in comparison to medication. But we cannot ignore the fact that medication alone often fails to address the issue of comorbidity just as we cannot ignore that children with ADHD suffer academically. It is doubtful that medication alone will significantly improve a child's study skills, organisational skills and time management abilities — all critical to success in school — to the same standard as children without ADHD. So while alternative treatments like CBT or SST may not be as successful in reducing the core symptoms of ADHD in the same fashion as medication, such treatments are known to help address the comorbid conditions and the other problems associated with ADHD. For instance, medication may reduce the core symptoms of hyperactivity and inattention in the child, which in turn may reduce the excessive movement of the child in the classroom, and it may help the child to stay focused a little longer. However, medication does not necessarily address the fact that the child might have a learning disorder, or depression, or an anxiety disorder. Also it seems there are mixed results in how successful medication might be at helping the child develop and maintain peer relationships. You might also remember that medication is not a cure and as soon as it is stopped or missed or wears off, the core symptoms quickly return. Keep in mind that ADHD is a neurological disorder so it is not necessarily a failure of the treatment as much as it is a result of the disorder, which is extremely resistant to current treatment. It is for this reason that I believe parents cannot afford to dismiss the evidence-based behavioural treatments presented in this book simply because they may not be as effective in reducing the core symptoms of ADHD.

ADHD is a complex disorder and therefore requires a multifaceted approach for maximum effectiveness. The greatest treatment effectiveness is most likely going to come from a combination of pharmacotherapy and behavioural interventions. Professionals will normally take a multi-modal treatment approach in an attempt to address all of the problems a child with ADHD will experience in each area of their life. A multi-modal treatment program typically includes the continued use of medication such as methylphenidate or atomoxetine, combined with family therapy or parent management training, school-based behavioural programs, organising academic support for the child, and quite often the professional will also put the child through a social skills training program. In the case where psychotherapy and medication is decided on as a combined treatment approach for an individual, it is referred to as psychopharmacology or a psychopharmacological treatment program. According to the Multimodal Treatment Study of Children with ADHD (1999):

> *... treatments are far from a magic bullet ... multi-modal therapy is, by definition, aimed at multiple targets designed to achieve multifaceted treatment effects, more like a shotgun than a magic bullet.*

So what does all this mean? Well, quite simply, we need only look again at the core features of ADHD to realise it has multifaceted problems or multiple impairments such as inattention, impulsivity and hyperactivity, not to mention the often associated problems with social relationships, with family members and peers, and general academic deficits, along with an array of comorbid conditions. Multi-modal programs are developed to specifically target problem behaviours in the home and in the classroom and school playground by teaching the child problem-solving skills and strategies, and by taking advantage of 'in-the-moment' teaching and instruction to reinforce the learning of applying those strategies when the child is faced with difficult situations. Then there are the family-based interventions or parent management training that will focus on the nature of the parent–child relationship, aid in developing a positive parent–child relationship and/or sibling to sibling relationship, and teach parents appropriate ways of controlling problematic behaviour and appropriate discipline methods rather than punishing the child in anger. And, of course, there will be extensive education on ADHD as even today there is still a lot of confusion about this disorder.

## WHAT DOES THE RESEARCH SAY?

Of all the available treatments used to treat ADHD there is one factor that has consistently and profoundly had a negative influence on any potential positive outcome — adherence to treatment and, specifically, parental adherence to treatment. Parents resisting the treatment and failing to continue with and complete the treatment:

- Experience more negative changes in their discipline.
- Influence the child's future anti-social behaviour.
- Often find their child being arrested.
- Often find their child is placed in out-of-home care.
- Encourage their child to drop out of treatment.

Research has demonstrated time and time again that medication alone is usually insufficient to address the issue of family relationships. However, it seems to be a very different story when medication is combined with behavioural interventions such as parent management training, social skills training and so on. One study had a 95 per cent success rate in reducing ADHD after they combined a child-training program with a parenting program. The changes in the child and the parent–child relationships were still evident one year after the study had concluded. However, very few differences were noted when only the parents or the child completed the program.

One of the largest ever studies conducted on the treatment of ADHD is the 1999 Multimodal Treatment Study of Children with ADHD (MTA). This study included children aged seven to ten years who were diagnosed with ADHD Combined Type. The study followed the children for fourteen months and produced some of the most extensive information about medication and alternative ADHD treatments to date. The MTA used four different types of therapy treatments:

1. A behavioural intervention that included the parents undergoing intensive treatment and training and education, training the teachers in classroom behavioural management, the child undergoing social skills training and computer-assisted instruction, and a summer treatment program.
2. The best possible medication management.
3. A combination of medication and behavioural intervention.
4. A group in community care that received no intervention.

The results of the four interventions were compared and revealed that children in all four groups experienced some reductions in the core ADHD symptoms. The children in the combined group and those receiving medication management had the same positive results and were far better off than the children in the community care group. The behavioural management therapies alone were less effective at reducing ADHD symptoms when compared to medications. However, when it came to anxiety symptoms, academic performance, parent–child relations and social skills, the combination of a medication and behavioural treatment was far more effective that just medication alone or behavioural treatment alone. Of particular interest was the discovery that when children's medication was carefully monitored and they were receiving the combined intervention, they ended up reducing their medication doses compared to the children just taking medication. The combined treatment group continued to show improvements ten months after the study had finished but only on the ADHD and ODD symptoms. Even though this was one of the most comprehensive studies to date, it still did not address all the problems associated with ADHD. For instance, at the end of the study, the children with ADHD were rated by their peers on several assessments. Unfortunately, the children in the study did not manage to develop *normal* friendships but instead still struggled with significant social impairments.

Other research has found that when medication was managed properly in combination with the child undergoing intensive behaviour therapy (this could include SST, CBT and even school interventions), there were significant decreases in the symptoms of comorbid conditions, there was academic improvement, healthier parent–child relationships and improved social skills, compared to just medication alone or behavioural therapy alone. Also, when families are involved in the combined treatment of properly managed medication and intensive behaviour therapy, parents reduced the use of ineffective and negative discipline at home and the children improved in their social skills at school.

As you can see there are a number of therapies that are quite effective for the various comorbid conditions of ADHD and some of the behavioural concerns such as poor social skills and poor academic performance. Unfortunately, you may find yourself in a position where some of these therapies are not offered and consequently this may require a greater responsibility on you to act as an advocate for your child. For instance, you may find your child's school does not have an effective program in place for children with ADHD or does not offer academic assistance. You may need to call a meeting with the teachers and principal and present to them the school-based therapies as discussed in this chapter. Depending on where you live, you might also gain great benefit from starting a support group for parents (and children) of children with ADHD. Such groups are not designed to offer therapy, but to support one another. In such a supportive group you are exposed to a wide range of parenting approaches and can learn such things as more effective parenting skills, discipline skills, or how to support your child academically and promote socially acceptable behaviour. Remember, you are not the only parent of a child with ADHD, and other parents may have worked out specific skills that are quite effective and that have worked for them across a range of different situations. Several years ago I was asked to attend one such meeting to discuss various parenting strategies and skills that parents could use to modify their child's problematic behaviour. You can contact professionals and invite them to join in on one of your meetings to discuss pretty much anything you, as a group, would like support with.

Of all the things you learned in this chapter, there are a few points to remember that will serve you well. No matter what therapy you believe is most suitable for you or your child there are a number of factors to consider:

1. The therapy must be suitable for use in every one of the child's environments (for example, home, school, grandparents' house, shopping centre).
2. Using the therapeutic skills or strategies in one environment only will not see a reduction of the symptoms in other environments.
3. You cannot stop using the therapy after a couple of weeks or even months, as the problematic behaviours will likely reappear very quickly.

4. Accept that ADHD is a disorder that will require long-term support. Just as if the child had a physical disability, children with ADHD will require ongoing professional support.

# CHAPTER 9

# ADHD sufferers tell their story

Have you ever been in a situation where you were bullied, ridiculed or put down; where people became angry with you because you made a silly mistake? Just suppose for a moment your boss asks you to prepare a report on the projected annual growth of the business for the next five years. Knowing this task is going to be difficult, you go away and give it everything you've got. The day comes when you have finally finished the report and with a mixed sense of pride and anxiety you approach your boss's office door. You knock first then carefully enter and as you walk across the room to hand him your report, your stomach is in knots. The boss looks up at you from his desk and with an excitement rarely seen he jumps to his feet and takes the report from you. As he begins to read it you can't help but notice his beaming smile slowly fading away. He looks back at you and with an angry face and stern voice demands of you, 'What the hell is this?' Stunned, you struggle to find an answer as your mind has gone blank. Your boss impatiently slams the report down on his desk and demands an answer. How would you feel in this situation?

Not so long ago I had a young wife sitting in my office crying as she thought her husband didn't love her anymore. In the beginning things were as you might imagine — they were in love, they did everything together and they went everywhere together. Life was sweet. One evening he surprised her with a special romantic dinner in a restaurant overlooking the bay. She described it as absolutely beautiful. It was a warm evening with a gentle sea breeze and they were seated where she could watch the sun set over the water. She could hear the water gently lapping at the edge of the sand and loved the way the yellow streetlights reflected off the water. After a wonderful night out, he drove her home and, taking her by the arm, escorted her to the front door. At the front porch he bent down on one knee and taking her by the hand he gazed up at her and said:

*Before I met you my life felt meaningless. I felt so lost and there were times when I thought the loneliness inside would consume me. Many times I questioned the purpose of my existence and wondered if I would ever meet someone I could really love. My life with you has been nothing but a blessing. I love your gentleness, your kindness and how you give people the benefit of the doubt. I love you.*

As the young wife recalled this night and how much it had touched her heart she sobbed and sobbed. The gentle man who had knelt before her that night and asked for her hand in marriage had changed. Today he was critical of everything she did, the clothes she wore, and everything she attempted. He criticised her cooking, the food she bought, the way she ironed *his* shirts. He even got angry at her one night because his dinner wasn't ready when he arrived home from work. He expected her to greet him at the front door each evening after work in her lingerie and he belittled her intelligence when she wanted to undertake a course of study to better her employment opportunities. This young wife began to question herself: what was wrong with her that her husband would treat her this way? In time she began to believe she was a failure because nothing she did was ever good enough, and she was beginning to undermine her own efforts. How would you feel if you were at the receiving end of all this criticism?

You might be asking yourself what these two examples have got to do with ADHD? Well everything, really. You see, when we are faced with difficult circumstances we seek out support from our friends and family. We sit down and complain about how unfair our boss has been and how hard we've worked only to be mistreated in this way. Equally, when we hear our friends say their life is falling apart, we feel sorry for them, we offer them our support, and we reassure them that everything is going to be okay. But what if something like this really did happen to you and everyone around you seemed to be angry and impatient with you all the time? What if your spouse teased you or belittled you when you told her what the boss had said? What if you had very few friends to turn to and if those relationships were strained at the best of times? What if everyone who had meaning in your life kept on sending you negative messages — like you're difficult to live with, that everything you do is sub-standard, that you're clumsy, lazy, stupid, rebellious and a failure? How would you feel? You know, it seems everywhere we look we see something negative about ADHD, from its presentation across different environments, to the problems schoolteachers face, to the problems parents face, to the negative media attention on medication and everything in between. But one thing we never seem to hear anything about is what it is like to live with ADHD. It seems as if all the focus is about whether or not the disorder is real and how best to treat it. In fact, when looking for information in the professional literature about this very issue, I was incredibly disappointed to find very few people had ever asked the child or adult, 'What is it like for you to have ADHD?'

---

Throughout their childhood and adolescence, participants acknowledged that they had a sense of feeling different from others, including their peers and family: the feeling of being different developed from being repeatedly told by others, including family members, friends, and teachers, that they were 'problem children' and that there was something wrong with them. More specifically, they were told that they were stupid, lazy, and disruptive ... The feeling of being different from others also developed from being compared unfavourably with their peers, often by family members and teachers. (Young, et al., 2008.)

Fortunately, there have been a few professionals who have stopped and asked the question. Virtually every study used in this book is a *quantitative* research design. Essentially this means that sophisticated data analysis is used to determine whether the results of their research are statistically significant. While this research is important, its very nature and design fails to take into account the individual's own perspectives, that is their thoughts and feelings about the disorder. *Qualitative* research, however, generally presents open-ended questions to the individual and allows them to provide rich information about a disorder because they can tell their own story in their own words. In this instance, qualitative research on ADHD can help us understand what it is like for an individual to live with ADHD, the meaning an individual may attach to the disorder, or what it felt like when they were diagnosed with the disorder or the experience of undertaking various treatments.

One qualitative study surveyed children with ADHD between the ages of nine and fourteen years. The authors stated their reason for conducting the study was because of the importance of understanding what it was like for young people to receive a diagnosis of ADHD. The results of the study revealed some troubling answers. The group as a whole felt there was a stigma attached to the diagnosis of ADHD even more than having to take the medication. However, when they had to take their medication, particularly at school, they felt exposed or vulnerable and different from other children in a negative way. They were called names like 'druggie' and 'tablet boy' and were bullied about their ADHD behaviours or diagnosis and their need for medication. The children recognised that the name calling and bullying had a negative impact on their sense of self that often resulted in feelings of low self-esteem. Generally speaking, these kids believed there was a lack of empathy and understanding from their peers for people with ADHD. They believed that the negative assumptions others had of them were very difficult to manage and that they received negative differential treatment because they had ADHD. All of the children in this study believed that being diagnosed with ADHD automatically gave them a bad reputation with other children, their teachers, and the parents of their peers. Sadly, the children believed there was a general agreement that people with ADHD were stupid and they often got into fights as a result of the bullying.

A second qualitative study was retrospective in nature asking adults about their experiences as children with ADHD. The research revealed some rather disturbing yet common factors: the adults had grown up with a sense of feeling different from others; there was an emotional impact on the adults after receiving an ADHD diagnosis; and a realisation that they would have to deal with the stigma of ADHD in the future. Let's take a closer look at these three points.

## Feeling different to others

The adults in the study revealed that all through their childhood and adolescent years they had a general feeling of being different from others. This included feeling different to their family members and peers. It turns out these feelings were directly related to constantly being told by their family and friends that they were problem children and that there was something wrong with them. Specifically, these adults clearly remembered being regularly called stupid, lazy and disruptive and that their behaviour was nothing more than naughtiness and attention-seeking. The feeling of being different for these adults was further compounded by the fact that family members and their schoolteachers would often make harsh comparisons between them and their siblings or their peers.

It seems that for the adults there were only two options for dealing with the criticisms from their parents, friends and teachers: they either accepted that what was said about them was absolute truth or they tried to ignore it. For those adults who believed the negative criticisms, some of them also believed they were less able than others, and they reported feeling confused and frustrated because they could not understand what was causing them such difficulties. One adult said, 'I didn't know what it was. I found it very distressing. I knew I couldn't do the things that normal people could do. I had the ability to do it but I just couldn't do it. I found it very frustrating'. While a second adult gives us a little more insight into the internal turmoil they must have been feeling, 'I got so angry with myself because I used to go to bed at night and think, "Tomorrow I'm going to be really good" but I actually didn't know what I was doing wrong'. This frustration, hurt and confusion often led to the adults struggling with both low self-esteem and low expectations of themselves and ultimately they had little faith in what they might achieve throughout their life. This almost sounds like a sense of hopelessness about oneself and about one's future — how devastating for the individual!

## The emotional impact of the diagnosis

As adults receiving a diagnosis of ADHD, they reported feeling a huge sense of relief and excitement that finally someone was listening to them and that they really knew what was 'wrong' with them. One person described a sense of joy at finally knowing what was going on, 'In one part of me, I felt elated. It was almost like, "Oh there's an actual reason why I acted like that".'

Unfortunately, up until the moment of diagnosis, a lot of the adults actually blamed themselves for the difficulties they had experienced during their childhood. Understanding that there was a reason for their difficulties provided a great sense of relief for these individuals that there wasn't something terribly wrong with them, that there was a reason for their difficulties. Perhaps an extremely important point of this research was that when the adults were finally diagnosed with ADHD, there was quite a bit of anger that a diagnosis had not come earlier in life. The adults were left to wonder what their life might have been like if they had received professional help at a younger age. For some of the adults there was also quite a bit of sadness as they felt as if they had wasted so many years believing they were 'destined to fail'. This is quite a burden to carry.

## Dealing with the stigma attached to ADHD

Once the adult had received a diagnosis of ADHD they began to take medication with some noticeable changes in their symptoms and attitudes about their future. However, of some concern for the adults was their awareness of the stigma attached to an ADHD diagnosis and that as a result of the diagnosis others might view them differently. I guess with a lifetime of exactly those experiences behind them this concern is completely understandable. But they were also very much aware of the changes due to medication. One of the prominent outcomes was that they didn't feel different from others, and because they were able to function as 'normal' people do, they were beginning to feel normal. They were able to hold conversations with others without interrupting them all the time. They were aware the medication had improved motivation, they were able to structure their life, make priorities, they felt their creative skills had been set free, and instead of believing they were underachievers with little hope for the future, they had a more positive attitude and outlook on life and many believed for the first time that they could actually reach their potential in life.

Other studies have also found that children and adolescents with ADHD:

- More often than not have low self-esteem.
- Really struggle with a general sense of hopelessness and underachievement.
- Have a general belief of being a failure primarily because they experienced many failures throughout their childhood and adolescence.
- Believe people do not understand them or the disorder.
- Often feel uncertain.
- Have a general sense of dissatisfaction because their problems remained unidentified, their symptoms misdiagnosed or because the symptoms remained undiagnosed and untreated.
- Some children felt teachers were unjustly focusing on their behaviour, assuming they would be more of a problem than other children.
- Some children felt their teachers were constantly watching their behaviour as though this were a sign the child had forgotten to take their medication.

It is important to understand what I consider to be a universal law when it comes to child-rearing practices, which is simply what you do today will matter tomorrow. Young children are helpless in the face of parental, sibling, other family and teacher criticism. This can have such a negative influence on their self-identity and self-esteem and in my own practice I have witnessed first-hand adults recalling painful memories about things their parents said to them as children. Perhaps one of the saddest moments I have witnessed in the clinic is witnessing a 75-year-old woman crying with a broken heart about how, as a young child, her mother had told her she was sorry for the day she had given birth to her, that she did not love her, and that it would be almost impossible for anyone to love her because she was a failure and worthless. Those words spoken by her mother had been with this lady her entire life.

# CHAPTER 10

# Is adult ADHD real?

The idea of adult ADHD is an interesting yet very controversial topic. Many people simply do not believe that adults can have ADHD and vigorously argue their point. And for a long time the professional world struggled to come to grips with a disorder that was thought to be exclusively limited to childhood and adolescence. In fact, the overwhelming view in the past was that children with ADHD would simply 'outgrow' the disorder by the time they reached puberty and adolescence. I remember having a discussion with a doctor not so long ago who proved to be extremely cynical when I suggested that one of his adult patients had ADHD. However, the evidence for adult ADHD has been clear for a long time. Remember George Still in Chapter 2 about the history of ADHD? Some specialists believe that George Still was the first to mention that ADHD might persist into adulthood. In recent years there has been an increasing body of research that portrays a very clear picture of the natural history of ADHD. We have reached a point where, just like childhood ADHD, adult ADHD is incontrovertible as the scientific literature continues to demonstrate adult ADHD is a real disorder.

Let's have a quick look at some of this research. In 1979, a very large longitudinal study followed 75 hyperactive children who were first evaluated from six years of age right through to 22 years of age. According to the researchers none of the children was treated with methylphenidate for the duration of the study. The results of this extensive study indicated that the participants struggled academically, had more car accidents, and moved house more often than people without ADHD.

Encouragingly, only a small percentage were still engaged in antisocial behaviour or evidenced severe psychopathology (mental illness) in adulthood. The final results indicated that the hyperactive children as adults were still demonstrating some symptoms from the diagnosis of 'hyperkinetic child syndrome' including 'impulsive personality traits' (remember ADHD has been known under different names). The same researchers were at it again in 1985, this time following 63 children with 'hyperactive child syndrome' for fifteen years. The results of this study indicated that about half of the participants still experienced mild to severely disabling symptoms of ADHD. About 23 per cent of the adults in the study struggled with antisocial behaviour, and tended to struggle in life more than people of the same age without ADHD.

However, the critics of adult ADHD do raise some interesting points. For instance, the section below discusses the prevalence rates among adults with ADHD, and as you will read for yourself, it could be argued that the prevalence rate is fairly low in adulthood. Further questions have also been raised such as, 'Why doesn't ADHD persist into adulthood in all cases?'. These are reasonable questions that deserve an answer. There are a number of possible explanations for this:

- Knowing how complex and involved assessing for ADHD is, you would be aware that an inexperienced or ill-trained individual could provide an incorrect diagnosis. This issue has already been extensively dealt with in Chapter 5.
- There may be a lack of age-appropriate criteria.
- As you will read, some of the symptoms remit as the individual grows older.
- We know that appropriate interventions during childhood can improve the condition by teaching coping skills.

## Prevalence rates

By now you would clearly understand the difficulties associated with providing exact figures on the prevalence rates for ADHD. Remember the issue of determining prevalence rates for childhood ADHD between countries using different diagnostic tools, different diagnostic parameters and, of course, the disorder being known under different names? However, the professional literature tends to agree that the prevalence rate of adult ADHD in the general population is around 4 per cent with up to 60 per cent of children diagnosed with ADHD still exhibiting symptoms in adulthood. Other studies have found that up to 85 per cent of children given a clinical diagnosis of ADHD will have the disorder in adolescence and up to 65 per cent will have ADHD in adulthood.

One author reported on the long-term outcomes of childhood ADHD studied in Montreal, New York and London. This most wide-ranging study did a follow-up of boys between the ages of six and twelve and found that 25 per cent of them still had symptoms when they were between the ages of sixteen and 23. By the time they reached 23 to 30 years of age, 8 per cent of the boys still struggled with ADHD symptoms. The Montreal study found that two-thirds of the participants claimed to be struggling with one or more of the core symptoms of ADHD when they were 25 years old and that around 34 per cent of the adults had moderate to severe hyperactive, impulsive and inattentive symptoms. Sadly adults with ADHD experience more than just the core symptoms of ADHD and, just like children, they often have to struggle with comorbid conditions.

## Comorbid conditions

A very disturbing fact is that research has found up to 87 per cent of adults with ADHD had at least one co-existing disorder and up to 56 per cent had two or more co-existing disorders, with many of these sharing similar features to ADHD. Comorbid conditions can include conduct disorder (CD), depression, anxiety disorders such as obsessive compulsive disorder (OCD), frustration, anger, sleep disturbance, substance abuse, bipolar disorder, personality disorders such as borderline personality disorder (BPD) and antisocial personality disorder (ASPD). In addition, an excessively high number of adults are involved with the criminal justice system. It has been estimated that adults with ADHD will have at least one lifetime comorbidity and these conditions need to be clearly understood and addressed as many adults often don't realise they may have depression, anxiety or any of the potential comorbid conditions. They know something is wrong, but they just can't put their finger on it and this can cause a lot of concern, fear and worry. Let's take a look at the more common adult comorbid conditions.

## DEPRESSION

Extremely severe depression is a disorder that I deal with almost every day in my clinic. Depression is a terrible illness that doesn't just affect the individual but also the loved ones in the individual's life; if left untreated it can have devastating consequences for all family members. Of all the horrible symptoms of depression it seems lethargy and lack of motivation are particularly debilitating for the individual. Someone with severe depression can sleep for hours and hours but still wake up feeling exhausted, almost as though they have had very little sleep. One patient was only 23 years of age and had been battling depression for about five years when he came to see me. The man told me that he needed on average about twelve hours of sleep every night just so he could get through each day. He would come home from work and sleep for about two hours, get up to have his evening meal, shower, watch television for a little while, and be back in bed again so he could get his twelve hours of sleep before facing another day. People often ask me about the ever-constant lethargy and exhaustion they battle with and the only way I can explain it in a way that makes sense is like this.

Depression is a bit like a leech. A leech can sneak up on you and attach itself to your body and who knows how long it has been sucking your blood before you realise something doesn't feel right. Depression can feel as if the life force is being sucked out of you, leaving you feeling exhausted all the time, that it's just too hard to concentrate, too hard to even try to make yourself do anything around the house, and so all the important stuff that needs your attention is ignored because the simplest things seem like the biggest to tackle. Then there are the horrible negative thinking patterns that constantly undermine you, telling you how you screw up everything, you never do anything right, and that basically you're a failure, you're not good enough, or you're just a worthless waste of space. This combination of feelings and beliefs often leads to an overwhelming sense of helplessness and hopelessness, and in my experience, when a severely depressed person is feeling that way, they are often struggling with suicidal ideation and if not caught soon enough this can lead to attempted or completed suicide.

Think about how profound the negative effects of depression can be on someone who already struggles with low self-esteem, who knows they don't perform as well as everyone else because their teachers, parents, siblings, friends and employers have constantly reminded them of all their failures and shortcomings. They have had an endless struggle with school, with keeping a job, they can't seem to concentrate or organise themselves like everyone else, and they can't seem to make their relationships or marriage work.

## ANXIETY DISORDERS

Unfortunately, anxiety is another one of those co-existing disorders with rates ranging from 25 to 40 per cent of adults with ADHD having a co-existing anxiety disorder. The more common co-existing anxiety disorders are obsessive compulsive disorder (OCD), social phobia, generalised anxiety disorder (GAD) and panic disorder. The high rates of comorbidity may be due in part to the ever-increasing demands on the individual in maintaining their responsibilities and the constant threat of negative outcomes in the family and the workplace. Don't forget, these individuals have now lived most of their lives with people all around them demanding they perform to a particular level or that they strive to be more committed in their work. How many parents have heard, 'He would do a lot better if he just put in more effort'? Also, genetic factors cannot be ruled out as we know anxiety is also hereditary.

Possibly one of the major problems faced by the adult with ADHD with co-existing anxiety is the negative impact that anxiety has on the person. Anxiety can intensify low self-esteem, intolerance to stressful situations or circumstances, and it can interfere with our working memory. There is a fairly significant concern for clinicians when an adult presents to a clinic and the diagnosis is looking like ADHD with anxiety. The issue here is that both disorders have a major impact on the individual's concentration. An understanding of the overlap between the two disorders can have major implications on the choice of treatment. For instance, if the anxiety is secondary to the inattention, the anxiety is likely to decrease with medication. However, a primary anxiety disorder with secondary inattention may actually see an increase in the anxiety symptoms if stimulant medication is used as the choice treatment.

## SUBSTANCE ABUSE

As noted earlier there is not only a major concern about the relationship between substance abuse and ADHD but also the high prevalence rate with which it occurs. In fact, the comorbidity of adult ADHD and substance abuse is almost expected by the clinician when the adult presents to a clinic. One study found that adults with ADHD were more likely to use cannabis and ecstasy while another study revealed just over 23 per cent of the adult participants with alcohol dependence also met the criteria for ADHD in childhood and 33 per cent of these participants still had ADHD as adults. This study further revealed that just over 76 per cent of the ADHD participants also had an 'average to high' use of nicotine. Further research has also found that alcohol abuse or dependence has a lifetime prevalence rate of 21 to 53 per cent while 8 to 32 per cent of adults with ADHD with a substance abuse disorder may use and abuse 'other' substances.

Why are there such high rates of substance abuse among adults with ADHD? One possible explanation that is often reported by the adult is that drugs, alcohol and nicotine are often used as a form of self-medication in an effort to treat their own symptoms of ADHD. Substance use can also develop as some drugs have a calming effect on some of the symptoms of ADHD in much the same way as methylphenidate reduces the core symptoms of ADHD. More disturbing, however, is that adults with ADHD have been found to slip into dependence much faster than adults without ADHD, and substance dependence is much harder to treat in adults with ADHD.

It seems researchers are increasingly finding that treating ADHD in childhood and adolescence can reduce the risk of adult substance use and abuse. For example, a recent study found that treating children with ADHD with stimulant medication such as methylphenidate significantly protected them against later substance use and smoking cigarettes. This type of research might also indicate that treating adults with ADHD with stimulant medication with substance abuse disorders might, in fact, help to control the substance use disorder as well as the ADHD.

Recently a 34-year-old male came in to see me because he was suffering from depression. It wasn't very long before I realised the man may have had ADHD and when I asked him he said, 'Oh yes. I was diagnosed as a child'. He continued to tell me that as a child he had been taking methylphenidate and that he and his parents didn't like the side effects so he simply stopped taking the medication. Since leaving school the man had been in and out of work, and he had been involved in numerous relationships, was totally disorganised and had been suffering from depression and anxiety as far back as he could remember. I asked him if he had been taking drugs to which he replied, 'Yeah. I smoke mainly cannabis because I feel calm and it helps me to get to sleep at night because I just can't sleep'. I asked him if he only smoked cannabis. 'No' he replied, 'I take ecstasy pills and I do ice and crack (extremely dangerous and highly addictive drugs) and I was drinking about six beers a night but I've slowed down on that'.

## BIPOLAR DISORDER

Bipolar disorder is another type of mood disorder which is described as a condition that is episodic in nature. The term 'bipolar' literally means 'two phases' as bipolar disorder is characterised by a swing between manic episodes and major depressive episodes. The manic phase is fairly obvious as the person tends to talk excessively, they appear to be easily distracted, they are constantly on the go, they are restless, and they appear to lose their normal social inhibitions. If this sounds a little like ADHD it's because these symptoms are very similar. People with bipolar disorder may not feel a need for sleep, they can exhibit psychotic symptoms, experience hallucinations, and possess an overinflated self-esteem.

Bipolar has been likened to a roller-coaster ride travelling from the peaks of elation to the depths of despair and possess is recognised by several key behaviours. For instance, during a full manic episode the individual may make silly and impulsive decisions like going on a spending spree and blowing all their money on the latest and greatest electronic gadgets. They will often deny they have a problem because they are so caught up in their excitement that their behaviour is perfectly rational to them. In a full manic episode, sometimes the person may even sound a little delusional. A couple of psychologists give us a fantastic example of what this might look like:

> *Whoo, whoo, whoo—on top of the world! ... It's going to be one great day! ... I'm incognito for the Lord God Almighty. I'm working for him. I have been for years. I'm a spy ... I can bring up the wind, I can bring the rain, I can bring the sunshine, I can do lots of things ... I love the outdoors. (Barlow & Durand, 2002)*

The depressive phase is defined by an extremely depressed mood for at least two weeks with severe disturbances in thoughts, such as feelings of worthlessness, disturbed sleep patterns, significant changes in appetite, an obvious lack of energy so that even a menial task requires a great amount of effort, and a loss of interest in once pleasurable activities and hobbies. The prevalence rate of ADHD and bipolar is estimated to range from 9 to 35 per cent.

## PERSONALITY DISORDERS

As we know, ADHD is highly hereditable and for those children whose parents might also have ADHD, other behavioural disorders are also likely to occur. Just as in children, oppositional defiant disorder (ODD) and conduct disorder (CD) are common comorbid conditions in adults. In fact, comorbidity rates between ADHD and ODD range from 29 to 53 per cent while the comorbidity rates between ADHD and CD range from 20 to 53 per cent. Antisocial personality disorder (ASPD) is also common in adults with ADHD, particularly when as children they were diagnosed with conduct disorder. This is because it appears that conduct disorder is a precursor to ASPD. One researcher has suggested that anywhere between 7 to 44 per cent of adults with ADHD referred to a specialist clinic are at risk of having ASPD.

In order to receive a diagnosis of ASPD it must be very clear that the individual had a persistent pattern of totally disregarding the rights of others and a continued pattern of violating those rights prior to the age of fifteen years. Remember, when we are talking about a diagnosable disorder, the symptoms are far outside what is considered average or 'normal'. So, there would need to be clear evidence of at least three of the following symptoms:

- Deceitfulness, in that the person is constantly deceiving and manipulating friends and family for their own gain to obtain money, sex and/or power without care or concern for the consequences of others.
- Lying to a pathological degree without care or concern for the consequences to others.
- Using an alias or conning others for their own profit or pleasure.
- Impulsivity and a general lack of being able to plan ahead.
- Irritability and aggressiveness that is typically marked by physical fights or assaulting others.
- A reckless disregard for the safety of others.
- Irresponsibility that goes well beyond normal that is demonstrated by failing to maintain consistent work behaviours and financial obligations.
- An almost complete lack of remorse in the individual where they really don't care that they hurt, mistreated or stole from someone else. In fact, they may even justify their behaviour.

## Other problems associated with adult ADHD

When we compare adults with ADHD to the rest of the population we see some rather disturbing trends. For instance, adults with ADHD have a higher rate of arrest; in fact, they are twice as likely to be arrested compared to adults without ADHD. Adult ADHD is also associated with significant problems with work performance and unemployment. The individual will more likely be dismissed from their job or quit their job due to a persistent need for changes in the working environment. This might alter, however, if there is a degree of autonomy in the workplace. Adults with ADHD have also been found to have poor driving records compared to adults without the disorder, and will more likely lose their driver's licence, receive more fines for violating traffic laws, and are at greater risk of having more motor vehicle accidents compared to adults without ADHD.

Just like children with ADHD, adults with ADHD really tend to face enormous problems in their day-to-day responsibilities, such as managing their finances, as they can be impulsive buyers, use their credit card excessively, fail to make repayments on debts and have very little savings. But the problems can be far-reaching, as the individual really struggles with social interactions and friendships, having fewer close friends and experiencing a great deal of difficulty in keeping the ones they do have. Unfortunately, adults with ADHD also tend to have higher rates of separation and divorce, generally tend to struggle with adjusting to married life and have more family problems compared to adults without ADHD. Finally, adults with ADHD tend to take more sexual risks, engage in sexual activity and intercourse earlier, and have more sexual partners and more casual sex with greater risk of partner pregnancies compared to adults without ADHD. One study that followed children with ADHD until they were between nineteen to 25 years of age found that 38 per cent would be more likely to become young parents based on their sexual activity compared to 4 per cent of young adults without ADHD, while 16 per cent would receive medical treatment for sexually transmitted diseases compared to 4 per cent of young adults without ADHD.

## Coping strategies

The core symptoms of inattention and impulsivity can make it much harder for the adult with ADHD to cope with stressful events. Most likely this is because they do not have adequate social supports to turn to for advice. Their issues with inattention can impede their ability to use adaptive strategies such as problem-solving or even hearing alternative perspectives from others, while the impulsivity can leave them in a position where they just respond to stressful events spontaneously and hastily with no forethought or planning. Unfortunately, such responses then are either aggressive or defensive in nature. One study wanted to work out how adults with ADHD might handle stressful situations compared to adults without ADHD. The study used a questionnaire where people described their coping styles to the most stressful events they had experienced in the previous month. The authors of the study described the eight strategies as:

1. Confrontative coping: aggressive efforts to alter the situation (for example, 'I stood my ground and fought for what I wanted.').

2. Distancing: efforts to detach oneself (for example, 'I went on as if nothing happened.').

3. Self-control: efforts to regulate one's own feelings (for example, 'I tried to keep my feelings to myself.').

4. Seeking social support: efforts to seek information for support (for example, 'I talked to someone to find out more about the situation.').

5. Accepting responsibility: acknowledging one's role in the problem (for example, 'I criticised or lectured myself.').

6. Escape–avoidance: wishful thinking and behavioural efforts to escape or avoid the situation (for example, 'I wished that the situation would go away'; avoided being with people in general).

7. Planful problem-solving: deliberate problem-focused efforts to alter the situation (for example, 'I made a plan of action and followed it.').

8. Positive reappraisal: efforts to create positive meaning by focusing on personal growth (for example, 'I changed or grew as a person in a good way.').

The results of this study indicated that adults with ADHD favoured using maladaptive coping strategies, particularly confrontative and escape–avoidance, and demonstrated pronounced deficits in planful problem-solving. This essentially means that when faced with stressful situations, the adult with ADHD may either react to it aggressively or do what they can to avoid the situation. The adults were also found to have lacked planful problem-solving skills, such as developing a plan of action and following it through. This could very well indicate that adults with ADHD may be unable to think and plan ahead and when faced with a stressful situation they can become confrontational. The results also showed that the better socialised an individual is, the more likely it is they will use adaptive problem-solving strategies.

The results of the study also found that there was a relationship between impulsivity and the ability to positively appraise a situation. This might suggest that adults with ADHD are able to reassess stressful situations, thus predisposing them to be resilient in the face of disappointments. Despite the pronounced disadvantages adults with ADHD experience, they may have an incredible ability to bounce back. This means the individual can continually assess, reassess, compensate and adapt to stressful life situations. This ability to adapt may be evident in creative and entrepreneurial qualities.

You may remember people with ADHD typically have very poor social skills. Deficits in social skills appear to negatively influence their ability to make use of planful problem-solving. This deficit is extended further, as failing to utilise planning has also been linked to impulsive responses, as evidenced by the lack of time people with ADHD spend thinking about a problem; and the more mistakes they make, the more complex the problem becomes. Overall the results of this research demonstrated that adults with ADHD have insufficient coping abilities and they utilise very rigid coping techniques. The ability to respond to stressful situations with flexibility is extremely important for healthy functioning. The lack of flexibility or the constant use of one coping style can prove to be extremely unhelpful for the individual. We need to be flexible in using a variety of possible coping strategies when faced with everyday demands and stressful situations. Given this, research found that adults with ADHD were still struggling on so many personal and social levels. The implications of this type of research to therapy provide us with a snapshot of why it is so important to get children the help they need as soon as possible. If you remember in Chapter 8, most of the evidence-based therapies focused on developing problem-solving skills and non-reactive responses: that is, learning how to appropriately appraise a situation, develop a solution and act on it.

## Problems with diagnosing adults

Part of the reason why many people don't accept adult ADHD is because of the changes in the presentation of the symptoms over time. One author stated, 'One of the most vexing aspects of ADHD for parents is that it evolves as a child grows up'. While still there, the hyperactive and impulsive symptoms become much less obvious as the child matures. However, these behaviours never return to 'normal', and inattention continues to remain a significant problem. Some theorise the decline in hyperactivity and impulsivity is because of how important adolescence is and the realisation that choices and decisions affect an individual's future. Also, while adolescents have a less structured environment, it is typically more demanding of them. Therefore, we cannot ignore the powerful influence peer groups have over the adolescent who has major issues with self-regulation. Finally, adolescence is a time when interpersonal changes take place and the teenager begins developing autonomy and learns to take responsibility for their actions. Interestingly, by the time an adolescent with ADHD reaches about 21, somewhere in the vicinity of 95 per cent will have stopped taking their medication. However, this is not necessarily representative of symptom remission.

Other confounding factors include the fact that the symptoms as listed in the DSM-5 simply do not match up with the symptoms displayed by the adult. For example, adults don't typically climb on furniture (unless you're Tom Cruise on *Oprah* declaring you're in love) and we don't often see adults butting in, calling out and talking over the top of other people all the time (unless, of course, you're watching question time in parliament on the television). In fact, the problems normally associated with hyperactivity can decline so much by adulthood that there is just a general feeling of restlessness and a need to keep busy. Instead, adult symptoms tend to occur around time management and organisational skills. Simply stated, the DSM-5 criteria were developed exclusively for diagnosing children. As the symptoms or severity of the symptoms change as the child matures and the symptoms may not be as evident across all domains, there are very real difficulties providing adults with an ADHD diagnosis.

Then there are the added problems due to the differences in the diagnostic criteria and the methodological differences between studies, which will inevitably include different populations, and differences in the age of participants in the studies at the final assessment stage. Finally, some research has indicated there are individuals who learn some pretty effective strategies and skills that help them overcome the day-to-day problems they face due to an ever-increasing ability to adapt to different environments and quite possibly due to earlier psychological interventions. Sadly for those who do not develop such skills, their symptoms tend to have a major impact on their ability to succeed in their adult lives. So, given all of these issues, how do we assess adults for ADHD?

## Assessing and diagnosing ADHD in adults

The Australian Guidelines on Attention Deficit Hyperactivity Disorder have recommended the best practices to assess and diagnose an adult ADHD as follows:

- The DSM-5 criteria are the minimum necessary for a diagnosis of ADHD.
- ADHD needs to be considered in adults who present with longstanding symptoms suggestive of ADHD (inattention, impulsivity, disorganisation) that appear to have started in childhood and are persisting into adult life.
- People with personality disorder and/or substance abuse accompanied by a significant level of impulsivity accompanied by inattention should be referred for evaluation of ADHD.
- Assessment of adults with suspected ADHD should include a comprehensive medical and psychosocial assessment, remembering there are 'other' medical conditions that can account for the symptoms of ADHD. A potential medical

condition must be ruled out before an ADHD diagnosis can be given.

- Assessment of adults with suspected ADHD should be undertaken by the best-qualified clinician available. This would usually be an adult psychiatrist (or psychologist) or a comprehensive psychiatric service with the training and skills required to assess and treat ADHD. This is due to the high incidence of comorbid psychiatric conditions and the overlap of clinical features of ADHD with other conditions such as bipolar disorder and personality disorders.
- Other possible diagnoses or comorbidities should be considered, via history; for example, acquired brain injury, a neurological condition or other DSM-5 diagnosis such as anxiety disorder or pervasive developmental disorder.
- Adult presentations may occur in the context of problems encountered with work and study. In such instances, vocational/intellectual assessments may be useful, not for diagnostic purposes, but to clarify the functional consequences of the diagnosis.
- For a diagnosis of ADHD in adults, input from multiple informants (for example, partners, family members) should be considered, where possible, in evaluating chronicity and pervasiveness of impairment.

As you can see there is a fairly comprehensive assessment required that involves both medical and psychiatric specialists. You will find, however, that those who specialise in adult ADHD will use more than just the above-listed criteria. For instance, clinicians will use questionnaires that reliably measure the core symptoms of ADHD and other important associated problems. Such questionnaires are said to have pronounced strengths as they draw on information obtained from both the individual being assessed and from an informant (for example, partners or parents). These questionnaires measure four domains:

1. ADHD symptoms such as inattention, hyperactivity and impulsivity.

2.  Emotional problems such as anxiety, depression, anger, and the impact these mood problems have on relationships.
3.  Delinquency, such as aggressive behaviours.
4.  Social functioning difficulties, such as engaging well with others.

Any adult assessment would include a thorough examination of the adult's history as provided by their parent, partner or spouse. Such a clinical interview would normally include seeking confirmation of a childhood diagnosis of ADHD, or a history suggesting childhood ADHD. There is a strong genetic component to ADHD so the clinician would be seeking a family history of ADHD. In addition, the adult's school history including academic problems and disciplinary problems would be examined. Part of the childhood history would also seek confirmation the disorder was present in the adult before age seven and that there was significant impairment beginning in childhood and evident throughout the lifespan in school, work and relationships.

In order to avoid a possible misdiagnosis some professionals suggest that in conjunction with the DSM-5, an absolute minimum requirement in the diagnostic phase would involve a history of hyperactivity in childhood and having access to informants who can provide reliable and accurate information about the adult as a child. Such informants typically include close relatives, a parent and any and all documentation such as medical, psychological and school reports.

One adult ADHD specialist reported that, in her clinic, if it is suspected an adult may have ADHD, they complete an extensive and comprehensive assessment before they will consider a diagnosis. Here's what they do:

- The adult must undergo a psychiatric assessment.
- The adult and their family member would be interviewed separately in order to:
  - determine any potential psychiatric problems not related to ADHD
  - complete a structured interview based on the DSM-5 diagnostic criteria
  - complete a personality assessment

- complete the Revised Conners Checklist based on the parents' recollections of the adult as a child (see Chapter 5).

This is followed by a reliable adult psychological assessment that would consider:

- ADHD features.
- The adult's educational achievement.
- The adult's occupational history.
- His or her general functioning.
- Drug use habits.
- Evidence of criminal activity, court and police records.

## Other causes of adult ADHD

There are a number of medical problems in childhood that may cause similar behaviours to the core symptoms of ADHD. It's no different for adult ADHD and this is one of the reasons why the assessment phase is so comprehensive. Medical or other conditions that may look like ADHD include:

- Hyperactivity as a side effect of some medications.
- As a result of seizures the person can appear as though they are daydreaming.
- Sleep disorders can be a cause of hyperactive behaviour and deficits in attention, concentration and short-term memory.
- Learning disabilities.
- Hypothyroidism.
- Anaemia.
- Lead toxicity.
- Autism.

Given there are medical factors that may present similar symptoms to ADHD, it is imperative that the assessment phase also includes a full physical check-up to rule out any medical conditions. As you can see, assessing an adult for ADHD is not taken lightly and involves a detailed and complex assessment phase.

# Medication

Generally speaking, the same classes of stimulant and non-stimulant medications used for childhood ADHD are just as effective for treating the symptoms of adult ADHD. However, the Australian guidelines inform us that not all people with ADHD would automatically be prescribed ADHD medication. In fact, we are told that medications should only be prescribed when the symptoms of ADHD are causing significant impairment or when the individual with moderate symptoms refuses or does not respond to psychological treatments. According to one paediatrician, while ADHD might have a genetic or neurological basis and is therefore a lifelong condition, most people will not need to take medication for their entire life. In fact, the suggestion was that 40 per cent of children will be off medication by middle school and a further 20 per cent by the time they start high school. This is not because the adult has 'outgrown' the disorder but more about the complexity of the brain and its ability to use or develop new pathways that will help people to overcome and compensate for the various kinds of problems associated with ADHD.

In Australia, the only medications currently available to treat ADHD in people over six years of age are Ritalin and Attenta (methylphenidate immediate-release), Ritalin LA and Concerta (extended-release formulations), dexamphetamine sulphate and Strattera (atomoxetine). Guidelines in a number of European countries recommend using methylphenidate as the first choice of treatment in adult ADHD. For instance, the National Institute for Health and Care Excellence (NICE) in the United Kingdom advises that methylphenidate should be the choice medication and used as the first line of treatment for adult ADHD. The only time atomoxetine might replace methylphenidate as a first-line treatment is simply when the adult has been unresponsive to or cannot tolerate methylphenidate, or if there is a concern the adult may abuse the drug. In the US and Canada there is a greater choice of medications for treating ADHD in adults, including Concerta XL (methylphenidate), Adderall XR (amphetamine mixed salts), Biphentin (methylphenidate) and Strattera (atomoxetine). The Canadian practice guidelines recommend using a long-acting medication such as Adderall XR, Biphentin, Concerta or Strattera.

## METHYLPHENIDATE

Professional literature suggests medications have profound effects on reducing the symptoms of ADHD across the lifespan. Unfortunately, medications may only be effective in about 50 per cent of adults with ADHD and this is likely due to the problem of comorbidities, side effects, only having a partial response to the medication or no response at all, or medical contraindications such as cardiovascular disease or a history of drug abuse. Therefore, the adult with ADHD must have their medication monitored very carefully. If you feel your medical professional is not adequately monitoring you, move on! Find someone who will be committed to you and who will help you work out the right dosage and administer any other medications you might need.

In the past it was difficult to determine the overall effects of methylphenidate for treating adult ADHD and while there were many reasons for this, thankfully in recent decades we have gathered some pretty impressive evidence that advocates the use of stimulant medication for use in adult ADHD. For instance, one researcher examined six different independent trials (a meta-analysis) of treating adult ADHD with methylphenidate. The results of the meta-analysis indicated that up to 78 per cent of the adults involved in the trials responded positively to methylphenidate. In general, professional research indicates the following:

- Methylphenidate reduces the core symptoms of adult ADHD.
- Methylphenidate is far superior to having no medication at all.
- Improvements in ADHD symptoms have been found with medication, regardless of gender, age or the individual's history of comorbidity.

### SIDE EFFECTS OF METHYLPHENIDATE

One researcher performed a comprehensive review of the evidence regarding how safe methylphenidate was for adults with ADHD. Evidence was collected from a number of different sources ending in a total of 26 trials. The duration of the trials included in the study was between one and twelve weeks with the dosage between 20 and 90 mg daily. Of the 811 patients receiving the drug, not one experienced such serious side effects that the drug was deemed to be life-threatening or to cause irreversible adverse side effects. Of the trials that did report problems, the side effects of individuals on methylphenidate were minor and included:

- a dry mouth
- decreased appetite
- emotional lability (intense mood swings or changes)
- jitteriness or tension
- depression or sadness
- weight loss
- vertigo.

Apparently these results indicated the known side effects of methylphenidate use in adults.

## ATOMOXETINE

As with methylphenidate there has been substantial research conducted on the efficacy of atomoxetine for treating adult ADHD. Such research has demonstrated that atomoxetine is effective in reducing the inattentive, hyperactive and impulsive symptoms of ADHD. But as most of you will know, there is a lot more to adult ADHD than just the core symptoms. There are also emotional difficulties and this has also been the subject of intense research. Studies have specifically looked at emotional dysregulation (as opposed to regulating emotional responses) in adult ADHD and the effectiveness of atomoxetine in treating these problems. One research design investigated the relationship between the symptoms of emotional dysregulation and ADHD. They assessed the individual's temper, emotional lability (exaggerated changes in mood or excessive emotional reactions), and the tendency to emotionally over-react. The results found that those adults with emotional lability experienced quite a reduction in the core symptoms of ADHD. Another study investigated how effective atomoxetine was in 442 adults with ADHD with comorbid social anxiety. The study lasted for twelve weeks and found that atomoxetine greatly reduced both the ADHD and social phobia symptoms in the adults.

## SIDE EFFECTS OF ATOMOXETINE

One large study of hundreds of adults with ADHD that were divided into two groups — one given atomoxetine for the duration of the trial; and the other a placebo (sugar pill) — reported the side effects for both groups as follows:

- Insomnia was reported in 20.8 per cent of the drug group and 8.7 per cent of the placebo group.
- A dry mouth was found in 21.2 per cent of the medicated group and 3.4 per cent of the placebo group.
- Constipation was experienced in 10.8 per cent of the drug group and 3.8 per cent of the placebo group.
- Blood pressure and heart rate was also found to have increased moderately when using atomoxetine.

It was recommended that anyone taking atomoxetine should be observed for agitation, irritability, suicidal ideation, self-harming behaviour or any unusual behaviour, particularly in the first few months of taking atomoxetine or when the dosage had been changed.

## HOW SAFE ARE ADHD MEDICATIONS?

Again, with any medication, there is the potential for side effects and misuse. There have been some concerns raised, however, of possible cardiovascular concerns in adults taking stimulant medication. The US Food and Drug Administration took this concern quite seriously and examined any deaths reported as being related to taking stimulants between 1992 and 2005. This examination revealed a total of eighteen deaths over the thirteen years that were related to methylphenidate treatments. However, of those eighteen deaths several people were found to have had very serious pre-existing heart problems or defects. Nevertheless, it should be obvious by now that a thorough medical examination ought to be completed to rule out any underlying medical concerns, including cardiovascular illness or disease that might place the individual at risk if taking medication for ADHD.

## Alternative treatments

As with childhood ADHD, pharmacotherapy (medication) has been shown time and time again to be the best treatment for reducing the core symptoms of adult ADHD. And just as with childhood ADHD, alternative treatments do not always bring about a reduction in the core symptoms of adult ADHD, but tend to be focused on teaching the adult coping skills and addressing the comorbid conditions. However, as good as the medication is, it does not work for everyone. In fact, it is estimated that ADHD medication only works for about half the adults taking it. As you might imagine, there is an increasing demand for effective therapies that are suitable for the adult. So while ADHD medication may reduce the core symptoms of ADHD, psychological treatments target specific impairments and teach the adult effective coping strategies they can use in their day-to-day lives.

Adults with ADHD often struggle with pessimistic and negative beliefs about their own abilities. They often have dysfunctional belief systems that are extremely destructive because they get caught in a web of self-defeating and self-undermining thoughts and belief systems. Such negativistic beliefs are frequently accompanied with distressing emotions that interfere with the ability to apply effective coping strategies. Such belief systems can also destroy the confidence the adult might have to actively apply new skills to make positive changes around them and can break down their sense of resiliency that might help them better manage ADHD. The ever-present, unrelenting and widespread negative effects of adult ADHD typically require comprehensive interventions to help them manage. Ideally, therapy would be directed at reducing symptoms and developing coping strategies that would also emphasise the individual's strengths and resources. Learning new strategies and skills to achieve positive changes may also result in developing a sense of control in their own life. It is hoped that taking this approach would also improve the adult's quality of life.

Any clinician faced with adult ADHD would be responsible for developing appropriate treatment goals for the individual. They would need to formulate an effective treatment plan, regularly monitor and evaluate the individual's progress, and ensure they are aware of any obstacles that may hinder the adult's success (this might also need to be accounted for in the intervention process). The clinician would need to prioritise and target any problem behaviour or other symptoms for intervention and teach the adult how to deal with procrastination. An individualised treatment program is probably going to have the greatest chance of success if the clinician is able to focus exclusively on the adult. However, there are benefits to group interventions as the individual has the added advantages of being encouraged by the entire group, learning about their coping strategies, and developing friendships. Whether it is individualised or group therapy, the intervention would normally include cognitive restructuring that focuses on altering negative self-undermining and self-defeating thought patterns. The therapy would also include:

- Targeting specific problems and developing coping strategies to manage those problems.
- Developing strategies to improve attention, such as using self-instructional training.
- Developing strategies to improve memory, such as using memory aids.
- Learning impulse control techniques, such as Stop, Think, Do.
- Learning time-management, organisational prioritisation and planning skills by using diaries and schedules.
- Learning problem-solving skills.
- Undertaking a sleep hygiene program to get sleep patterns back on track.
- Learning social skills.
- Learning how to self-monitor.
- Learning emotion control.
- Learning how to manage different moods like anger and frustration.
- Learning appropriate ways of responding to people through assertiveness training.

Cognitive behavioural therapy (CBT) is quite possibly one of the most researched forms of therapy due to its widespread application across so many different disorders and the promising results it often achieves. While CBT may not address the core issues of ADHD, apart from being one of *the most* effective treatments for depression and anxiety disorders, it is also very helpful for the adult with ADHD as it typically addresses the above-noted skills and strategies. Furthermore, CBT directly targets those negativistic thoughts and beliefs through cognitive restructuring and reframing the past, and teaches the individual how to recognise irrational and faulty thinking patterns, evaluate cognitive distortions, and effectively challenge those negative thoughts. See Chapter 8 for more information on cognitive behavioural therapy.

## WHAT DOES THE RESEARCH SAY?

Overall CBT as an effective adjunct to medication for treating adult ADHD is well supported both in clinical trials and in established community clinics. This is likely due to the fact that adults are more receptive to outside help.

One study aimed to explore the effectiveness of a group cognitive behavioural treatment program that had been specifically developed to treat ADHD symptoms and the more common comorbid conditions. Adults who were on medication were randomly assigned to one of two groups: those who would also receive CBT and those on the usual treatment of medication. The two central goals of this study were to see if the program brought about changes in ADHD symptoms and whether or not there were any measurable differences in anxiety, depression, emotional control, social functioning and antisocial behaviour. Overall, it was expected that the group on medication who also received the CBT training would show significantly greater improvements than the medication-only group both in ADHD symptoms and the co-existing problems. It was also expected that any changes in the medication plus CBT group would still be evident months later.

The program comprised fifteen CBT sessions developed specifically for adolescents and adults with ADHD and antisocial behaviour. The program was very structured and aimed to improve social, problem-solving, and organisational skills by teaching the subjects to:

- Control their attention, memory, impulse control and planning abilities.
- Problem-solve by developing skilled thinking, identifying problems, thinking of alternative options or approaches to a situation and the likely consequences, and learning how to manage conflict and make appropriate choices.
- Control one's emotions by learning how to manage feelings of anxiety and anger.
- Develop appropriate social skills by learning to recognise the thoughts and feelings of others, to show empathy, and to learn how to negotiate social situations and resolve conflict.
- Reason by weighing up one's options and assessing effective behavioural skills.

The program not only offered group therapy but also individual treatments where the adults were assigned a coach who met with them between sessions. The coach's role was to support the adults in their attempts at applying the new skills they were being taught in therapy in their daily lives. The authors reported on two very important outcomes of this program: first, and possibly most significant of all, were the noticeable improvements in core ADHD symptoms by the end of the program; and secondly, there were still noticeable improvements in ADHD symptoms months later. On the down side it appears that hyperactivity–impulsivity didn't change too much.

This investigation showed that while the ADHD symptoms may have been more under control, the adults were still struggling with 'residual symptoms' that were successfully improved by the CBT intervention. Three months after the program finished the adults were asked to complete a self-report questionnaire where it was found they were still experiencing the same improvements. The adults' self-reports were corroborated by independent evaluations. The adults even suggested that the effect the program had on ADHD symptoms was even greater at the three-month follow-up. It seems the program was also very successful at treating the common comorbid problems of anxiety, depression, antisocial behaviour and social functioning. That changes were stable three months after the course had finished, and had even continued to improve in time, was a result of the adults continuing to apply the strategies they had learned in therapy after they had finished the course. This is an extremely important point to remember — all the training in the world with the best clinician offering the best programs will mean absolutely nothing if the individual does not engage in the program and continue to use their new skills once therapy is over.

Another trial found that combining CBT and medication led to a moderate to significant reduction in ADHD symptoms in up to 70 per cent of the participants. This same group also reported significant improvements in depression, anxiety and that overwhelming sense of hopelessness.

We can go on and on listing trial after trial demonstrating how effective CBT is for the adult with ADHD. The bottom line is that a well-structured CBT program will take into account the aforementioned difficulties and administer a program that deals directly with both the difficulties and comorbidities that the unique individual is battling with.

## A word of encouragement

There is an awful lot of negativity and stigma about ADHD in popular media, in the pseudo-professional field and even in some corners of the professional world, not to mention the general public. But if there is just one thing you take from this book, please let it be this — don't be sucked in by the 'doom and gloom' statements of others who suggest that because you have ADHD you will not succeed at anything in life. Many people with ADHD can and do succeed. After reading this book you might be feeling the future looks both helpless and hopeless and you might even question what kind of a future you or your child might have. But this does not have to be the case because knowledge is power and the information contained in this book was designed to provide you with knowledge about the disorder to empower you to recognise why you might feel a certain way or act differently to others. You have learned about some of the common pitfalls like substance use and abuse and this gives you the power to make healthier choices for your life, steering clear of the mistakes you have read about in this book. You have learned about comorbid conditions, giving you the power to choose professional help to get through it. You have learned that maintaining relationships might be difficult for you at times, but this gives you the power to begin working collaboratively with your partner or spouse on a plan to address the more serious issues or again to seek professional assistance to help you manage a relationship effectively. You might have wanted to do a course of study but felt you couldn't because of problems like concentration. Now that you understand these difficulties you have the power to choose a course that would be more suited to your needs or develop a plan of study that would help you get through the course.

Take heart because some of the symptoms of ADHD are not necessarily a disadvantage. For instance, you might have energy levels that others only dream of, which can be channelled and used to your advantage in different fields of employment thus offering you fulfilling employment opportunities. During the course of writing this book I have read so many personal testimonies and reports of people with ADHD really getting somewhere in life from managing companies to being highly successful in various sports. I met a man who at the age of 38 presented at my clinic complaining of moodiness, irritability and days when he just felt down. To cut a long story short, he grew up in a very difficult part of town and he never knew his father until he was 25. He struggled all the way through school and can only remember one teacher who was kind, patient and helpful and 'would not take any shit from me ... That was a good class'. He recognised a number of difficulties during childhood including anger and frustration and as a child he was pretty much left to roam free. Sitting in my office he explained how he had always struggled with anxiety, even as a child. But he also recognised that he was very good at sport and growing up he put all his energy into different sports. As a child he would be outside playing football or cricket until dark with the other children in the neighbourhood. When he was older he joined a local football team and excelled in the game. As an adult he had become quite successful in life as he owned three houses, was in a paid part-time position as a football coach, and he held a sub-contract position with some major companies and had his own business. He had been with his wife for twenty years and after they married they had two daughters. This man was eventually diagnosed with adult ADHD.

It is important to keep this disorder in perspective, because although you might have some disadvantages in some areas, it does not mean you have nothing to offer. For you, as it is for everyone, it is a case of working out your needs and strengths and finding social, relational and employment opportunities that meet those needs. ADHD is not a curse and you should never allow it to be the single most important thing in your life because there are many positive things about you and who you are. Here are just some of the positive aspects of ADHD:

- You can be very creative.
- You can be spontaneous.
- You have energy levels that other people only dream of having.
- You can be very funny with a great sense of humour.
- You can be very resilient and instead of being crushed by a disappointment you can bounce back very quickly.
- You can be incredibly caring and compassionate.
- Seeking out new and exciting activities is not a problem for you. You get to experience exciting things in life that others will miss out on.
- You can be very sensitive, insightful and perceptive.
- You have a willingness to take risks (this can be a huge asset to you).
- You are enthusiastic.
- You can be flexible and not bogged down by traditional methods.
- You can be very forgiving.
- Everyone around you knows you have an amazing ability to think quickly.

# CHAPTER 11

# Where to from here?

Wow, what an incredible journey you have just been on. You may remember from the introduction that my reason for writing this book was a deep desire to teach you the truth about ADHD and what it *really* is. This was because I have grown so tired of the myths being preached as fact through various media outlets and how the information they provide is often so very wrong. I am just so tired of people misunderstanding ADHD and blaming the individual, their parents, or some other reason for the individual's behaviour, because as we know this disorder goes far beyond 'normal' childhood misbehaviour and poses a significant risk to the person's physical and mental health.

The ignorance attached to ADHD is so frustrating and hurtful for the individual and their families who have to live with the disorder day in and day out. This is why I wanted to teach you about the symptoms of ADHD, to separate the myths and media hype from the facts of the disorder, and to prepare you for the assessment phase. I also wanted to show parents that ADHD is not a result of something they did or didn't do, and that they are not a failure as a parent. Parents do not need to carry that burden! I wanted to provide some insight for the sufferer so they could understand what is going on in their life and that they are not crazy or worthless or a failure, and with the appropriate treatment they can learn to manage this disorder and get on with giving to the world all those positive things they have to offer. You don't have to be burdened down by ADHD, but you can learn what your strengths are and get on with enjoying your life.

The information I have presented has come from the evidence of mainstream research from various professional fields such as psychology, psychiatry, pharmacology, neurology and other medical sciences. It is founded in solid research and not based on my or any other person's opinions. We have looked at the three core symptoms of ADHD — inattention, hyperactivity and impulsiveness — and how they impact a child, adolescent or adult in almost every area of their life. Such negative impacts range from poor academic performance, poor concentration and the inability to organise oneself to poor peer friendships, to difficult parent–child relationships, problems with employment, and risks of developing numerous comorbid conditions.

You have seen that ADHD is not a new disorder or something that is just purely a Western phenomenon, but rather a condition that has been around for a very long time, albeit under different names. We have been thoroughly introduced to the causes of ADHD from smoking and drinking alcohol during pregnancy through to other toxic causes and to the areas of the brain that are the most likely culprits behind the disorder. Then we examined the assessment of ADHD and what is involved in this phase and what you and your child could expect. This was an important chapter as many parents and children can feel frightened and vulnerable when they are asked by the professional to sit a gamut of assessments followed by the diagnosis of ADHD. This chapter also covered another important point: that of seeking appropriately qualified and experienced professionals who have access to the necessary assessments and are well experienced in using them. We also looked at a rather saddening chapter on comorbidity and the many other problems that often accompany ADHD and the difficult issue of deciding whether or not to medicate your child and what other mainstream therapies are available that have been shown to be most effective with the symptoms of ADHD.

Perhaps you or someone you know has ADHD and after reading this book a lot of behaviours, feelings and thoughts are beginning to make sense to you. Perhaps you can identify with what you have read and after gaining so much new information the question is where to from here? A good place to start is seeking the services of someone who specialises in the disorder as they will support you and offer some very practical strategies in managing this disorder and they will also map out the most appropriate form of therapy for you. When seeking a specialist you can contact professional organisations such as medical associations, psychological and psychiatric societies and associations, and request the contact details of their members in and around your suburb who specialise in ADHD. You could also ask your family doctor or a paediatrician if they know of a specialist he or she could refer you to.

But you should also know that therapy may require you to make some changes to your life choices and lifestyle. As parents, you may need to complete a parent management training program to help you better deal with your child's behaviour and equip you to meet their emotional and psychological needs. Your child may need to undertake a social skills training program to help them learn how to appropriately interact with others in order to make and keep friends, and you may need to advocate for them at school. To give you a bit of an idea of the kind of changes you may need to make, presented below are some of the steps you would need to consider if your child has ADHD:

- Once a diagnosis is determined from a complete assessment phase you may need to request that a written report be sent to your child's school outlining the findings and any recommendations the specialist has in terms of supporting your child socially and academically.
- You may need to call a meeting with your child's schoolteacher and ask them exactly how they intend to support your child.
- You may need to have your professional involved with your child's schoolteachers in order to meet your child's educational needs.
- If your school is unable or unwilling to offer you appropriate support you may need to consider changing to a school that will support your family.
- Your mental health specialist should help you develop a therapeutic program for your child. Because they will have the results of all the assessments, and a thorough knowledge of your child's developmental, psychiatric and medical history,

they are the best person to do this.

- Your child would begin a social skills program.
- You may undertake a parent management training program designed to help you meet your child's needs and manage their difficult behaviour.
- You would also request the specialist teach you how to encourage your child in their efforts with the social skills program and how to reinforce relevant skills and strategies across different environments.
- You would also need to discuss with a medical specialist whether medication is an option for your child.

Many parents have told me they see the loneliness and the hurt their child feels because they have few if any friends. As we know, this is a major issue of concern and needs to be dealt with. One way you can help your child make friends is to get them involved in an after-school sports program. Not only is this good for their incredible energy levels but it exposes them to social situations and the possibility of forming new friendships. While your child is completing the social skills training program they will have plenty of opportunities to practise their new skills while you as the parent can take the opportunity to be the social skills coach and reinforce their learning and encourage their attempts. You could also invite one or maybe two of their new friends over to your house for a fun-filled day.

Adults may also need to consider making some changes in their lives. For example, I have dealt with many adults who refuse to take medication because as a child they may have had a negative experience with stimulant medication. While that may be understandable, the concern is that quite a few of the adults replaced stimulant medication with illicit drug use in an effort to gain some relief from the symptoms of ADHD. We know, for example, that ADHD often interferes with one's sleep and it is not uncommon for adults to drink alcohol to excess or use drugs to help them sleep at night. There is a clear danger of developing an addiction to these drugs. I talk to them about the different medications that are now available and discuss all their concerns and offer them a multi-modal approach. As most of the adults with ADHD I have dealt with also have depression, depending on how severe it is, I suggest it may be necessary to undertake a course of anti-depressants. When it comes to issues around medication for the adult with ADHD I will often refer the person to a psychiatrist as they specialise in mental health medications and know what will be the best medications to provide. They will monitor the medications and will request follow-up reviews with the person which provide the individual with the opportunity to discuss any concerns they may have regarding any aspect of the medication.

While professionals have to study for many years to get their credentials, and work incredibly hard to offer you their very best, on occasion our different personalities might get in the way or there are times when we can get it wrong. I tell everyone who comes to my clinic that if they feel I have misunderstood them or just got it wrong, they need to tell me otherwise we are wasting each other's time and they are wasting their money. You have this right and ought to exercise it if you feel your specialist hasn't understood you or if for any reason you feel they are not hearing you. Don't just walk away and give up. Find another person who will listen to you. My clients have every right to request I refer them to another equally qualified and experienced professional and I encourage you to make that request if needed. Your health and wellbeing is our utmost concern and priority.

## Acknowledgements

To my precious wife and children, I thank you for your patience and undying support with this project and my endeavours. How blessed I am that you continue to teach me how to be a better father and husband.

My deepest gratitude to my friend and colleague, Noni. You have supported and encouraged me with your knowledge and professionalism and I am eternally thankful for your insights and your friendship.

To my father. You have always been there for me, you have watched in silence when needed, you have offered wise advice, you have supported me, stretched and challenged me, and you have always encouraged me. I dedicate this book to you.

# References

## CHAPTER 1

American Psychiatric Association 2013, *Diagnostic and statistical manual of mental disorders* (DSM), 5th edn, American Psychiatric Association, Arlington, Virginia.

Barkley, RA 1998, *Attention-deficit hyperactivity disorder: A handbook for diagnosis and treatment*, 2nd edn, The Guilford Press, New York.

Daly, BP, Creed, T, Xanthopoulos, M & Brown, RT 2007, 'Psychosocial treatments for children with attention deficit/hyperactivity disorder', *Neuropsychological Review Journal*, vol. 17(1), pp. 73–89.

Lahey, BB, Pelham, WE, Loney, J, Lee, SS & Willcutt, E 2005, 'Instability of the DSM-IV subtypes of ADHD from preschool through elementary school', *Archives of General Psychiatry*, vol. 62(8), pp. 896–902.

Lee, SI, Schachar, RJ, Chen, SX, Ornstein, TJ, Charach, A, Barr, C & Ickowicz, A 2008, 'Predictive validity of DSM-IV and ICD-10 criteria for ADHD and hyperkinetic disorder', *Journal of Child Psychology and Psychiatry*, vol. 49(1), pp. 70–8.

Loe, IM & Feldman, HM 2007, 'Academic and educational outcomes of children with ADHD', *Journal of Paediatric Psychology*, vol. 32(6), pp. 643–54.

Mikami, AY, Huang-Pollock, CL, Pfiffner, LJ, McBurnett, K & Hangai, D 2007, 'Social skills differences among attention-deficit/hyperactivity disorder types in a chat room assessment task', *Journal of Abnormal Child Psychology*, vol. 35(4), pp. 509–21.

Sadock, BJ, & Sadock, VA 2003, *Synopsis of psychiatry: Behavioural sciences/clinical psychiatry*, 9th edn, Lippincott Williams & Wilkins, Philadelphia.

Schachar, R, Chen, S, Crosbie, J, Goos, L, Ickowicz, A & Charach, A 2007, 'Comparison of the predictive validity of hyperkinetic disorder and attention deficit hyperactivity disorder', *Journal of the Canadian Academy of Child and Adolescent Psychiatry*, vol. 16(2), pp. 90–100.

Stolzer, JM 2009, 'Attention Deficit Hyperactivity Disorder: Valid medical condition or culturally constructed myth?', *Ethical Human Psychology and Psychiatry*, vol. 11(1), pp. 5–15.

Widiger, TA & Samuel, DB 2005, 'Diagnostic categories or dimensions? A question for the Diagnostic and Statistical Manual of Mental Disorders — Fifth Edition', *Journal of Abnormal Psychology*, vol. 114(4), pp. 494–504.

Wilmshurst, L 2005, *The essentials of child psychopathology*, John Wiley & Sons Inc., Hoboken, New Jersey.

## CHAPTER 2

Millichap, JG 2010, *Attention deficit hyperactivity disorder handbook: A physician's guide to ADHD*, 2nd edn, Springer, New York.

Palmer, ED & Finger, S 2001, 'An early description of ADHD (Inattentive Subtype): Dr Alexander Crichton and "Mental Restlessness" (1798)', *Child and Adolescent Mental Health*, vol. 6, pp. 66–73.

Sharkey, L & Fitzgerald, M 2007, 'The history of attention deficit hyperactivity disorder', in *Handbook of attention deficit hyperactivity disorder*, Michael Fitzgerald, Mark Bellgrove and Michael Gill (eds.), John Wiley & Sons Ltd, Chichester.

Singh, I 2008, 'ADHD, culture and education', *Early Child Development and Care*, vol. 178(4), pp. 347–61.

# CHAPTER 3

Barkley, RA 2002, 'International consensus statement on ADHD', *Clinical Child and Family Psychology Review*, vol. 5(2), pp. 89–111.

Barzam, DH, Fieler, L & Sallee, FR 2004, 'Attention-deficit hyperactivity disorder diagnosis and treatment', *The Journal of Legal Medicine*, vol. 25, pp. 23–38.

Biederman, J, Wilens, T, Mick, E, Spencer, T & Faraone, SV 1999, 'Pharmacotherapy of attention/deficit hyperactivity disorder reduces risk for substance use disorder', *Pediatrics*, vol. 104(2), e20.

Comings, DE, Chen, TJ, Blum, K, Mengucci, JF, Blum, SH & Meshkin, B 2005, 'Neurogenetic interactions and aberrant behavioral co-morbidity of attention deficit hyperactivity disorder (ADHD): dispelling myths', *Theoretical Biology and Medical Modelling*, vol. 23(2), p. 50.

Davari-Ashtiani, R, Shahrbabaki, ME, Razjouyan, K, Amini, H & Mazhabdar, H 2010, 'Buspirone versus methylphenidate in the treatment of attention deficit hyperactivity disorder: A double-blind and randomized trial', *Child Psychiatry and Human Development*, vol. 41(6), pp. 641–8.

Faraone, SV & Biederman, J 2000, 'Nature, nurture and attention deficit hyperactivity disorder', *Developmental Review*, vol. 20, pp. 568–81.

Faraone, SV, Sergeant, J, Gillberg, C & Biederman, J 2003, 'The worldwide prevalence of ADHD: Is it an American condition?', *World Psychiatry*, vol. 2(2), pp. 104–13.

Fritz, GK 2000, 'The time is right to dispel myths about ADHD', *The Brown University Child and Adolescent Behavior Letter*, vol. 16(9), p. 8.

Gadow, KD, Nolan, EE, Litcher, L, Carlson, GA, Panina, N, Golovakha, E, Sprafkin, J & Bromet, EJ 2000, 'Comparison of attention-deficit/hyperactivity disorder symptom subtypes in Ukrainian schoolchildren', *Journal of the American Academy of Child and Adolescent Psychiatry*, vol. 39(12), pp. 1520–7.

Spencer, TJ, Biederman, J & Mick, E 2007, 'Attention-deficit/hyperactivity disorder: Diagnosis, lifespan, comorbidities, and neurobiology', *Journal of Paediatric Psychology*, vol. 32(6), pp. 631–42.

Stolzer, JM 2005, 'ADHD in America: A bioecological analysis', *Ethical Human Psychology & Psychiatry*, vol. 7, pp. 65–75.

Stolzer, JM 2007, 'The ADHD epidemic in America', *Ethical Human Psychology & Psychiatry*, vol. 9(2), pp. 109–16.

Stolzer, JM 2009, 'Attention deficit hyperactivity disorder: Valid medical condition or culturally constructed myth?', *Ethical Human Psychology and Psychiatry*, vol. 11(1), pp. 5–15.

Weyandt, LL 2007, *An ADHD Primer*, 2nd edn, Lawrence Erlbaum Associates Inc., New Jersey.

Wilmshurst, L 2005, *The essentials of child psychopathology*, John Wiley & Sons, Hoboken, New Jersey.

World Health Organization 1992, *International classification of diseases version 10.* (ICD-10).

# CHAPTER 4

Barkley, RA 1997, *Defiant children: A clinician's manual for parent training*, The Guilford Press, New York.

Barkley, RA 1998, *Attention deficit hyperactivity disorder: A handbook for diagnosis and treatment*, 2nd edn, The Guilford Press, New York.

Barkley, RA 2002, 'International consensus statement on ADHD', *Clinical Child and Family Psychology Review*, vol. 5(2), pp. 89–111.

Beaumont, JG 2008, *Introduction to neuropsychology*, 2nd edn, The Guilford Press, New York.

Bennett, FC, Brown, RT, Craver, J & Anderson, D 1999, 'Stimulant medication for the child with attention-deficit/hyperactivity disorder', *Pediatric Clinics of North America*, vol. 46(5), pp. 929–44.

Biederman, J, Monuteaux, MC, Doyle, AE, Seidman, LJ, Wilens, TE, Ferrero, F, Morgan, CL & Faraone, SV 2004, 'Impact of executive function deficits and attention-deficit/hyperactivity disorder (ADHD) on academic outcomes in children', *Journal of Consulting and Clinical Psychology*, vol. 72(5), pp. 757–66.

Biederman, J 2005, 'Advancing the neuroscience of ADHD: Attention-deficit/hyperactivity disorder: A selective overview', *Biological Psychiatry*, vol. 57(11), pp. 1215–20.

Brennan, AR & Arnsten, AF 2008, 'Neuronal mechanisms underlying attention deficit hyperactivity disorder: The Influence of arousal on prefrontal cortical function', *Annals of the New York Academy of Sciences*, vol. 1129, pp. 236–45.

Brown, TE 2005, *Attention deficit disorder: The unfocused mind in children and adults*, Yale University Press, New Haven.

Castellanos, FX, Lee, PP, Sharp, W, Jeffries, NO et al. 2002, 'Developmental trajectories of brain volume abnormalities in children and adolescents with attention-deficit/hyperactivity disorder', *Journal of the American Medical Association*, vol. 288(14), pp. 1740–8.

Chandler, C 2010, *The science of ADHD: A guide for parents and professionals*, John Wiley & Sons Ltd, Chichester.

Daly, BP, Creed, T, Xanthopoulos, M & Brown, RT 2007, 'Psychosocial treatments for children with attention deficit/hyperactivity disorder', *Neuropsychological Review Journal*, vol. 17(1), pp. 73–89.

Green, RL & Ostrander, RL 2009, *Neuroanatomy for students of behavioral disorders*, WW Norton & Company, New York.

Haber, JS 2003, *ADHD: The great misdiagnosis*, revised edn, Taylor Trade Publishing, Maryland.

Kraly, FS 2009, *The unwell brain: Understanding the psychobiology of mental health*, WW Norton & Company, New York.

Linnet KM, Wisborg K, Obel C et al. 2005, 'Smoking during pregnancy and the risk for hyperkinetic disorder in offspring', *Journal of the Academy of Pediatrics*, vol. 116(2), pp. 462–7.

Needleman, HL, Schell, A, Bellinger, D, Leviton, A & Allred, EN 1990, 'The long-term effects of exposure to low doses of lead in childhood. An 11-year follow-up report', *New England Journal of Medicine*, vol. 322(2), pp. 83–8.

Pastor, PN & Reuben, CA 2008, 'Diagnosed attention deficit hyperactivity disorder and learning disability: United States, 2004–2006', *Vital Health Statistics*, series 10, pp. 1–14.

Premkumar, K 2004, *The massage connection: Anatomy and physiology*, 2nd edn, Lippincott Williams & Wilkins, Baltimore.

Ramsay, JR & Rostain, A 2007, *Cognitive Behavioral Therapy for adult ADHD: An integrative psychosocial and medical approach*, Routledge, New York.

Sparrow, EP 2010, *Essentials of Conners behavior assessments*. John Wiley & Sons, Hoboken, New Jersey.

Thibodeau, GA & Patton, KT 2004, *Structure & function of the body*, 12th edn, Mosby, St Louis.

Tortora, GJ & Derrickson, B 2012, *Principles of anatomy & physiology*, 13th edn, John Wiley & Sons Inc., Hoboken, New Jersey.

Wilmshurst, L 2005, *The essentials of child psychopathology*, John Wiley & Sons Inc., Hoboken, New Jersey.

## WEBSITES

The Australian Heart Foundation 2012, viewed 18 July 2012 and 25 July 2012, www.heartfoundation.org.au.

Presentation by Dr Russell Barkley 2012, viewed August 2012, www.caddac.ca.

## CHAPTER 5

Achenbach, TM & Ruffle, TM 2000, 'The Child Behavior Checklist and related forms for assessing behavioral/emotional problems and competencies', *Pediatrics in Review*, vol. 21(8), pp. 265–71.

American Psychiatric Association 2013, *Diagnostic and statistical manual of mental disorders* (DSM), 5th edn, American Psychiatric Association, Arlington, Virginia.

Barkley, RA 1998, *Attention deficit hyperactivity disorder: A handbook for diagnosis and treatment*, 2nd edn, The Guilford Press, New York.

Barzam, DH, Fieler, L & Sallee, FR 2004, 'Attention-deficit hyperactivity disorder diagnosis and treatment', *The Journal of Legal Medicine*, vol. 25(1), pp. 23–38.

Greenbaum, PE, Dedrick, RF & Lipien, L 2004, 'Childhood and adolescent assessment instruments', in MJ Hilsenroth, DL Segal & M Hersen (eds.), *Comprehensive handbook of psychological assessment*, vol. 2, pp. 188–191, John Wiley & Sons Ltd, New Jersey.

Mayes, SD & Calhoun, SL 2006, 'WISC-IV and WISC-III profiles in children with ADHD', *Journal of Attention Disorders*, vol. 9(3), pp. 486–93.

Prifitera, A, Saklofske, DH & Weiss, LG (eds) 2005, *WISC-IV: Clinical use and interpretation. Scientist-practitioner perspectives*, Elsevier Academic Press, Boston.

Sattler, JA 2008, *Assessment of children: Cognitive foundations*, 5th edn, Jerome M. Sattler, San Diego.

Schachar, R, Chen, S, Crosbie, J, Goos, L, Ickowicz, A & Charach, A 2007, 'Comparison of the predictive validity of hyperkinetic disorder and attention deficit hyperactivity disorder', *Journal of the Canadian Academy of Child and Adolescent Psychiatry*, vol. 16(2), pp. 90–100.

Schwean, VL & Saklofske, DH 2005, 'Assessment of attention deficit hyperactivity disorder with the WISC-IV', in A Prifitera, DH Saklofski & LG Weiss (eds.), *WISC-IV clinical use and interpretation: Scientist-practitioner perspectives*, Elsevier Academic Press, Boston.

Sparrow, EP 2010, *Essentials of Conners behavior assessments*. John Wiley & Sons, Hoboken, New Jersey.

Stolzer, JM 2005, 'ADHD in America: A bioecological analysis', *Ethical Human Psychology & Psychiatry*, vol. 7, pp. 65–75.

Stolzer, JM 2009, 'Attention deficit hyperactivity disorder: Valid medical condition or culturally constructed myth?', *Ethical Human Psychology and Psychiatry*, vol. 11(1), pp. 5–15.

## WEBSITES

American Academy of Pediatrics 2011, viewed 10 August 2011, www.healthychildren.org/English/health-issues/conditions/adhd/pages/AAP-Recommendations-Diagnostic-Guidelines-for-ADHD.aspx.

Australian Government National Health and Medical Research Council 2011, Draft Australian Guidelines on ADHD, viewed 10 August 2011, www. nhmrc.gov.au.

Australian Psychological Society 2011, 'Understanding and Managing ADHD in children', viewed 23 November 2011, www.psychology.org.au.

## CHAPTER 6

American Psychiatric Association 2013, *Diagnostic and statistical manual of mental disorders* (DSM), 5th edn, American Psychiatric Association, Arlington, Virginia.

Bowen, R, Chavira, DA, Bailey, K, Stein, MT & Stein, MB 2008, 'Nature of anxiety comorbid with attention deficit hyperactivity disorder in children from a pediatric primary care setting', *Psychiatry Research*, vol. 157(1–3), pp. 201–9.

Bruce, B, Thernlund, G & Nettelbladt, U 2006, 'ADHD and language impairment: A study of the parent questionnaire FTF (Five to Fifteen)', *European Child and Adolescent Psychiatry*, vol. 15(1), pp. 52–60.

Buschgens, CJ, van Aken, MA, Swinkels, SH, Altink, ME, Fliers, EA, Rommelse, NN et al. 2008, 'Differential family and peer environmental factors are related to severity and comorbidity in children with ADHD', *Journal of Neural Transmission*, vol. 115(2), pp. 177–86.

Dabrick, DA, Gadow, KD & Sprafkin, J 2006, 'Co-occurrence of conduct disorder and depression in a clinic-based sample of boys with ADHD', *Journal of Child Psychology and Psychiatry*, vol. 47(8), pp. 766–74.

Daviss, WB & Diler, R 2012, 'Does comorbid depression predict subsequent adverse life events in youth with attention-deficit/hyperactivity disorders?', *Journal of Child and Adolescent Psychopharmacology*, vol. 22(1), pp. 65–71.

Engelhardt, PE, Ferreira, F & Nigg, JT 2011, 'Language production strategies and disfluencies in multi-clause network descriptions: A study of adult attention-deficit/hyperactivity disorder', *Neuropsychology*, vol. 25(4), pp. 442–53.

Gau, SS, Ni, HC, Shang, CY, Soong, WT, Wu, YY, Lin, LY & Chiu, YN 2010, 'Psychiatric comorbidity among children and adolescents with and without persistent attention-deficit hyperactivity disorder', *Australian and New Zealand Journal of Psychiatry*, vol. 44(2), pp. 135–43.

Hammerness, P, Geller, D, Petty, C, Lamb, A, Bristol, E & Biederman, J 2010, 'Does ADHD moderate the manifestation of anxiety disorders in children?', *European Child and Adolescent Psychiatry*, vol. 19(2), pp. 107–12.

Humphreys, KL, Aguirre, VP & Lee, SS 2012, 'Association of anxiety and ODD/CD in children with and without ADHD', *Journal of Clinical Child and Adolescent Psychology*, vol. 41(3), pp. 370–7.

Jensen, PS, Hinshaw, SP, Kraemer, HC, Lenora, N, Newcorn, JH, Abikoff, HB et al. 2001, 'ADHD comorbidity findings from the MTA study: Comparing comorbid subgroups', *Journal of the American Academy of Child and Adolescent Psychiatry*, vol. 40(2), pp. 147–58.

Jensen, PS, Martin, D & Cantwell, DP 1997, 'Comorbidity in ADHD: Implications for research, practice, and DSM-V', *Journal of the American Academy of Child and Adolescent Psychiatry*, vol. 36(8), pp. 1065–79.

Keenan, K, Wroblewski, K, Hipwell, A, Loeber, R, Stouthamer-Loeber, M 2010, 'Age of onset, symptom threshold, and expansion of the nosology of conduct disorder for girls', *Journal of Abnormal Psychology*, vol. 119(4), pp. 689–98.

Kim, DK, Eunyoung J, Sora, L, Kijyung, K, Boongnyun, K & Ienai 2011, 'A synthesis on the research of the comorbidity of ADHD and LD in Korea: perspective and trend', *Asia Pacific Education Review*, vol. 12, pp. 581–91.

Lebowitz, ER, Motlagh, MG, Katsovich, L, King, RA et al., 2012, 'Tourette syndrome in youth with and without obsessive compulsive disorder and attention deficit hyperactivity disorder', *European Child and Adolescent Psychiatry*, vol. 21(8), pp. 451–7.

Linnet KM, Wisborg K, Obel C et al. 2005, 'Smoking during pregnancy and the risk for hyperkinetic disorder in offspring', *Journal of the Academy of Pediatrics*, vol. 116(2), pp. 462–7.

Maughan, B, Rowe, R, Messer, J, Goodman, R & Meltzer, H 2004, 'Conduct disorder and oppositional defiant disorder in a national sample: Developmental epidemiology', *Journal of Child Psychology and Psychiatry, and Allied Disciplines*, vol. 45(3), pp. 609–21.

Sibley, MH, Pelham, WE, Molina, BS, Gnagy, EM, et al., 2010, 'The delinquency outcomes of boys with ADHD with and without comorbidity', *Journal of Abnormal Child Psychology*, vol. 39(1), pp. 21–32.

Silver, LB 2003, *Attention-deficit/hyperactivity disorder: A clinical guide to diagnosis and treatment for health and mental health professionals*, 3rd edn, American Psychiatric Publishing Inc., Washington, DC.

Sørensen, L, Plessen, KJ, Nicholas, J & Lundervold, AJ 2011, 'Is behavioral regulation in children with ADHD aggravated by comorbid anxiety disorder?', *Journal of Attention Disorders*, vol. 15(1), pp. 56–66.

Takeda, T, Ambrosini, PJ, deBerardinis, R, Elia, J 2012, 'What can ADHD without comorbidity teach us about comorbidity?', *Research in Developmental Disabilities*, vol. 33(2), pp. 419–25.

Torok, M, Darke, S & Kaye, S 2012, 'Attention deficit hyperactivity disorder and severity of substance use: The role of comorbid psychopathology', *Psychology of Addictive Behaviors*, vol. 26(4), pp. 974–9.

Young, S & Gudjonsson, GH 2006, 'ADHD symptomatology and its relationship with emotional, social and delinquency problems', *Psychology, Crime and Law*, vol. 12, pp. 463–71.

## WEBSITES

US Centers for Disease Control and Prevention, www.cdc.gov.

## CHAPTER 7

Arnsten, AF 2006, 'Stimulants: Therapeutic actions in ADHD', *Neuropsychopharmacology*, vol. 31(11), pp. 2376–83.

Barkley, RA & Cunningham, CE 1978, 'Do stimulant drugs improve academic performance of hyperkinetic children? A review of outcome studies', *Clinical Pediatrics*, vol. 17(1), pp. 85–92.

Bennett, FC, Brown, RT, Craver, J & Anderson, D 1999, 'Stimulant medication for the child with attention-deficit/hyperactivity disorder', *Pediatric Clinics of North America*, vol. 46, pp. 929–43.

Biederman, J 2003, 'Pharmacotherapy for attention-deficit/hyperactivity disorder (ADHD) decreases the risk for substance abuse: Findings from a longitudinal follow-up of youths with and without ADHD', *Journal of Clinical Psychiatry*, vol. 64, pp. 3–8.

Breggin, P & Breggin, GR 1995, 'The hazards of treating "Attention-deficit/hyperactivity disorder" with methylphenidate (Ritalin)', *Journal of College Student Psychotherapy*, vol. 10(2), pp. 55–72.

Brown, RT & Daly, BP (in press), 'Neuropsychological effects of stimulant medication on children's learning and behavior', in CR Reynolds & E Fletcher-Janzen (eds), *Handbook of clinical neuropsychology*, Plenum, New York.

Brown University Psychopharmacology Update 2009, 'Your medication information: methylphenidate immediate release (IR) (generic)', vol. 20, pp. 1–2.

Brown University Child & Adolescent Psychopharmacology Update 2011, vol. 13, pp. 1–3.

Cheng, JY, Chen, RY, Ko, JS & Ng, EM 2007, 'Efficacy and safety of atomoxetine for attention-deficit/hyperactivity disorder in children and adolescents — meta-analysis and meta-regression analysis', *Psychopharmacology*, vol. 194(2), pp. 197–209.

Connor, DF, Glatt, SJ, Lopez, ID, Jackson, D & Melloni, RH 2002, 'Psychopharmacology and aggression. I: A meta-analysis of stimulant effects on overt/covert aggression-related behaviors in ADHD', *Journal of the American Academy of Child and Adolescent Psychiatry*, vol. 41(3), pp. 253–61.

Crick, NR & Dodge, KA 1996, 'Social information-processing mechanisms in reactive and proactive aggression', *Child Development*, vol. 67(3), pp. 993–1002.

Croxtall, JD 2011, 'Clonidine extended-release: In attention-deficit hyperactivity disorder', *Pediatric Drugs*, vol. 13(5), pp. 329–36.

Daly, BP, Creed, T, Xanthopoulos, M & Brown, RT 2007, 'Psychosocial treatments for children with attention deficit/hyperactivity disorder', *Neuropsychological Review Journal*, vol. 17(1), pp. 73–89.

Dodge, KA 1991, 'The structure and function of reactive and proactive aggression', in DJ Pepler & KH Rubin (eds), *The development and treatment of childhood aggression*, Erlbaum, Hillsdale, New Jersey.

Epstein, JN, Casey, BJ, Tonev, ST, Davidson, MC, et al., 2007, 'ADHD- and medication-related brain activation effects in concordantly affected parent–child dyads with ADHD', *Journal of Child Psychology and Psychiatry*, vol. 48(9), pp. 899–913.

Firestone, P, Musten, LM, Pisterman, S, Mercer, J & Bennett, S 1998, 'Short-term side effects of stimulant medication are increased in preschool children with attention-deficit/hyperactivity disorder: A double-blind placebo-controlled study', *Journal of Child and Adolescent Psychopharmacology*, vol. 8(1), pp. 13–25.

Greenhill, LL, Halperin, JM & Abikoff, H 1999, 'Stimulant medications', *Journal of the American Academy of Child and Adolescent Psychiatry*, vol. 38(5), pp. 503–12.

Gualtieri, CT & Johnson, LG 2008, 'Medications do not necessarily normalize cognition in ADHD patients', *Journal of Attention Disorders*, vol. 11(4), pp. 459–69.

Haber, JS 2003, *ADHD: The great misdiagnosis*, revised edn, Taylor Trade Publishing, Maryland.

Hinshaw, SP 1991, 'Stimulant medication and the treatment of aggression in children with attentional deficits', *Journal of Clinical Child Psychology*, vol. 20, pp. 301–12.

Hinshaw, SP & Lee, SS 2000, 'Ritalin effects on aggression and antisocial behavior', in LL Greenhill & BB Osman (eds), *Ritalin: Theory and patient management*, 2nd edn, Mary Ann Liebert, Larchmont, New York.

Hodgkins, P, Sasane, R & Meijer, WM 2011, 'Pharmacologic treatment of attention-deficit/hyperactivity disorder in children: Incidence, prevalence, and treatment patterns in the Netherlands', *Clinical Therapeutics*, vol. 33(2), pp. 188–203.

Hollingworth, SA, Nissen, LM, Stathis, SS, Siskind, DJ, Varghese, JM & Scott, JG 2010, 'Australian national trends in stimulant dispensing: 2002-2009', *Australian and New Zealand Journal of Psychiatry*, vol. 45(4), pp. 332–6.

Kratochvil, CJ, Wilens, TE, Greenhill, LL, Gao, H, Baker, KD, Feldman, PD & Gelowitz, DL 2006, 'Effects of long-term atomoxetine treatment for young children with attention-deficit/hyperactivity disorder', *Journal of the American Academy of Child & Adolescent Psychiatry*, vol. 45(8), pp. 919–27.

Jadad, AR, Booker, L, Gauld, M, Kakuma, R, Boyle, M, Cunningham, CE et al. 1999, 'The treatment of attention-deficit hyperactivity disorder: An annotated bibliography and critical appraisal of published systematic reviews and meta-analyses', *Canadian Journal of Psychiatry*, vol. 44(10), pp. 1025–35.

King, S, Waschbusch, DA, Pelham, WE, Frankland, BW, Corkum, PV, Jacques, S 2009, 'Subtypes of aggression in children with attention deficit hyperactivity disorder: Medication effects and comparison with typical children', *Journal of Clinical Child & Adolescent Psychology*, vol. 38(5), pp. 619–29.

Loe, IM & Feldman, HM 2007, 'Academic and educational outcomes of children with ADHD', *Journal of Paediatric Psychology*, vol. 32(6), pp. 643–54.

McCormick, LH 2003, 'ADHD treatment and academic performance: A case series', *Journal of Family Practice*, vol. 52(8), pp. 620–4; 626.

McManus, P, Mant, A, Mitchell, PB, Montgomery, WS, Marley, J & Auland, ME 2000, 'Recent trends in the use of antidepressant drugs in Australia, 1990-1998', *Medical Journal of Australia*, vol. 173(9), pp. 458–61.

Michelson D, Adler L, Spencer T, Reimherr FW, West SA, Allen AJ, Kelsey D, Wernicke

J, Dietrich A, Milton D 2003, 'Atomoxetine in adults with ADHD: Two randomized, placebo-controlled studies', *Biological Psychiatry*, vol. 53(2), pp. 112–20.

Michelson, D, Allen, AJ, Busner, J, Casat, C, Dunn, D, Kratochvil, C et al. 2002, 'Once-daily atomoxetine treatment for children and adolescents with attention deficit hyperactivity disorder: A randomized, placebo-controlled study', *The American Journal of Psychiatry*, vol. 159(11), pp. 1896–901.

MTA Cooperative Group 1999b, 'Moderators and mediators of treatment response for children with attention-deficit/hyperactivity disorder: The multimodal treatment study of children with attention-deficit/hyperactivity disorder', *Archives of General Psychiatry*, vol. 56(12), pp. 1088–96.

'Noteworthy briefs from the field, Psychiatric Dispatches, 2009', *Primary Psychiatry*, vol. 16, pp. 17–18.

Perwien AR, Faries, DE, Kratochvil, CJ, Sumner, CR, Kelsey, DK & Allen, AJ 2004, 'Improvement in health-related quality of life in children with ADHD: An analysis of placebo controlled studies of atomoxetine', *Journal of Developmental and Behavioral Pediatrics*, vol. 25(4), pp. 264–71.

Pliszka, SR 2003, 'Non-stimulant treatment of attention-deficit/hyperactivity disorder', *CNS Spectrums*, vol. 8(4), pp. 253–8.

Prosser, B & Reid, R 2009, 'Changes in use of psychostimulant medication for ADHD in South Australia (1990-2006)', *Australian and New Zealand Journal of Psychiatry*, vol. 43(4), pp. 340–7.

Ramsay, JR & Rostain, A 2007, *Cognitive Behavioral Therapy for adult ADHD: An integrative psychosocial and medical approach*, Routledge, New York.

Rapport, MD & Moffitt, C 2002, 'Attention deficit/hyperactivity disorder and methylphenidate: A review of height/weight, cardiovascular and somatic complaint side effects', *Clinical Psychology Review*, vol. 22(8), pp. 1107–31.

Ruff, ME 2005, 'Attention deficit disorder and stimulant use: An epidemic of modernity', *Clinical Paediatrics*, vol. 44(7), pp. 557–63.

Santosh, PJ, Sattar, S & Canagaratnam, M 2011, 'Efficacy and tolerability of pharmacotherapies for attention-deficit hyperactivity disorder in adults', *CNS Drugs*, vol. 25(9), pp. 737–63.

Semrud-Clikeman, M, Pliszka, S & Liotti, M 2008, 'Executive functioning in children with attention-deficit/hyperactivity disorder: Combined type with and without a stimulant medication history', *Neuropsychology*, vol. 22(3), pp. 329–40.

Smith, BH, Barkley, RA & Shapiro CJ 2006, 'Attention-deficit/hyperactivity disorder', in EJ Mash & RA Barkley (eds), *Treatment of Childhood Disorders*, 3rd edn, The Guilford Press, New York.

Spencer, TJ, Biederman, J & Mick, E 2007, 'Attention-deficit/hyperactivity disorder: Diagnosis, lifespan, comorbidities, and neurobiology', *Journal of Paediatric Psychology*, vol. 32(6), pp. 631–42.

Ter-Stepanian, M, Grizenko, N, Zappitelli, M & Joober, R 2010, 'Clinical response to methylphenidate in children diagnosed with attention-deficit hyperactivity disorder and comorbid psychiatric disorders', *The Canadian Journal of Psychiatry*, vol. 55(5), pp. 305–12.

Thorell, LB, Dahlström, K 2009, 'Children's self-reports on perceived effects on taking stimulant medication for ADHD', *Journal of Attentional Disorders*, vol. 12(5), pp. 460–8.

Toh, S 2006, 'Datapoints: Trends in ADHD and stimulant use among children, 1993–2003', *Psychiatric Services*, vol. 57(8), pp. 1091–8.

Vaughan, B, Roberts, HJ & Needleman, HL 2009, 'Current medications for the treatment of attention-deficit/hyperactivity disorder', *Psychology in the Schools*, vol. 46, pp. 846–56.

Waschbusch, DA, Pelham, WE Jr, Jennings, JR, Greiner, AR, Tarter, RE & Moss, HB 2002, 'Reactive aggression in boys with disruptive behavior disorders: Behavior, physiology, and affect', *Journal of Abnormal Child Psychology*, vol. 30(6), pp. 641–56.

Waschbusch, DA, Willoughby, MT & Pelham, WE Jr 1998, 'Criterion validity and the utility of reactive and proactive aggression: Comparisons to attention deficit hyperactivity disorder, oppositional defiant disorder, conduct disorder, and other measures of functioning', *Journal of Clinical Child Psychology*, vol. 27(4), pp. 396–405.

Wigal, SB 2009, 'Efficacy and safety limitations of attention-deficit hyperactivity disorder pharmacotherapy in children and adults', *CNS Drugs*, vol. 23, suppl. 1, pp.21–31.

Wood, JG, Crager, JL, Delap, CM & Heiskell, KD 2007, 'Beyond methylphenidate: Nonstimulant medications for youth with ADHD', *Journal of Attention Disorders*, vol. 11(3), pp. 341–50.

## WEBSITES

Australian Bureau of Statistics 2012, viewed 25 July 2012, www.abs.gov.au.

Australian Institute of Health and Welfare 2012, viewed 25 July 2012, www.aihw.gov.au.

US Food and Drug Administration 2011, viewed May 2011, www.fda.gov/medwatch/SAFETY/2004/Strattera-PI.pdf.

The Heart Foundation 2012, viewed 25 July 2012, www.heartfoundation.org.au.

## CHAPTER 8

Abikoff, H 1991, 'Cognitive training in ADHD children: Less to it than meets the eye', *Journal of Learning Disabilities*, vol. 24(4), pp. 205–9.

Abikoff, H, Hechtman, L, Klein, RG, Gallagher, R, Fleiss, K, Etcovitch, J et al. 2004, 'Social functioning in children with ADHD treated with long-term methylphenidate and multimodal psychosocial treatment', *Journal of the American Academy of Child & Adolescent Psychiatry*, vol. 43(7), pp. 820–9.

Barkley, RA 1992, 'Is EEG biofeedback effective for ADHD children? Proceed with much caution', Attention Deficit Disorder Advocacy Group newsletter.

Barkley, RA 1997, *Defiant children: A clinician's manual for parent training*, The Guilford Press, New York.

Barkley, RA 2000, 'Commentary: Issues in training parents to manage children with behavior problems', *Journal of the American Academy of Child and Adolescent Psychiatry*, vol. 39(8), pp. 1004–7.

Barkley, RA 2002, 'Psychosocial treatments for attention deficit/hyperactivity disorder in children', *Journal of Clinical Psychiatry*, vol. 63, pp. 36–43.

Barkley, RA & Cunningham, CE 1978, 'Do stimulant drugs improve academic performance of hyperkinetic children? A review of outcome studies', *Clinical Pediatrics*, vol. 17(1), pp. 85–92.

Barkley, RA, Edwards, G, Laneri, M, Fletcher, K & Metevia, L 2001, 'The efficacy of problem-solving communication training alone, behaviour management training alone, and their combination for parent–adolescent conflict in teenagers with ADHD and ODD', *Journal of Consulting and Clinical Psychology*, vol. 69(6), pp. 926–41.

Barkley, RA, Fischer, M, Edelbrock, CS & Smallish, L 1990, 'The adolescent outcome of hyperactive children diagnosed by research criteria: I. An 8-year prospective follow-up study', *Journal of the American Academy of Child and Adolescent Psychiatry*, vol. 29(4), pp. 546–57.

Barkley, RA, Fischer, M, Smallish, L & Fletcher, K 2004, 'Young adult follow-up of hyperactive children: Antisocial activities and drug use', *Journal of Child Psychology and Psychiatry, and Allied Disciplines*, vol. 45(2), pp. 195–211.

Barkley, RA, Guevremont, DC, Anastopoulos, AD & Fletcher, KE 1992, 'A comparison of three family therapy programs for treating family conflicts in adolescents with attention-deficit hyperactivity disorder', *Journal of Consulting and Clinical Psychology*, vol. 60(3), pp. 450–62.

Beck, JS 1995, *Cognitive therapy: Basics and beyond*, The Guilford Press, New York.

Bloomquist, ML 2006, *Skills training for children with behavior problems: A parent and practitioner guidebook*, revised edn, The Guilford Press, New York.

Boon, HJ 2007, 'Low- and high-achieving Australian secondary school students: Their parenting, motivations and academic achievement', *Australian Psychologist*, vol. 42, pp. 212–25.

Brown, RT & Daly, BP (in press), 'Neuropsychological effects of stimulant medication on children's learning and behavior', in CR Reynolds & E Fletcher-Janzen (eds.), *Handbook of clinical neuropsychology*, Plenum, New York.

Chandler, C 2010, *The science of ADHD: A guide for parents and professionals*, John Wiley & Sons Ltd, Chichester.

Chronis, AM, Jones, HA & Raggi, VL 2006, 'Evidence-based psychosocial treatments for children and adolescents with attention-deficit/hyperactivity disorder', *Clinical Psychology Review*, vol. 26(4), pp. 486–502.

Conlon, KE, Strassle, CG, Vinh, D & Trout, G 2008, 'Family management styles and ADHD: Utility and treatment implications', *Journal of Family Nursing*, vol. 14(2), pp. 181–200.

Daly, BP, Creed, T, Xanthopoulos, M & Brown, RT 2007, 'Psychosocial treatments for children with attention deficit/hyperactivity disorder', *Neuropsychological Review Journal*, vol. 17(1), pp. 73–89.

DuPaul, GJ & Eckert, TL 1998, 'Academic interventions for students with attention deficit/ hyperactivity disorder: A review of the literature', *Reading and Writing Quarterly*, vol. 14, pp. 59–82.

Fabiano, GA, Pelham, WE Jr, Coles, EK, Gnagy, EM, Chronis-Tuscano, AC & O'Connor, BC 2009, 'A meta-analysis of behavioral treatments for attention-deficit/hyperactivity disorder', *Clinical Psychology Review*, vol. 29(2), pp. 129–40.

Farmer, RF & Chapman, AL 2008, *Behavioural interventions in cognitive behaviour therapy: Practical guidance for putting theory into action*, American Psychological Association, Washington, DC.

Forness, SR, Walker, HM & Kavale, KA 2003, 'Disorders and treatments: A primer for teachers', *Teaching Exceptional Children*, vol. 36, pp. 42–9.

Germer, CK, Seigel, RD & Fulton, PR (eds.) 2005, *Mindfulness and psychotherapy*, The Guilford Press, New York.

Hagen, KA, Ogden, T & Bjørnebekk, G 2011, 'Treatment outcomes and mediators of parent management training: A one-year follow-up of children with conduct problems', *Journal of Clinical Child & Adolescent Psychology*, vol. 40(2), pp. 165–78.

Heriot, SA, Evans, IM & Foster, TM 2008, 'Critical influences affecting response to various treatments in young children with ADHD: A case series', *Child Care, Health and Development*, vol. 34(1), pp. 121–33.

Hinshaw, SP 2006, 'Treatment for children and adolescents with attention-deficit/hyperactivity disorder', in PC Kendall (ed.), *Child and adolescent therapy: Cognitive-behavioral procedures*, 3rd edn, The Guilford Press, New York.

Hodgens, JB, Cole, J & Boldizar, J 2000, 'Peer-based differences among boys with ADHD', *Journal of Clinical Child Psychology*, vol. 29(3), pp. 443–52.

Kazdin, AE 2005, *Parent management training: Treatment for oppositional, aggressive, and antisocial behavior in children and adolescents*, Oxford University Press, New York.

Kazdin, AE 2007, 'Progress in treating children referred for severe aggressive and antisocial behavior', *NYS Psychologist*, vol. 19(5), pp. 7–12.

Kendall, PC & Braswell, L 1993, *Cognitive-behavioral therapy for impulsive children*, The Guilford Press, New York.

Landau, S & Moore, LA 1991, 'Social skill deficits in children with attention-deficit/hyperactivity disorder', *School Psychology Review*, vol. 20, pp. 235–51.

Lee, SW 1991, 'Biofeedback as a treatment for childhood hyperactivity: A critical review of the literature', *Psychological Reports*, vol. 68(1), pp. 163–92.

Loe, IM & Feldman, HM 2007, 'Academic and educational outcomes of children with ADHD', *Journal of Paediatric Psychology*, vol. 32(6), pp. 643–54.

Loo, SK & Barkley, RA 2005, 'Clinical utility of EEG in attention deficit hyperactivity disorder', *Applied Neuropsychology*, vol. 12(2), pp. 64–76.

Lubar, JF 1991, 'Discourse on the development of EEG diagnostics and biofeedback for attention-deficit/hyperactivity disorders', *Biofeedback and Self-Regulation*, vol. 16(3), pp. 201–25.

Lundahl, B, Risser, HJ & Lovejoy, MC 2006, 'A meta-analysis of parent training: Moderators and follow-up effects', *Clinical Psychology Review*, vol. 26(1), pp. 86–104.

Mace, C 2008, *Mindfulness and mental health: Therapy, theory and science*, Routledge/Taylor & Francis Group, New York.

McCormick, LH 2003, 'ADHD treatment and academic performance: A case series', *Journal of Family Practice*, vol. 52(8), pp. 620–4; 626.

Miller, M & Hinshaw, SP 2012, 'Attention deficit hyperactivity disorder', in PC Kendall (ed.), *Child and adolescent therapy: Cognitive-behavioral procedures*, 4th edn, The Guilford Press, New York.

MTA Cooperative Group 1999a, 'A 14-month randomized clinical trial of treatment strategies for attention-deficit hyperactivity disorder: Multimodal treatment study of children with ADHD', *Archives of General Psychiatry*, vol. 56(12), pp. 1073–86.

Conners, CK, Epstein JN, March, JS et al., 'Multimodal treatment of ADHD in the MTA: An alternative outcome analysis', *Journal of the American Academy of Child and Adolescent Psychiatry*, vol. 40(2), pp. 159–67.

Myers, R 2007, 'Evidence-based psychological treatment for children with ADHD', *A child development institute white paper*, Orange, California, pp 1–8.

Owens, JS, Murphy, CE, Richerson, L, Girio, EL & Himawan, LK 2008, 'Science to practice in underserved communities: The effectiveness of school mental health programming', *Journal of Clinical Child and Adolescent Psychology*, vol. 37(2), pp. 434–47.

Pear, ES 2009, 'Parent management training for reducing oppositional and aggressive behaviour in pre-schoolers', *Journal of Aggression and Violent Behaviour*, vol. 14, pp. 295–305.

Pfiffner, LJ, Calzada, E & McBurnett, K 2000, 'Interventions to enhance social competence', *Child and Adolescent Psychiatric Clinics of North America*, vol. 9(3), pp. 689–709.

Pfiffner, LJ & McBurnett, K 1997, 'Social skills training with parent generalization: Treatment effects for children with attention deficit disorder', *Journal of Consulting and Clinical Psychology*, vol. 65(5), pp. 749–57.

Pfiffner, LJ, Yee Mikami, A, Huang-Pollock, C, Easterlin, B, Zalecki, C & McBurnett, K 2007, 'A randomized, controlled trial of integrated home-school behavioural treatment for ADHD, predominantly inattentive type', *Journal of the American Academy of Child and Adolescent Psychiatry*, vol. 46(8), pp. 1041–50.

Ramsay, JR 2010, 'CBT for adult ADHD: Adaptations and hypothesized mechanisms of change', *Journal of Cognitive Psychotherapy*, vol. 24, pp. 37–45.

Ramsey, JR 2010, *Nonmedication treatments for adult ADHD: Evaluating impact on daily functioning and well-being*, 1st edn, American Psychological Association, Washington, DC.

Ramsay, JR & Rostain, A 2007, *Cognitive-behavioral therapy for adult ADHD: An integrative psychosocial and medical approach*, Routledge, New York.

Riccio, CA & French, CL 2004, 'The status of empirical support for treatments of attention deficits', *The Clinical Neuropsychologist*, vol. 18(4), pp. 528–58.

Sacco, WP & Beck, AT 1995, 'Cognitive theory and therapy', in Ernest Edward Beckham, William R. Leber (eds.), *Handbook of depression*, 2nd edn, The Guilford Press, New York.

Schultz, BK, Storer, J, Watabe, Y, Sadler, J & Evans, SW 2011, 'School-based treatment of attention-deficit/hyperactivity disorder', *Psychology in the Schools*, vol. 48, pp. 252–64.

Singh, NN, Singh, AN, Lancioni, GE, Singh, J, Winton, ASW & Adkins, AD 2010, 'Mindfulness training for parents and their children with ADHD increases the children's compliance', *Journal of Child and Family Studies*, vol. 19, pp. 157–66.

Smith, BH, Barkley, RA & Shapiro, CJ 2006, 'Attention-deficit/hyperactivity disorder', in EJ Mash & RA Barkley (eds), *Treatment of childhood disorders*, 3rd edn, The Guilford Press, New York.

Springer, C & Peddy, LA 2010, 'Measuring parental treatment adherence in a multimodal treatment program for children with ADHD: A preliminary investigation', *Child and Family Behavior Therapy*, vol. 32, pp. 72–290.

Toplak, ME, Connors, L, Shuster, J, Knezevic, B & Parks, S 2008, 'Review of cognitive, cognitive-behavioral, and neural-based interventions for attention-deficit/hyperactivity disorder (ADHD)', *Clinical Psychology Review*, vol. 28(5), pp. 801–23.

Tyrka, AR, Wyche, MC, Kelly, MM, Price, LH & Carpenter, LL 2009, 'Childhood maltreatment and adult personality disorder symptoms: Influence of maltreatment type', *Psychiatry Research*, vol. 165(3), pp. 281–7.

van der Oord, S, Bögels, SM & Peijnenburg, D 2011, 'The effectiveness of mindfulness training for children with ADHD and mindful parenting for their parents', *Journal of Child and Family Studies*, vol. 21(1), pp. 139–47.

Webster-Stratton, C & Hammond, M 1997, 'Treating children with early-onset conduct problems: A comparison of child and parent training interventions', *Journal of Consulting and Clinical Psychology*, vol. 65(1), pp. 93–109.

Webster-Stratton, C, Reid, J & Hammond, M 2001, 'Social skills and problem-solving training for children with early-onset conduct problems: Who benefits?', *Journal of Child Psychology and Psychiatry, and Allied Disciplines*, vol. 42(7), pp. 943–52.

Weyandt, LL 2007, *An ADHD primer*, 2nd edn, Lawrence Erlbaum Associates Inc., New Jersey.

Wilkenson, W and Lagendijk, M 2007, in M. Fitzgerald, M. Bellgrove & M. Gill (eds.). *Handbook of attention deficit hyperactivity disorder*, John Wiley & Sons Ltd, Chichester.

Wilmhurst, L 2005, *Essential of child psychopathology*, John Wiley & Sons Ltd, New Jersey.

Young, S 1999, 'Psychological therapy for adults with attention deficit hyperactivity disorder', *Counselling Psychology Quarterly*, vol. 12, pp. 183–90.

Young, S 2007, 'Cognitive behavioural treatment of ADHD', in M Fitzgerald, M Belgrove & M Gill (eds.), *Handbook of attention hyperactivity disorder*, John Wiley & Sons Ltd, Chichester.

Young, S & Amarasinghe, JM 2010, 'Practitioner review: Non-pharmacological treatments for ADHD: A lifespan approach', *Journal of Child Psychology and Psychiatry*, vol. 51(2), pp. 116–33.

Zylowska, L, Ackerman, DL, Yang, MH, Futrell, JL, Horton, NL, Hale, TS, Pataki, C & Smalley, SL 2008, 'Mindfulness meditation training in adults and adolescents with ADHD: A feasibility study', *Journal of Attention Disorders*, vol. 11(6), pp. 737–46.

Zylowska, L, Smalley, SL & Schwartz, JM 2009, 'Mindfulness awareness and ADHD', in F Didonna (ed), *Clinical handbook of mindfulness*, Springer Science and Business Media, New York.

## CHAPTER 9

Singh, I 2008, 'ADHD, culture and education', *Early Child Development and Care*, vol. 178, pp. 347–61.

Singh, I, Kendall, T, Taylor, C, Mears, A, Hollis, C, Batty, M & Keenan, S 2004, 'Young people's experience of ADHD and stimulant medication: A qualitative study for the NICE Guideline', *Child and Adolescent Mental Health*, vol. 15, pp. 186–92.

Kendall, J, Hatton, D, Beckett, A & Leo, M 2003, 'Children's accounts of attention-deficit/ hyperactivity disorder', *Advances in Nursing Science*, vol. 26(2), pp. 114–30.

Young, S 2007, 'Cognitive behavioural treatment of ADHD', in M Fitzgerald, M Belgrove & M Gill (eds.), *Handbook of attention hyperactivity disorder*, John Wiley & Sons Ltd, Chichester.

Young, S, Bramham, J, Gray, K & Rose, E 2008, 'The experience of receiving a diagnosis and treatment of ADHD in adulthood: A qualitative study of clinically referred patients using interpretative phenomenological analysis', *Journal of Attention Disorders*, vol. 11(4), pp. 493–503.

# CHAPTER 10

Albrecht, AT 2010, *100 questions and answers about adult attention-deficit hyperactivity disorder (ADHD)*, Jones and Bartlett Publishers, Massachusetts.

American Psychiatric Association 2013, *Diagnostic and statistical manual of mental disorders* (DSM), 5th edn, American Psychiatric Association, Arlington, Virginia.

Barkley, RA 2005, *Take charge of ADHD: The complete, authoritative guide for parents*, Hinkler Books Pty Ltd, Victoria.

Barkley, RA 2010, *Taking charge of adult ADHD*, The Guilford Press, New York.

Barkley RA, Cox D 2007, 'A review of driving risks and impairments associated with attention-deficit/hyperactivity disorder and the effects of stimulant medication on driving performance', *Journal of Safety Research*, vol. 38(1), pp. 113–28.

Barkley RA, Fischer M, Smallish L, Fletcher K 2006, 'Young adult outcome of hyperactive children: Adaptive functioning in major life activities', *Journal of the American Academy of Child and Adolescent Psychiatry*, vol. 45(2), pp. 192–202.

Barkley, RA, Murphy, KR & Fischer, M 2008, *ADHD in adults: What the science says*, The Guilford Press, New York.

Barkley, RA, Murphy, KR, Dupaul, GI, Bush, T 2002, 'Driving in young adults with attention-deficit/hyperactivity disorder: Knowledge, performance, adverse outcomes, and the role of executive functioning', *Journal of the International Neuropsychological Society*, vol. 8, pp. 655–72.

Barlow, DH & Durand, VM 2002, *Abnormal psychology: an integrative approach*, 3rd edn, Wadsworth/Thomson Learning, Belmont.

Biederman, J, Faraone, SV, Spencer, T, Wilens, T, Norman, D, Lapey, KA, Mick, E, Lehman, BK & Doyle, A 1993, 'Patterns of psychiatric comorbidity, cognition, and psychosocial functioning in adults with attention deficit hyperactivity disorder', *American Journal of Psychiatry*, vol. 150(12), pp. 1792–8.

Eakin, L, Minde, K, Hechtman, L, Ochs, E, Krane, E, Bouffard, R, Greenfield, B & Looper K 2004, 'The marital and family functioning of adults with ADHD and their spouses', *Journal of Attention Disorders*, vol. 8(1), pp. 1–10.

Emilsson, B, Gudjonsson, G, Sigurdsson, JF, Baldursson, G, Einarsson, E, Olafsdottir, H & Young, S 2011, 'Cognitive behaviour therapy in medication-treated adults with ADHD and persistent symptoms: A randomized controlled trial', *BMC Psychiatry*, vol. 11, p. 116.

Faraone, SV & Biederman, J 2004, 'A controlled study of functional impairments in 500 ADHD adults', Paper presented at the 157th annual APA meeting; 6 May 2004, New York.

Faraone, SV, Spencer, T, Aleardi, M, Pagano, C & Biederman, J 2004, 'Meta-analysis of the efficacy of methylphenidate for treating adult attention-deficit/hyperactivity disorder', *Journal of Clinical Psychopharmacology*, vol. 24(1), pp. 24–9.

Fischer, M & Barkley, RA 2006, 'Young adult outcomes of children with hyperactivity: Leisure, financial, and social activities', *International Journal of Disability, Development and Education*, vol. 53, pp. 229–45.

Fischer, AG, Bau, CH, Grevet, EH, Salgado, CA, Victor, MM, Kalil, KL, Sousa, NO, Garcia, CR & Belmonte-de-Abreu, P 2007, 'The role of comorbid major depressive disorder in the clinical presentation of adult ADHD', *Journal of Psychiatric Research*, vol. 41(12), pp. 991–6.

Flory, K, Molina, BS, Pelham, WE Jr, Gnagy, E & Smith, B 2006, 'Childhood ADHD predicts risky sexual behavior in young adulthood', *Journal of Clinical Child and Adolescent Psychology*, vol. 35(4), pp. 571–7.

Godfrey, J 2009, 'Safety of therapeutic methylphenidate in adults: A systematic review of the evidence', *Journal of Psychopharmacology*, vol. 23(2), pp. 194–205.

Jerome, L, Segal, A & Habinski, L 2006, 'What we know about ADHD and driving risk: A literature review, meta-analysis and critique', *Journal of the Canadian Academy of Child and Adolescent Psychiatry*, vol. 15(3), pp. 105–25.

Mannuzza, S, Klein, RG & Addalli, KA 1991, 'Young adult mental status of hyperactive boys and their brothers: A prospective follow-up study', *Journal of the American Academy of Child and Adolescent Psychiatry*, vol. 30(5), pp. 743–51.

Mannuzza, S, Klein, RG, Bessler, A, Malloy, P & LaPadula, M 1993, 'Adult outcome of hyperactive boys: Educational achievement, occupational rank, and psychiatric status', *Archives of General Psychiatry*, vol. 50(7), pp. 565–76.

McGillivray, JA & Baker, KL 2009, 'Effects of comorbid ADHD with learning disabilities on anxiety, depression, and aggression in adults', *Journal of Attention Disorders*, vol. 12(6), pp. 525–31.

McGough, JJ, Smalley, SL, McCracken, JT, Yang, M et al. 2005, 'Psychiatric comorbidity in adult attention deficit hyperactivity disorder: Findings from multiplex families', *American Journal of Psychiatry*, vol. 162(9), pp. 1621–7.

Minde, K, Eakin, L, Hechtman, L, Ochs, E, Bouffard, R et al. 2003, 'The psychosocial functioning of children and spouses of adults with ADHD', *Journal of Child Psychology and Psychiatry*, vol. 44(4), pp. 637–46.

Murphy, KR, Barkley, RA & Bush, T 2002, 'Young adults with attention deficit hyperactivity disorder: Subtype differences in comorbidity, educational, and clinical history', *Journal of Nervous and Mental Disease*, vol. 190(3), pp. 147–57.

Ohlmeier, MD, Peters, K, Kordon, A, Seifert, J, Wildt, BT, Wiese, B, Ziegenbein, M, Emrich, HM, Schneider, U 2007, 'Nicotine and alcohol dependence in patients with comorbid attention-deficit/hyperactivity disorder (ADHD)', *Alcohol and Alcoholism*, vol. 42(6), pp. 539–43.

Ramsay, JR 2010, 'CBT for Adult ADHD: Adaptations and hypothesized mechanisms of change', *Journal of Cognitive Psychotherapy*, vol. 24, pp. 37–45.

Ramsey, JR 2010, *Nonmedication treatments for adult ADHD: Evaluating impact on daily functioning and well-being*, 1st edn, American Psychological Association, Washington, DC.

Ramsay, JR & Rostain, A 2007, *Cognitive-behavioral therapy for adult ADHD: An integrative psychosocial and medical approach*, Routledge, New York.

Reimherr, FW, Marchant, BK, Strong, RE, Hedges, DW, Adler, L, Spencer, TJ, West, SA & Soni, P, 'Emotional dysregulation in adult ADHD and response to atomoxetine', *Biological Psychiatry*, vol. 58(2), pp. 125–31.

Rostain, AL & Ramsay, JR 2006, 'A combined treatment approach for adults with ADHD — results of an open study of 43 patients', *Journal of Attention Disorders*, vol. 10(2), pp. 150–9.

Santosh, PJ, Sattar, S & Canagaratnam, M 2011, 'Efficacy and tolerability of pharmacotherapies for attention-deficit hyperactivity disorder in adults', *CNS Drugs*, vol. 25(9), pp. 737–63.

Safren, SA, Otto, MW, Sprich, S, Winett, CL, Wilens, TE & Biederman, J 2005, 'Cognitive-behavioural therapy for ADHD in medication-treated adults with continued symptoms', *Behaviour Research and Therapy*, vol. 43(7), pp. 831–42.

Stein, MA 2007, 'The complexity of ADHD: Diagnosis and treatment of the adult patient with comorbidities', *CNS Spectrums*, vol. 12(8), pp. 1–16.

Taylor, E, Chadwick, O, Heptinstall, E & Danckaerts, M 1996, 'Hyperactivity and conduct problems as risk factors for adolescent development', *Journal of the American Academy of Child and Adolescent Psychiatry*, vol. 35(9), pp. 1213–26.

Tamam, L, Karakus, G & Ozpoyraz, N 2008, 'Comorbidity of adult attention-deficit hyperactivity disorder and bipolar disorder: Prevalence and clinical correlates', *European Archives of Psychiatry and Clinical Neuroscience*, vol. 258(7), pp. 385–93.

Tannock, R 2000, 'Attention deficit disorders with anxiety disorders', in S Brown (ed), *Attention deficit disorders and comorbidities in children, adolescents and adults*, American Psychiatric Press, New York.

The Royal College of Australasian Physicians 2009, *Australian guidelines on attention deficit hyperactivity disorder (ADHD)*.

Toner, M, O'Donoghue, T & Houghton, S 2006, 'Living in chaos and striving for control: How adults with attention deficit hyperactivity disorder deal with their disorder', *International Journal of Disability, Development and Education*, vol. 53, pp. 247–61.

van der Linden, G, Young, S, Ryan, P & Toone, B 2000, 'Attention deficit hyperactivity disorder in adults: Experience of the first National Health Service clinic in the United Kingdom', *Journal of Mental Health*, vol. 9, pp. 527–35.

Weiss, G, Hechtman, L, Perlman, T, Hopkins, J & Wener, A 1979, 'Hyperactives as young adults: A controlled prospective ten-year follow-up of 75 children', *Archives of General Psychiatry*, vol. 36(6), pp. 675–81.

Weiss, G, Hechtman, L, Milroy, T & Perlman, T 1985, 'Psychiatric status of hyperactives as adults: A controlled perspective 15-year follow-up of 63 hyperactive children', *Journal of the American Academy of Child Psychiatry*, vol. 24(2), pp. 211–20.

Weiss, G & Hechtman, LT 1986, *Hyperactive children grown up: Empirical findings and theoretical considerations*, The Guilford Press, New York.

Wender, PH 2001, *ADHD: Attention-deficit hyperactivity disorder in children, adolescents and adults*, Oxford University Press, New York.

Weyandt, LL 2007, *An ADHD primer*, 2nd edn, Lawrence Erlbaum Associates Inc., New Jersey.

Wilens, TE 2004, 'Impact of ADHD and its treatment on substance abuse in adults', *Journal of Clinical Psychiatry*, vol. 65, pp. 38–45.

Wilens, TE, Adamson, J, Monuteaux, MC, Faraone, SV, Schillinger, M et al. 2008, 'Effect of prior stimulant treatment for attention-deficit/hyperactivity disorder on subsequent risk for cigarette smoking and alcohol and drug use disorders in adolescents', *Archives of Pediatrics and Adolescent Medicine*, vol. 162(10), pp. 916–21.

Wingo, AP, Ghaemi, SN 2007, 'A systematic review of rates and diagnostic validity of comorbid adult attention-deficit/hyperactivity disorder and bipolar disorder', *Journal of Clinical Psychiatry*, vol. 68(11), pp. 1776–84.

Young, S 1999, 'Psychological therapy for adults with attention deficit hyperactivity disorder', *Counselling Psychology Quarterly*, vol. 12, pp. 183–90.

Young, S 2000, 'ADHD children grown up: An empirical review', *Counselling Psychology Quarterly*, vol. 13, pp. 191–200.

Young, S 2005, 'Coping strategies used by adults with ADHD', *Personality and Individual Differences*, vol. 38, pp. 809–16.

Young, S 2007, 'Cognitive behavioural treatment of ADHD', in M Fitzgerald, M Belgrove & M Gill (eds), *Handbook of attention hyperactivity disorder*, John Wiley & Sons Ltd, Chichester.

Young, S & Amarasinghe, JM 2010, 'Practitioner review: Non-pharmacological treatments for ADHD: A lifespan approach', *Journal of Child Psychology and Psychiatry*, vol. 51(2), pp. 116–33.

Young, S & Bramham, J 2006, *ADHD in adults: A psychological guide to practice*, John Wiley & Sons Ltd, Chichester.

Young, S, Bramham, J, Gray, K & Rose, E 2008, 'The experience of receiving a diagnosis and treatment of ADHD in adulthood: A qualitative study of clinically referred patients using interpretative phenomenological analysis', *Journal of Attention Disorders*, vol. 11(4), pp. 493–503.

Young, S & Gudjonsson, GH 2006, 'ADHD symptomatology and its relationship with emotional, social and delinquency problems', *Psychology, Crime and Law*, vol. 12, pp. 463–71.

Young, S & Toone, B 2000, 'Attention deficit hyperactivity disorder in adults: Clinical issues. A report from the first NHS clinic in the UK', *Counselling Psychology Quarterly*, vol. 13, pp. 313–9.

# Useful websites

Below is a list of potentially helpful websites that appear to be based on the facts of ADHD.

ADDults with ADHD (NSW) Inc. (also provides links to other states)
www.adultadhd.org.au

American Academy of Child and Adolescent Psychiatry (type in 'ADHD' in the Search box)
www.aacap.org

Attention Disorders Association of South Australia Inc.
www.adasa.com.au

Children and Adults with Attention-Deficit/Hyperactivity Disorder (CHADD)
www.chadd.org

The Hyperactive Children's Association of Victoria Incorporated Association
www.vicnet.net.au

Learning and Attentional Disorders Society of Western Australia (Inc.)
www.ladswa.com.au

The National Attention Deficit Disorder Information and Support Services (ADDISS)
www.addiss.co.uk

National Resource Center on AD/HD: A Program of CHADD
www.help4adhd.org

NYU Child Study Center
www.aboutourkids.org

# INDEX

behaviour regulation, prefrontal cortex
46–8
behavioural goals 172
behavioural interventions 157–61
behavioural programs
    common core factors 160
    research results 161
behavioural report cards 172–3
behavioural social skills 169
behaviours
    aggressive 114–5, 151, 155–6, 203
    anger 36–7
    avoidance 4
    deficit in 'moral control' 14
    delinquent 96
    generic labels 151
    identified by Still 14
belief systems, dysfunctional 216
beta waves 141
biofeeback 140–2
biphasic action, medications 108
bipolar disorder 201–2
birth defects, alcohol while pregnant
34–5
blame for having ADHD 223
brain
    as control centre 40–3
    regions implicated in ADHD 40, 43–5
    see also executive functions (EFs)
brain injuries 15, 39
brain structure
    anterior cingulate cortex 53–4
    basal ganglia 49, 52, 54
    Broca's area 46
    caudate nucleus 49
    cerebellum 48
    cerebral cortex 45
    corpus callosum 45
    diagram of 44
    frontal limbic circuit 55
    frontal lobe 45–8, 51
    frontal-striatal circuit 54
    left hemisphere 43
    prefrontal cortex 46–8
    primary motor cortex 53–4
    right hemisphere 43–5
brain studies 56–9
brainwaves 141
bribery 158
Broca's area of the brain 46

## C

Canada, choice of medications 212
cardiovascular disease 33
caudate nucleus 49
causes of ADHD 32–9, 224
CBCL (Child Behaviour Checklist) 80–2
CBT see cognitive behavioural therapy
    (CBT)
central nervous system 41–3, 42
cerebellum 48
cerebral cortex 45
Chernobyl nuclear power plant 23–4
Child Behaviour Checklist (CBCL) 80–2
childhood disintegration disorder 99
children
    attending PMT sessions 152
    mindfulness steps 136
    mindfulness training 136–40
class sizes 177
classroom behaviour, helpful strategies
    174–7
classroom breaks 179–80
classroom environment, reducing
    distractions 177–8
clinic visit behaviour 73–4
clonidine 121–3
coercive parenting 143–4, 146
cognitive behavioural therapy (CBT)
    for adulthood ADHD 218–20
    explained 161–6
    gro8up treatment program 218–9
    limitations of 166
cognitive distortions 162–6
cognitive reframing 162–5
cognitive remediation techniques (CRT)
    165
Combined Type ADHD
    core symptoms 2
    disorder of EFs 51–2
    MTA study 183–4
communication disorder 100–1
communication strategies 166
comorbid conditions
    adulthood ADHD 197–203, 209
    atomoxetine treatment 120
    CBT as therapy 164
    common conditions 83, 93
    explained 67, 93
    good news 102
    with learning disorders 101

tics 99–100
Tourette syndrome (TS) 99–100
toxins
    alcohol 35
    in cigarettes 34
    environmental 33–4, 36
    lead 34, 36
twins, studies using 38

## U

Ukrainian children 23–4
United States, choice of medications 212

## V

Verbal Comprehension Index (VCI,
    WISC-IV) 89, 90
vocal tics 100

## W

Waldron, Dr Karen 176
Wechsler Adult Intelligence Scale
    (WAIS) 75
Wechsler Intelligence Scale for Children
    (WISC-IV)
    four domains 88–9
    test completion time 91
Western phenomenon, ADHD 21–4
words of encouragement 220–2
working memory
    core deficit 91
    disorder of 51–2
    function 54–5
Working Memory Index (WMI, WISC-
    IV) 89, 91
Working With Children Check 132

## Y

Young-Bramham Programme 165
Youth Self-Report (YSR 11-18, CBCL) 81

## Raising Stress-Proof Kids

*Parenting today's children for tomorrow's world*

Shelley Davidow MSEd

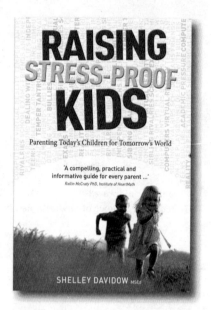

Stress is rising alarmingly in our children, both at school and at home. Across the world, hearts are racing, faces are pale — and most of the time we're unaware that many of our children are chronically stressed.

Drawing on cutting-edge research from the Institute of HeartMath, California, as well as Shelley Davidow's extensive experience in working with children and teens, *Raising Stress-Proof Kids* explores the powerful and potentially long-term effects of stress on our children. Most importantly, it offers simple but effective steps that parents can take to minimise the impact of stress at home and at school. These include tools from the author's 'Restorative Parenting Toolbox', empowering parents with the necessary skills to:

- resolve behaviour issues
- deal with temper tantrums
- resolve sibling rivalries
- handle bullying
- cope with teenagers testing their independence
- navigate the challenges posed by the virtual world, and
- provide firm, effective guidance when problems arise.

A must-read for every parent who wants to raise smart, emotionally stable, responsible, stress-proof kids!

ISBN 978 1 921966 40 8